WORKING AND WINNING IN CHINA

WORLD FORTUNE

500 CEOS

TALK ABOUT CHINA

By China Daily

新世界出版社
NEW WORLD PRESS

First Edition 2008
By China Daily
Edited by Li Shujuan
Cover Design by Wang Tianyi

ISBN 978-7-80228-497-5

Published by
NEW WORLD PRESS
24 Baiwanzhuang Road, Beijing 100037, China

Distributed by
NEW WORLD PRESS
24 Baiwanzhuang Road, Beijing 100037, China
Tel: 86-10-68995968
Fax: 86-10-68998705
Website: www.newworld-press.com
E-mail: frank@nwp.com.cn

Printed in the People's Republic of China

Foreword

2007 could well go down as the year of paradigm shift for multinationals in China.

In March, a single, uniform corporate income tax was set for domestic and foreign-invested enterprises, ending years of preferential tax treatment multinationals and other foreign-invested companies enjoyed. At the same time, the Property Law was enacted, giving equal protection in law to public and private property. These two moves sent out a clear yet powerful message to foreign investors: The country has shifted gears from courting foreign capital at any cost to promoting a favorable investment climate that will automatically draw international investors, who will now have to be content with a level playing field.

The reasons for this policy shift are not far to seek. Multinationals today need China as much as China needs them, if not more. The country is already among the top 10 markets for most MNCs while many have drawn up a timetable to make sure that it is among their top 5. For, an MNC's billing in the world market today depends on its performance in China. With the country emerging as the driving force of the world economy, any company that fails to keep pace with the rapidly expanding market here is doomed to lose the race to those who do, and eventually run the risk of losing their exalted global status.

But chasing Chinese consumers is a far more difficult exercise today. With more global companies converging on the Chinese market and domestic companies quickly picking up the tricks of the trade, MNCs are under constant pressure to localize and innovate in order to survive in the face of fierce competition. The search for new survival strategies has opened up new vistas within the Chinese market itself, with second- and third-tier cities emerging as hot favorites both for their cost advantages and for their untapped purchasing power. But selling wares to a regionally diverse clientele can be a far more difficult proposition than peddling them to homogeneous city dwellers, requiring MNCs to localize even deeper.

New challenges also confront multinationals for which China is more important as producer than buyer. There are increasing signs that policymakers are not satisfied with China's "world's factory" tag and are pushing the country to move up the value chain rather than produce the most basic of things, often causing grave threats to the country's resources and environment.

Issues such as these and more crop up in the following pages as MNC bosses tell us about their goals, challenges, and plans to grow with China. They discuss the opportunities new China throws up and shed light on the rules of engagement in this changing business climate. We hope these interviews and profiles, put together with other recent MNC stories, will help you understand where multinationals stand in today's China.

Zhu Ling
Editor-in-Chief
China Daily

Contents

Airbus Flies High in Soaring Market

An Interview with Laurence Barron,
President of Airbus China

aurence Barron was probably the proudest executive at Airbus' annual global meeting in Toulouse at the beginning of 2007.

"We (the China team) were like the stars of the show," recalls Barron. "We've had the best results in terms of volume and market share, and very encouraging future prospects. China is clearly at the forefront of people's attention."

With a double-digit annual growth rate, China has become the world's second-largest aviation market after the United States. The country's soaring economic development is fueling the surging demand for air travel.

China's three largest airline groups have been traditional opponents for plane manufacturers such as Airbus and Boeing. But emerging markets in the country are now attracting Barron's attention. He points out two new trends: the growth of start-up air carriers, and Chinese companies' increasing interest in the aircraft leasing business.

Start-up Opportunities

Ever since the Chinese government gave the nod to private investors to set up airlines two years ago, six private airlines have been flying in China's skies. The six start-up companies all have ambitious plans to expand their fleets.

Shanghai-based Spring Airlines, operating four planes, ordered 10 A320s at the end of 2006. Tianjin-headquartered Okay Airways, flying three passenger jets and one freighter, plans to expand its fleet to eight jets in 2007. Sichuan-based United Eagle Airlines plans to increase its fleet from 4 to 10 this year. Shanghai-based Juneyao Airlines will go from 3 to 10 this year, Central China's East Star Airlines from 2 to 10 by 2010 and Guizhou-based China Express from 1 to 30 in the next five years.

"An aircraft manufacturer should not neglect this market," says Liu Weimin, Director of the Aviation Laws Research Center at the Civil Aviation Management Institute of China.

Currently, four out of the six private carriers in China fly Airbus A320 family aircraft.

"Our strategy is to establish stable relationships with all customers, from the biggest to the smallest, from major airlines to regional airlines and start-ups," says Barron.

A major reason for Airbus' success with China's private airlines, he says, is its close partnership with international leasing companies such as GECAS (GE Commercial Aviation Services) and ILFC (International Lease Finance Corp). The four Chinese start-up airlines began business by leasing Airbus aircraft.

About one-third of Airbus A320 family aircraft are sold to international leasing companies, Barron says. The single-aisle A320 family jets have received 5,016 orders.

"One problem we have now is that we have sold so many aircraft that it is difficult to respond to short-term needs; the production positions are basically sold out till 2010," says Barron. "Start-up companies always want to start operating as soon as they get their certificates. It is difficult for manufacturers to supply new aircraft directly on sales."

Airbus' long-term partnerships with leasing companies have paid off, he adds, since leasing companies can have aircraft available much sooner. (Barron specialized in aircraft financing at Airbus for more than 10 years.)

Chinese Leasing Boom

About 40 percent of the 900-plus aircraft in service in China are leased airplanes. Leasing is a popular and economical way for airlines to expand their fleet

quicker and with less money. International leasing companies control almost 90 percent of China's aircraft leasing market.

But Chinese financial institutions and companies are beginning to show increasing interest in the aircraft leasing business. A good example is the Bank of China's takeover of Singapore Aircraft Leasing Enterprise Private Ltd (SALE) in December 2006, the first major acquisition by a state-owned Chinese bank.

The Bank of China paid $965 million in cash to acquire 100 percent of SALE, the leading Asia-based aircraft leasing company. SALE has been profitable every year since its establishment in 1993. The bank says the acquisition is part of its strategy to diversify into non-interest income.

The China Aviation Industry Corp I (AVIC I) established an aircraft leasing company at the beginning of 2007. AVIC I, China's leading airplane manufacturer, holds a controlling stake in the new company, with the rest of the stakes shared by 13 domestic aviation enterprises and scientific research institutes.

The China Aviation Supplies Import & Export Group Corporation (CASGC), which handles most of China's commercial aircraft imports, set up a leasing joint venture in October 2006, with Netherlands-based AerCap and France's Calyon

Airfinance. The venture comprises Dragon Aviation Leasing Co Ltd, based in Beijing, and AerDragon Aviation Partners, based in Shannon, Ireland.

"This is clearly an indication of the trend that Chinese institutions are looking to aircraft leasing as a future source of business development for them," says Barron.

"This new trend would probably become significant in the next 10 years, so we want to work closely with these new developments and hope to do business with them."

China Strategy Unchanged

During the second half of 2006, Barron had to fly back to Airbus headquarters in Toulouse more frequently, to update top management with the latest on China's development. The A380 delivery delays spurred a series of management shake-ups, with three chief executives resigning in four months.

"Despite the management changes in Toulouse, there is absolutely no change in our strategies in China," says Barron. "We even have a stronger desire to continue our strategies."

Besides maintaining stable relationships with Chinese airlines, having a close industrial partnership with the Chinese aviation industry is another key component of Airbus' strategies in China, he affirms.

"It is about building for the future, with the Chinese industry being more and more integrated into our industrial organization, and not just supplying parts. It is based on win-win principles."

Airbus' industrial partnership with China ranges from subcontracting basic parts of aircraft to a joint venture engineering center that will design five percent of the airframe of the A350 to the final assembly of A320s in Tianjin.

The Tianjin plant will start to assemble A320s in early 2009. The factory is Airbus' first final assembly line outside of Europe.

"The Tianjin plant is the logical next step. But it won't be the last," says Barron.

Barron's Guide to Airbus' China Plan

Airbus sold its first plane to China in 1985, while Boeing had a 13-year head start. But the European company has steadily ramped up its fleet in China, with its market share increasing from seven percent in 1995 to 35 percent at the end of 2006. A close industrial partnership with the Chinese aviation industry is a key part of Airbus' strategy in China. The final assembly of Airbus A320 in Tianjin is "the logical next step" for Airbus' development in China, the company says. Laurence Barron, President of Airbus China, tells the reporter more about the project in this exclusive interview.

Q: How did you convince your headquarters and colleagues in Europe about the importance of the Chinese project at a time when Airbus is exercising the Power 8 Plan, cutting costs and workforce?

A: It's important to understand that with Power 8, we are not reducing our production capacity. The job cuts in Europe are not in the area of production. We are increasing our production right now. We produce 32 A320s a month and have committed to 36 a month. We are studying (the possibility of producing) 38 to even 40 a month. So we can't reduce the number of people working in the factories producing aircraft. The Tianjin project will be about production. We are not taking away jobs from Europe and transferring them to China. Production demand is growing bigger and the project will help us meet some of that demand.

Q: The Tianjin factory will be able to assemble four aircraft a month by 2011. Will all the aircraft assembled there be delivered to Chinese airlines?

A: Four aircraft a month means up to 50 aircraft will be produced every year. But based on existing orders, we expect to deliver 80 to 90 A320 family aircraft per year to our Chinese customers from 2009 onwards. So the final assembly line in Tianjin will only meet part of the local demand.

Q: Why was Tianjin chosen as the site for your first assembly line outside Europe?

A: The Chinese government asked us to evaluate four cities. We decided two cities, including Tianjin, were viable with regard to seaport and logistics facilities, airport facilities, airspace for flight tests and so on. The Chinese government then selected Tianjin from the two sites we pre-selected. The Tianjin plant will be a copy of the assembly line in Hamburg.

Q: How many employees does the Tianjin factory need? How many of them will be Chinese? How is the recruitment process coming along?

A: So far over 150 Chinese employees have been recruited, including white- and blue-collar workers. They have been divided into groups to receive language and basic training in China for half a year, and will be sent to the existing final assembly lines in Hamburg and Toulouse to receive on-the-job training and work together with experienced Airbus workers and experts. We expect to employ about 500 people, mainly blue-collar workers. Once we fully train the Chinese employees, we will only have a core team of expatriate specialists here. In the end, over 90 percent of the employees in Tianjin will be Chinese.

Q: China has announced its plan to make large commercial aircraft by 2020. As the world's largest aircraft manufacturer, what do you think of that decision?

A: There's no doubt China can build a large aircraft. The challenge is not to build the aircraft, but to sell it and support it. The question is whether it can be a commercial success. It's a tough and very competitive business.

Q: How can China benefit from this project? Will it help China make its own large aircraft?

A: Final assembly is considered one of the core competences of an aircraft manufacturer. Clearly, this will increase the areas in which the Chinese industry will have access to core competences and the essential skills. But whether the technology will be similar enough and be used in other programs will really depend on the technical decisions made by China in terms of the new large aircraft. It might be assembled in a totally different way. It's more a question of overall production efficiency and processes, rather than a specific technology. This project should have significant positive spin-offs for the aviation industry because it will encourage other industry suppliers to make their presence bigger in China.

By Lu Haoting
(2007-03, 2007-05)

Super Link

1. Airbus Inks Tianjin Plant Deal

Airbus plans to assemble about 300 A320 aircraft in Tianjin by the beginning of 2016, a senior company official said yesterday.

Marc Bertiaux, Airbus Vice-President for Cooperation and Partnership with China, told the reporter in an exclusive interview that if the Tianjin factory met that target, Airbus would consider further cooperation with the northern port city.

Airbus and a Chinese consortium that includes China's two leading aviation manufacturers yesterday signed a joint venture contract to operate the Tianjin factory, which will start assembling the A320 family jet next summer.

The joint venture is 51 percent controlled by Airbus. The remaining shares are split between Tianjin Free Trade Zone Investment, representing the Tianjin government, which holds a 60 percent stake, and the China Aviation Industry Corp I (AVIC I) and China Aviation Industry Corp II (AVIC II), each of which holds 20 percent.

Neither side of the joint venture released the investment volume.

Bertiaux said both sides had achieved "a good result by optimizing the costs." Profit would be shared according to the respective shareholdings, he added. The Tianjin plant is expected to deliver the first A320 in the first half of 2009 and assemble four jets per month by 2011.

The factory will likely be used to fill Airbus' two major Chinese orders it clinched over the past two years, said Li Lei, an aviation analyst with CITIC China Securities.

Airbus signed two orders with China in December 2005 and October 2006 for a total of 300 A320s.

Analysts said the Tianjin assembly line will not be initially profitable due to the relatively high costs and low profit margins of aircraft assembly. Bertiaux said the cost to assemble aircraft in Tianjin would be "slightly higher than that in Europe".

"The local labor costs will be lower, but other costs are much higher," he said.

High cost factors include transporting the aircraft sections from Europe, hiring expatriate experts, and the "learning curve" that the Chinese workers and engineers will face.

Li said China was not looking for profits from the venture, but to improve its aircraft manufacturing capabilities.

The joint venture's general manager would come from Airbus France, and the Chinese consortium would nominate a deputy general manager, Bertiaux added.

"The operation and quality management of the factory, which requires our know-how, will be in hands of Airbus," he said. "Anything related to human resources, support and services will be arranged by our Chinese partners."

AVIC I and AVIC II will deploy up to 80 people to serve the joint venture for five years.

"They have promised that they will not send people we can easily find in Tianjin," said Bertiaux, adding that the factory will hire about 500 employees.

China has expressed a strong ambition to establish its own commercial aircraft industry; AVIC I and AVIC II have been the two pillars of the Chinese aviation manufacturing industry.

By Lu Haoting
(2007-06-29)

2. Airbus Comes to Tianjin

Construction for Airbus' first aircraft assembly plant outside Europe kicked off in Tianjin yesterday.

The factory, which will start assembling the popular A320 family jet next summer, will be operated by a joint venture to be launched next month. It will be 51 percent controlled by Airbus. A consortium of Chinese enterprises, including the China AVIC I and AVIC II, will hold the remaining shares.

The plant is expected to deliver the first A320 in the first half of 2009 and assemble four jets per month in 2011.

"I believe this project will not only enhance the further development of the aviation industries of China and the European Union, but also help promote Sino-EU economic and trade cooperation," said State Councilor Tang Jiaxuan at the groundbreaking ceremony. "It provides a win-win result and represents a new achievement in the China-EU strategic partnership."

The project, occupying about 600,000 square meters of land, includes assembly workshops, a paint shop and outdoor facilities. An aircraft delivery center wholly owned by Airbus will also be constructed. The main body of the factory will be completed by the end of this year.

"The new top management of Airbus fully backs this very important development of our presence in this country," said Fabrice Bregier, Airbus Chief Operating Officer (COO). "We are determined to do everything in our power to ensure the aircraft assembled in Tianjin will be delivered on time and to the same quality standards as those delivered in Toulouse, France, and Hamburg, Germany."

Bregier became Airbus COO in November 2006, shortly after the appointment of new Airbus President and CEO Louis Gallois.

The Tianjin project is a strategic part of Airbus' plans to ramp up production of A320s from 32 jets per month to 36 by the end of 2008 to meet the strong demand for the aircraft. The single-aisle A320 family aircraft is the company's most successful model. It has received more than 5,000 orders and has a backlog of over 2,000 jets. China has more than 370 A320 family jets on order and now operates over 270, accounting for more than 80 percent of Airbus' total fleet in the country.

Airbus declined to specify the total investment in the project. It was reported earlier that it would cost 8 billion to 10 billion yuan.

The factory, located in the Tianjin Binhai New Area, is 30 km from the Tianjin Port and 13 km southeast of the northern coast city's downtown.

By Lu Haoting
(2007-05-16)

Alcoa Looks to Greener Growth in Aluminum

An Interview with Chen Jinya,
President for the Asia-Pacific Region of Alcoa

Today China's demand for aluminum is soaring, making for a potentially enormous market for global aluminum giant Alcoa. As the government attaches mounting importance to energy efficiency and emission reduction, Alcoa is offering advice on how to save energy and protect the environment, while at the same time expanding production to meet demand. Chen Jinya, newly appointed President for the Asia-Pacific Region of Alcoa, shares with the reporter some of the company's commitments to and strategies in China.

Q: It is said that Alcoa is looking for expansion opportunities both upstream and downstream in the aluminum industry. Does this still hold true, especially as the government is sparing no effort to save energy and control emissions?

A: Alcoa views and treats China as a high priority because the country represents a major growth opportunity for all major aluminum companies. Alcoa came to China in 1993 and has since invested over $700 million. It is Alcoa's commitment to the Chinese aluminum industry to bring in new technologies, energy saving practices and environmental standards.

As a strong indication of Alcoa's commitment, the company has continued to expand investment in its largest facility in China, our Bohai operation. Some new products will be on stream from the Bohai facility by the middle of next year (2008). Specific products include lithographic sheets, can body stock and sheets for use in the commercial transportation industry.

Q: We have learned that Alcoa was looking for merger and acquisition (M & A) opportunities in China. What is your top priority right now concerning potential M & As?

A: We will keep our doors open for any growth option in China, including potential M & As. But we would rather keep tight-lipped on possible M & As right now.

Alcoa is committed to working in China for the long term, and will do everything necessary to improve and enhance its strategic vision and productivity in the market. As a prudent business, Alcoa's priority is also improvement of its current business and productivity. The global aluminum industry is projected to double in the next 14 years. By the year 2020, China will consume as much aluminum as the rest of the world does today. With that foundation of opportunity, it is up to Alcoa to explore options so we can grow in order to support and foster this growth.

Q: What are your views on the development of China's aluminum industry?

A: China's aluminum industry is growing with the growth of its economy. If one looks at aluminum consumption per capita, it is obvious that aluminum use is very closely related to the stages of economic growth. For example, as of today, the aluminum consumption per capita in the US and Japan is between 28 to 30 kg. But in China, aluminum consumption is in its developing stage, with a figure of 6.67 kg per capita, although this is a big jump from a much lower number 10 years ago. China's growth needs aluminum, and the aluminum industry can do more to grow further.

China's aluminum industry is growing at a rate of 24 percent annually. From January to May, 2007, aluminum production increased by 36 percent, reaching 4.68 million tons, while alumina production increased to 7.62 million tons, up by 55 percent. The aluminum industry is full of potential and Alcoa will continue to be part of the growth and development.

Q: What is the most crucial factor in the aluminum sector in making sustainable and environmentally-friendly development possible? Is it technology, investment or something else?

A: The most crucial factor in the industry that would make sustainable growth and environmentally-friendly development feasible is a paradigm shift. We must change our concepts for developing the aluminum industry. China needs a great amount of aluminum supplied and the aluminum industry must grow with lower emissions and energy consumption. At Alcoa, sustainability is a core value. The environment and energy will first be considered whenever a project is built or a plant is operated.

It should also be pointed out that aluminum has a unique selling position versus all the other materials and industries in this regard — the aluminum industry is projected to be greenhouse gas (GHG) neutral by the year 2020, simply through the projected growth of aluminum used in transportation industries (such as autos, airplanes, trucking, rail and marine craft). That means the aluminum used in transportation vehicles results in lower GHG emissions, which offset the GHG created when the material is produced. Aluminum is the only industry anywhere in the world that can make this claim, which certainly bodes well for the material as concerns about climate change grow each day.

Q: How does Alcoa manage to save energy and protect the environment while expanding production to meeting soaring demand?

A: These are not two contradictory processes. Growth and expansion must be based on energy saving and emission control. Again, there must be a paradigm shift. It is Alcoa's value that the environment comes first if there is any conflict between production, profit and environment protection. Alcoa has reduced GHG by 26 percent after 1990, several years ahead of our goal, while it has increased production. It can be done.

Q: How do you see China's long-term target to trim per-unit-GDP energy consumption and cut pollutant emissions?

A: We believe the efforts made by the Chinese government on environmental protection and energy saving make good sense. Any reduction in emissions and efforts to save energy must be recognized.

By Wang Yu
(2007-07-31)

Full Steam Ahead

An Interview with Bob Larson, President of Alcoa China Rolled Products

Alcoa, the global aluminium giant, is busy seeking parallel development opportunities across both the up- and down-stream of the aluminium industry, while fueling the construction and expansion of existing facilities in China. This development involves mergers with and acquisitions (M & As) of local counterparts.

"In addition to our existing projects in China, we are eyeing additional opportunities in the primary aluminium segment of the industry. Of course, we will not let chances slip in the downstream," says Bob Larson, President of Alcoa China Rolled Products. The executive reveals Alcoa will "give careful thought to more M & As" in the fledgling Chinese market, but he is tight lipped on details concerning future programs. However, he does make it clear that Alcoa will not drag its feet if appropriate business opportunities emerge.

"While we are focused on boosting the capacity of our current facilities, we will continue to look for other development options," explains Larson. "We will not wait till our current projects are completed. It will be a parallel approach."

Currently, the construction and capacity expansion of Alcoa's Bohai and Kunshan joint venture facilities are in full swing. The Bohai venture, located in Qinhuangdao, currently produces aluminium foil. The facility is scheduled to expand into sheet products in mid-2008.

Alcoa will not wait until 2008 to launch new projects, Larson says, because the firm cannot afford to waste precious time.

Alcoa expects to witness double-digit business growth for many of its aluminium applications in the Chinese market, although the country's industrial watchdog has issued tightening policies, reining in over-development of certain overheated industrial sectors, including alumina and primary aluminium.

"There currently is a supply-demand imbalance across the alumina and smelting segments of our industry," says Ren Binyan, Vice President of China, Alcoa Asia Pacific. "As the country's economy drives forward and electricity shortage is relieved, we foresee that the aluminium upstream sector will experience better fundamentals, especially for large and efficient producers."

Giants Win

In the downstream of the aluminium industry, the problem of over supply is a headache for small- and medium-sized aluminium manufacturers, but not for giants.

Within the Chinese aluminium flat-rolled products segment, there are many small and medium-sized manufacturers, who mainly target the domestic market. As global counterparts flood into the market, they will have to face severe competition.

To ensure unified sourcing quality and standards, multinationals scattered in various industrial sectors bring their global suppliers to China. It is also the case with sectors using aluminium as materials, such as the aerospace and automobile sectors.

"Our global position helps us understand the requirements of multinationals moving to China," says Larson, who believes this will give Alcoa an upper hand, competing effectively with rivals who do not have a global footprint.

Asked whether there will be an inevitable trend for consolidation within the downstream sector of the aluminium industry, Larson responds in a diplomatic way: "The marketplace will dictate who succeeds in this type of environment and this dynamic is what spurs such things as consolidation and M & As."

Larson elucidates Alcoa's principles on further expanding business in China, revealing that his company will adopt a prudent approach in conducting more M & As. The golden rule for Alcoa to take control of potential projects is to develop in a profitable way, he says.

"We are not interested in growth for the sake of growth," he states. "We are seeking profitable growth. We believe in a prudent pace that targets segments where we bring in a high degree of product and technology differentiation."

Wen Xianjun, Director of the Aluminium Department of the China Nonferrous Metals Industry Association, says that as a result of the nation's macroeconomic structural adjustment, the upstream of the aluminium industry will not witness astonishing growth as it did several years ago, but will expand and upgrade existing facilities.

"Since its hard for new facilities to be approved, expansions can be obtained by expanding existing ventures," Wen says. "Foreign giant conglomerates may seek more market share by acquiring smaller Chinese counterparts."

However, Wen points out, the golden period for M & As within the upstream sector is over, because unlike the year 2005, both the alumina and electrolytic aluminium business are gradually recovering from the industrial reshuffle. As for the downstream sector, Wen says China lacks quality foreign investors like Alcoa to meet local demand and to enhance the technological capability of the local aluminium industry.

"Alcoa's new facilities, such as the Bohai one, do boast advanced technologies and leading manufacturing capacity," Wen affirms. "Its products, which Chinese players cannot make, will enjoy bright sales prospects."

Past Deals

Alcoa hammered out a deal with China International Trust & Investment Corp (CITIC) late in 2005, setting up the Alcoa Bohai Aluminium Industries Company Ltd to expand from foil to aluminium sheet production in Qinhuangdao, Hebei Province.

Alcoa is injecting more than $200 million in the Bohai facility, which includes a technologically advanced hot rolling mill and related equipment. The company anticipates having the mill commissioned by 2008. With the hot mill on line, the Bohai project will be able to produce high quality aluminium sheet and foil products, such as can body stock, lithographic sheets and commercial transportation products. Total capacity will reach 223,000 metric tons per year to meet market demand and fill the gap for high quality aluminium plates and foil in the Chinese aluminium industry.

The Bohai project is "on schedule and within budget," with all the construction work in full swing, according to Larson.

Larson is also upbeat about the market prospects of the project.

"We are positive about the market potential for the Bohai facility. We believe it will turn out to be a profitable investment," he says.

Alcoa's investment in the Bohai facility lays the foundation for Alcoa's global flat-rolled products growth strategy in China, according to Larson.

"The Bohai venture is part of our global rolling business, which includes similar facilities in Europe, North America and Australia. Alcoa's facilities here are targeted primarily to serve China, as well as certain segments of the broader Asian market," says Larson.

Alcoa's latest investment in China is the Kunshan joint venture, formed near Shanghai in April with the Shanxi Yuncheng Engraving Group of China to produce aluminium brazing sheets. The total investment here is more than $95 million.

The Kunshan venture is part of Alcoa's global flat-rolled products strategy to provide customers with a portfolio of products worldwide supplied by regional manufacturing assets. This investment will give Alcoa the ability to supply up to 50,000 metric tons per year of aluminium brazing sheet primarily to automotive customers serving the Asian market. The company's capability will complement Alcoa's existing brazing sheet production centers in the United States and Hungary.

Alcoa is the world leader in aluminium smelting capacity, and the world's second largest producer of aluminium. Alcoa also leads the world in alumina production and capacity.

By Wang Yu
(2006-10-23)

Super Link

Alcoa Plans to Quadruple Investment

Alcoa Inc, the world's largest aluminium producer, plans to quadruple its investment in China by 2014, aiming to break into the country's upstream smelting and alumina sector.

"With the country's aluminium consumption expected to grow more than 10 percent annually over the next three years, our investment is estimated to quadruple by 2014," the company said in its China sustainability report.

Since it started business in the country in 1993, Alcoa has invested 5.3 billion yuan ($662.5 million) in China (up to the end of 2005).

"We would like to invest, and will look into any area (in both the upstream and downstream sectors of the aluminium industry) that might give good economic returns," Lloyd H Jones, President of Alcoa Asia-Pacific, told the reporter in an interview.

But the total spending indicated in the report is an estimate, Jones added. "It is hard to give a fixed figure concerning future investments; it is a one-by-one thing, all depending on each individual opportunity we have."

The company has also showed interest in China's upstream smelting and alumina sector. Alcoa currently has 15 ventures in China relating to downstream fabrication such as rolled components for cars.

"We would like to invest in one or more smelters here, and also (get into) the alumina business if opportunities present (themselves)," Jones said.

China is the world's biggest aluminium producer, but is short on alumina, a white powder used to produce aluminium.

Alcoa must take a long-term perspective of at least 30 years to enter China's smelting and alumina business, Jones added, citing additional factors such as the ability to get economic returns and minimize environmental and community impact.

He admitted that under the current policy it would be a long and complicated process to get government approval in China.

"But we remain optimistic (about starting the upstream business in China), and we will work our way out," he said. "It will depend on finding the right opportunity and working closely with both the national and provincial governments in China."

"China is a good place to invest in smelting given the availability of energy, relatively cheap construction costs and the growing market," he stated.

Although the Chinese Government was determined to fight overcapacity in many energy-intensive sectors including aluminium production, Jones said, the country aimed to close down small and inefficient plants, and new technology and products would help China improve efficiency and save energy.

Alcoa is expected to establish three ventures in China's downstream sector, which would more than triple its capacity of fabricated products by 2008. These ventures comprise two new plants in Kunshan near Shanghai and Suzhou in East China's Jiangsu Province, and an expansion of its joint venture with CITIC in Qinhuangdao of North China's Hebei Province.

"The three ventures will boost our fabricated goods capacity from the current 80,000 tons (a year) to 340,000 tons (a year)," Jones said.

The company is also looking into opportunities to build greenfield plants and take over existing ones to expand its business in China.

Alcoa's total revenue in China in 2005 was $700 million, compared with global sales of $26 billion.

By Wang Ying
(2006-06-15)

Reactor Rivalry

An Interview with Arnaud de Bourayne,
President of Areva China

Paris-based Areva, one of the world's largest reactor builders, is prepared to transfer its latest nuclear technology to Chinese partners to win a contract for four new Chinese nuclear reactors.

"Areva has put in everything that is designed to satisfy the requirements of the Chinese Government, both the transfer of know-how and the manufacturing process," says Arnaud de Bourayne, President of Areva China.

The French company is betting on the deal to maintain its lead in China's nuclear market, in which Areva and its competitors, particularly US-based Westinghouse Electric Co, are vying for orders worth up to 400 billion yuan ($50 billion) before 2020.

Areva and Westinghouse are now bidding for the contracts of four third-generation nuclear reactors: Two in East China's Zhejiang Province's Sanmen and a pair in Yangjiang of South China's Guangdong Province. The two companies submitted their bids last February (2005) and are still awaiting the result of the $8 billion deal, which was supposed to be announced last October (2005). Winning the bid is considered vital for nuclear power equipment vendors, as the Chinese Government has said it will adopt a unified, standardized design for the third generation nuclear reactors across its nuclear industry. So the winner may easily gain access to the huge nuclear power investment planned in the nation.

The Chinese Government has announced plans to spend 400 billion yuan ($50 billion) to increase nuclear power generation capacity from 8.7 million kilowatts now to 40 million kilowatts in the next 14 years. That massive investment will be used to build more than 30 nuclear plants in the nation by 2020, mostly located along the rapidly industrializing coastal area such as the Guangdong and Shandong provinces.

China currently has only nine operating reactors, using technology from France, Canada, Japan and Russia in its nuclear plants in the Guangdong and Zhejiang provinces.

"China is the largest potential market for the nuclear industry in the coming years," says de Bourayne, adding the market is critical for Areva to obtain one-third of the world's nuclear energy market.

Having established its presence in China in 1986, the French builder has supplied four of China's nine working nuclear plants — more than any other company, including State-owned China National Nuclear Corp.

"There are two main reasons for our current status in China," says de Bourayne. "First, we agreed in the late 1980s to be the supplier for the Chinese nuclear industry, a time when most other companies were reluctant or unable to do so.

"We not only provided reactors for the Chinese nuclear industry but also technology during the years. We also prepared solutions for our partners to local-ize the manufacturing process, which helped the development of China's own nuclear industry."

Areva has transferred its technologies to between 14 and 20 Chinese nuclear power producers so far. Its technology has been adopted in reactors in Ling'ao and Dayawan, both in Guangdong Province, and in the Qinshan phase II units in Zhejiang Province.

China, now the world's second-largest energy user, has started to look for alternatives to oil and coal to meet the surging demand for electricity, in order to sustain its fast economic and industrial growth. With the surge in reactor con-struction, nuclear power will account for only 4 percent of China's electricity output by 2020, compared with 1.6 percentage points now. Yet, it's far below the 17 percent average among countries with nuclear power plants.

Areva is now facing fierce competition from Westinghouse in the bid for the four new nuclear reactors in East China and South China. Westinghouse, whose designs run half the world's nuclear reactors, is now in a head-to-head race with the French builder. During the past two decades, Westinghouse has not won any power plant contract in China, due to the US government's restriction on exports in the area till the end of last century.

Westinghouse is counting on its pressurized water reactor AP1000 to tap into the Chinese market. Westinghouse said its new reactor is much safer than the 1970s-era reactors that are dominant in China and elsewhere. The US company got $5 billion in combined loans from the US Export-Import Bank to help it bid for the four reactors.

Toshiba Corp, Japan's largest maker of nuclear power plant equipment, bought Westinghouse for $5.4 billion this February to bolster its position in the nuclear power industry. The Tokyo-based company is also seeking a shortcut to tap the opportunities in China's nuclear power sector through the deal.

Les Echos, a French business newspaper, reported in March that Areva was put out of the tender after refusing to match Westinghouse's offer for access to the reactor designs. According to *Les Echos*, Westinghouse has proposed selling its plans for $400 million as well as receiving royalties of $15 million per year for each reactor. That figure is much smaller than the 8-billion-euro figure that Areva pitched to build the four reactors.

"We are confident of winning the bid, despite being unable to quantify the possibility of winning," says de Bourayne, noting his company is still in the running for the bid.

According to de Bourayne, the company's third generation reactor, European Pressurized Reactor (EPR), has 1,700 mw of capacity per unit, compared with the 1,000 mw of capacity per unit of the proposed Westinghouse reactor.

"Our product is quite advanced," he says.

Areva won the contract for its EPR reactor in 2003 in Finland, which paid $3.7 billion for a model from Areva's Framatome ANP nuclear-reactor unit, a venture with Germany's Siemens AG. That one is the only third generation reactor being built in the world so far.

"We understand that China want to become self-sufficient in nuclear power as it's a strategic issue," says de Bourayne. "And as in many other countries, the nuclear technology has to be Chinese no matter where it is developed."

By Wang Xu
(2006-07-17)

AREVA   23

Super Link

1. Areva T & D to Double Capacity

France-based Areva's transmission and distribution (T & D) arm has announced its plans to spend 50 million euros ($63 million) in the next three years to double its manufacturing capacity in China.

Areva T & D, one of the world's top three electricity transmission and distribution businesses, which also includes ABB and Siemens, aims to double sales to 500 million euros ($630 million) by 2009, according to Philippe Guillemot, CEO of Areva T & D, who spoke to this reporter in the city of Xiamen, in East China's Fujian Province.

"China is among the world's most competitive markets," Guillemot said. "The country now represents 20 percent of the global market in T & D product sales, totaling 24 billion euros ($30.2 billion). But with the fast growth of the Chinese market, the proportion is expected to further increase to 25 percent within three years."

The company will seek opportunities to increase its production plants in China. Currently it has seven such facilities in Beijing, Shanghai, Xiamen of Fujian Province, and Suzhou of Jiangsu Province.

"The new ventures will include both greenfield ones and existing plants in which Areva expects to buy a stake," said Arnaud de Bourayne, President of Areva (Group) China.

The Areva group set up its T & D division in 2004 by taking over Alstom T & D to diversify its business portfolio, which previously focused on nuclear energy development. Areva T & D announced the official opening of two new factories in Xiamen, which have a combined investment of 10 million euros ($12.6 million). The two plants produce vacuum interrupters and switchgears for the domestic electricity equipment market.

In 2005 the Xiamen vacuum interrupter venture brought in a revenue of 170 million yuan ($21.3 million), which is expected to almost double to 300 million yuan ($37.5 million) this year, according to Sher Hock Guan, a board member of the Xiamen-based firm.

To meet increasing demand, Areva plans to further expand the Xiamen plant's capacity during the second phase of development, Guillemot told a press briefing on Friday, without elaborating further.

Two other new factories for the production of GIS (gas installation sub-stations) and disconnectors (equipment used in electricity grid construction) are also being developed at Suzhou, near Shanghai, Arnaud de Bourayne disclosed.

Another Areva official who did not want to be named told the reporter, without specifying the location, that the company is also planning to build a third factory to produce instrument transformers.

As the nation speeded up its efforts to improve the electricity distribution network, Guillemot said, the company expected to gain more market share by providing products and transferring technology.

By Wang Ying
(2006-06-24)

2. Areva Teams Up with Tsinghua for Research

France-based Areva Transmission & Distribution (T & D) established its first major research center in China on Tuesday at Tsinghua University to spur its aggressive expansion in the domestic market.

One of the world's leading players in power T & D, competing with rivals ABB and Siemens, Areva T & D this year (2005) plans to pump half a million euros ($625,000) into five research projects through its partnership with experts from Tsinghua, the country's leading engineering university.

Phillipe Guillemot, CEO of Areva T & D, said the firm's research projects will cover all aspects of the sector.

The company has already set up research bodies in India and Xi'an in China, but the Tsinghua center is designed to be the most strategically important, Marius Vossoille, Executive Vice-President of Areva T & D, told the reporter.

The research base will be the launch pad for targeted annual domestic sales growth of 25 percent over the next four years.

Areva T & D, which contributed one third of the Areva energy group's revenue in 2004, has vowed to double its sales performance in China to 400 million euros ($500 million) by 2007. The T & D division collected 3.2 billion euros ($4 billion) in global sales, while the group notched up 11.1 billion euros ($13.8 billion) in 2004.

"It (the Tsinghua Research Center) will play a key role in the future T & D strategy of Areva T & D," said Guillemot. "Its research results will help China's modernization and also serve our global market."

Soaring electricity demand in China has attracted a slew of foreign investment in the power transmission and distribution sector.

Areva T & D will advance its research, production and services to secure a strong footing in the domestic market, Guillemot added.

Earlier this year the company opened two factories in Xiamen in Fujian Province to produce interrupters and circuit breakers. It plans to add more manufacturing companies to localize its full range of products, on the basis of its five existing sales offices, seven manufacturing sites and one research center nationwide.

By Wang Ying
(2005-6-22)

Hello, Avon

An Interview with SK Kao,
President of Avon China

Last year (2006) was a landmark year for Avon's operation in China: It acquired the nation's first direct selling license, restructured its massive distribution framework and worked to maintain revenue growth along with its new business mode.

Now the world's largest direct seller of beauty products is ready to take off in the Chinese market.

Avon China recently announced the launch of the second phase of its direct-selling rollout, which will include a series of new direct-selling services and technologies. These developments are part of Avon's new "Hello Tomorrow" global marketing campaign, which is scheduled to launch next month (March 2007).

SK Kao, President of Avon China, says that the launch of the "Hello Tomorrow" campaign in China will enhance product ordering systems through the introduction of "m-commerce", which will allow the company's sales promoters to lodge orders via mobile phone. The company also plans to establish an additional call center to improve nationwide support for sales promoters, service centers and customers. The enhancements are expected to shorten the average product delivery timeline from 72 hours to 48, while supporting the ongoing rollout of new products.

"Delivering products within two days in big cities might sound easy but

it's a challenge to achieve in small rural counties," Kao says. "Sometimes even horses are included."

Avon will also launch new consumer and recruiting advertising campaigns next month (March 2007).

"We will increase advertising investment and targeted marketing campaigns," says Kao, "and all of the new moves reflect Avon's increased commitment to the Chinese market."

So far Avon is still the only company to receive a truly national direct selling license from the Ministry of Commerce. Its major competitor, Amway, has the license in only 24 Chinese provinces and municipalities.

"It was an honor to be awarded the first and only nationwide license," says Kao. "We intend to continue leveraging our first-mover advantage in the marketplace. This year, the firm will introduce a greater range of initiatives to boost business, provide stronger earning opportunities to sales promoters and service centers, and increase excellence in its products and services."

To this end, the firm will launch a new version of its Anew series, placing more focus on whitening and anti-aging properties. It will also promote a "skin management package". "All of the new products can lead the market for two to three years," says Kao.

By the end of 2006, Avon had recruited 351,556 sales promoters and transitioned more than 5,400 of its beauty boutiques into service centers for sales promoters and customers. This expanded presence covered 23 provinces, five autonomous regions and four municipalities.

The company also completed a technology upgrade in 2006. Since this upgrade, 95 percent of product orders have been placed online and filled via a door-to-door product delivery network.

"We are confident in the progress we made in 2006, and our new initiatives this year will keep Avon at the forefront of the official direct-selling industry in China," says Kao .

China is a key growth engine for Avon. The market underwent a sales growth of 9 percent to $49.3 million in the third quarter of 2006. In the 2005 fiscal year, which ended in March, 2006, the company's revenues in China were $207 million.

Compared with its global sales of $8.15 billion in 2005, China is still a small market for the beauty product provider. However, the firm has high hopes for the Chinese market. At the end of 2005, the firm launched a new global operating structure, which increased the number of geographic business units from four to six. China became a stand-alone operating unit, as did North America, Latin America, Western Europe, the Middle East, Africa, Central and Eastern Europe, and the Asia Pacific region.

Andrea Jung, Shanghai's Avon Chairman and Chief Executive Officer, says: "As phase two of our direct selling rollout in China begins, we are very excited that we will be creating a new future for our customers, sales promoters and beauty boutique owners in the country."

Avon recently announced that it has become the official sponsor of the China National Diving Team through a two-year agreement which makes Avon the team's designate and exclusive provider of cosmetics and health food. As the official sponsor, Avon will feature the whole China National Diving Team in advertising and marketing initiatives until 2008.

AVON

Its rival Amway announced on the same day that it signed a worldwide endorsement contract with Olympic hurdler champion Liu Xiang.

As the world's largest direct seller, Avon markets to women in more than 100 countries through more than five million independent Avon sales representatives. Its product line includes beauty products, fashion jewelry and apparel.

By Jiang Jingjing
(2007-02-12)

Super Link

1. Avon Wins First Direct Sales Licence

US cosmetics giant Avon Products Inc was awarded China's first licence for direct sales, after the country lifted a seven-year ban on the business on December 1, 2005.

On February 22, 2006, the Ministry of Commerce approved Avon's application on direct selling, allowing the company to hire independent promoters to sell products directly to consumers, according to the website of the department of foreign investment administration of the Ministry of Commerce.

The ministry also granted certificates to seven of Avon's employees, allowing them to train door-to-door vendors for the company.

Information on the Ministry of Commerce's website shows that Avon is the only company approved for the direct selling business so far. Other foreign direct sellers are still preparing their applications. US-based Nu Skin Enterprises, for instance, sent its application to the Ministry of Commerce around two weeks ago and is waiting for approval, a company official told the reporter.

In the meantime, Amway, a US company selling cosmetics and nutrition products, is still under the county-level application process. "We need to get approval from the commercial offices of most of China's 2,300 counties as the first step," said a company official, declining to be named.

The company will then hand in materials to the provincial governments, and finally to the Ministry of Commerce. "It will take time," said the official. "We will do it step by step, and we are confident we will get the licence within the year."

China is allowing foreign-funded companies like Amway — which has been adopting a business model of selling goods through retail outlets and "non-employee" sales representatives since 1998 — to continue their current practice till December 1, 2006.

Because of this, some companies are not rushing to get licences. These foreign companies are experiencing troubled times, as they adjust their business practices according to the new regulations on direct selling issued last September (2005). Companies like Avon, Amway and Nu Skin all saw business decline in China in 2005. Avon said its revenue in China fell 22 percent in the fourth quarter as its Beauty Boutique owners placed smaller orders in anticipation of direct selling return in the country.

Avon's business in China has kept falling since it started a pilot direct selling scheme in April 2005. The company posted a year-on-year 19 percent decline in revenue for the second quarter and a 16 percent decrease for the third quarter. Nu Skin said in its fiscal report that revenue in Greater China was $55.5 million for the fourth quarter of 2005, compared to $62.8 million for the same period in 2004. Its number of active distributors was down 17 percent in 2005, and executive distributors decreased 19 percent compared to the prior year, primarily as a result of declines in the mainland.

"It is unavoidable during the business restructuring period," said the Amway official, who did not reveal the company's performance details.

However, these companies are confident they will weather troubled times and are hopeful for the Chinese market prospects.

"We expect sales in China will grow at least 10 percent this year," said Nu Skin.

In addition to foreign companies, domestic firms like Tiens, a Tianjin-based health care products seller, are also preparing for the licence applications.

It is uncertain how many licences the Ministry of Commerce will issue this year.

By Zhang Lu
(2006-02-28)

2. Makeover

The doorbell rings. You open the door to find a person's arms loaded down with brochures, as he explains beauty aids and greets you with the exuberance of someone eager to make a sale.

"Avon calling," says the face of one of the world's best-known cosmetics companies. "Would you like to see our products?" The sales rep reaches for the company's catalogue.

This could soon be a common scene in parts of China, as the central government has approved a direct-selling pilot programme. The move comes several years after the government banned this sales mode to clamp down on "pyramid-selling" schemes.

Avon will be the only company participating in the programme. The initiative will be limited to Beijing, Tianjin and Guangdong Province.

Although Avon, arguably the world's best-known direct-seller, plans to adopt direct-selling as part of its distribution system in China, this does not mean the company intends to abandon its thousands of boutiques across the country.

"They (boutiques) are Avon's babies. How could Avon let them disappear?" asks Smith Chen, Avon China's Chief Operating Officer. "I can promise all of Avon's boutique owners we will definitely keep the business mode in China."

Chen's comments are in response to widespread rumors that Avon will gradually give up its boutiques. In April China's Ministry of Commerce announced that direct-selling would resume on a trial basis in the country. The move took effect that month.

China banned direct-selling in 1998.

"Avon will have three modes of distribution in China: counters, boutiques and sales promoters," says Chen.

In 2004, Avon China's sales volume was $220 million, of which 70 percent was earned by the company's boutiques. Revenues from boutiques will remain Avon's main income source for the next several years, Chen predicts.

"After five years, the boutiques may not be our primary moneymakers, but they will still be a very important platform for direct-selling," states Chen.

He adds that the boutiques will continue to play a major, and complementary, role to counters and sales promoters.

"The objective is to improve the earning potential of every Avon entrepreneur, regardless of the sales channel they choose," he continues. "Our distribution network, which consists of more than 6,300 boutiques and 1,700 counters at shopping centers and supermarkets, is a precious source of wealth for the company. It ensures rapid delivery of all products to every corner of the country."

Chen says proudly that Avon is one of three entities in China that has such a highly developed distribution network. The other two are China's post office and US-based Eastman Kodak.

While Avon vows not to close its outlets, experts suggest the company will slow the development of new boutiques.

"Avon has the advantage of direct-selling, and once that door re-opens in China, the firm will devote its attention to tapping the potential of direct-selling," says Sun Xuanzhong, a professor with the College of Commerce affiliated with the China University of Political Science and Law.

"In some cities, Avon may reduce the number of boutiques," he says, "but the company will never eliminate all of its boutiques in China. The existence of boutiques will help customers trust Avon's sales promoters. The market disorder that resulted from 'pyramid selling' has affected customers' trust in the direct-selling mode."

Avon plans to launch an image-transformation project for its beauty boutiques in Beijing, Shanghai, Guangzhou and many other key cities. The makeover will begin this month. Chen expects that Avon will upgrade the outlook of its 6,300 boutiques in China within three years.

"The move will not only improve the images of our boutiques in consumers' minds and strengthen their sense of brand loyalty, but will also reflect Avon's promise to ensure the steady development of such outlets," says Chen.

That image makeover, he adds, will create the fourth generation of Avon's boutiques since the government banned direct-selling.

China decided in the late 1990s to prohibit direct-selling because authorities were having a hard time distinguishing between legitimate direct-selling companies and illegal "pyramid-selling" schemes, which resulted in widespread economic losses and social disorder. Avon was one of 10 foreign-funded direct-sellers allowed to continue operating in China. But it was required to change its sales mode, and to focus on retail outlets and sales representatives.

"Since we shifted our focus to retailing we have cultivated an experienced and loyal sales team," says Chen. "With the fierce market competition and customers' increasing demands, Avon's sales group in China will play a more significant role in promoting the company's image."

A generation of cosmetics stores generally has a lifespan of two years, especially in such fierce market competition, he adds, and Avon must continually upgrade its shops to survive in the market. Almost all of the world's famous brands have entered China and are competing for customers.

"Making a good first impression, through our shops and products, is crucial. That's why we decided to carry out the makeover," says Chen.

Under the plan, Avon's boutiques will provide beauty treatment, including facial massages, nail polishing and various spa-related services. Avon's boutiques previously offered free after-sales services, such as facial massages. But Chen observes that the new services will be of a higher standard.

For example, each shop will have two professional, certified masseuses on staff. Avon's outlets will also have relevant licences. As part of the makeover, Avon's boutique owners will be required to spend tens of thousands of yuan on redecoration. Chen acknowledges the boutiques' owners may be initially reluctant to join the programme, but he says he is confident they will realize the new image will bring in more business.

"We have conducted a survey that indicates new shops attract more customers and make customers stay longer, compared with the older stores," he affirms. "We need to guarantee the quality of each boutique."

As for the future stores, the threshold will be much higher than before. Avon's franchise fee will double from the existing 50,000 yuan ($6,039). The new boutiques will provide more relaxing and customized services. For example, customers will be able to receive one-on-one consultations with beauticians, who will provide customized services and/or treatments, Chen says.

Luo Xielong, President of the China Beauty and Cosmetic Chamber, an industry association, says a growing number of cosmetics companies are expanding their services to include beauty treatments.

"Customers who shop in boutiques and at counters tend to be from the lower end of the market, while those who receive services from salons are from the upper end of the market," says Luo. "China's beauty salon industry is worth about 220 billion yuan ($26.57 billion) each year. Leading brands, such as L'Oreal, P&G, Shiseido and Kanebo, are offering beauty treatments."

The Promoters

It has been more than a month since Avon unveiled its plans for the direct-selling pilot programme.

Chen says only three people in Beijing have received Avon's sales promoter permits to date. "That is within our expectations," says Chen. "The first person to receive a direct-selling permit told me it is such a complicated procedure to become a direct-seller. Before 1998, applicants only needed to provide an identity card but now they need to not only show educational certificates, but also complete various training and tests."

Avon currently pays its sales promoters a 25 percent commission, compared with 30 percent paid to its boutiques.

Chen admits that sales promoters may try to make their purchases through the boutiques to increase their profits, and that the company has put much effort into preventing such fraud.

A reputation for quality will be crucial, as the sales promoters will not have products for customers to test, Chen says.

"They will only have a brochure with pictures and text. That's why we make a trial of the high-end products for direct-sellers."

By Jiang Jingjing
(2005-05-30)

Seller's Block

An Interview with Bryan D. Ellis,
President of DirectGroup China

In the summer of 2004, Bryan D. Ellis's meeting with his boss in New York had a surprise ending.

"You're being promoted," his boss said, "but you must move all the way across the world to take the job."

Ellis, who had worked for Bertelsmann in the United States for six years, was promoted to General Manager of the Bertelsmann China Book Club in August 2004, and President of DirectGroup China in February 2006.

"Just before that, my wife and I had bought a house and two cars, and also had a baby boy," recalls Ellis. "We had planned a stable life in New York but then things changed."

In 1997, when the Bertelsmann Book Club was launched, the business model was an immediate hit. The clubs became popular with students from schools and universities. Currently, the Bertelsmann Book Club, through a multi-channel sale system composed of a catalog, website (www.bol.com.cn) and nationwide store chain, is playing an active role in both the offline and online retailing market for books and audiovisual products. In 1999, the website of BOL-China was set up, providing readers an online channel to buy books.

But Bertelsmann has to crack a lot of problems before it can achieve success in the local book market: rules and regulations, fierce competition from online retailers like Dangdang and Joyo, younger target readers and lower price and profit margins.

Ellis says that the biggest value he has created for Bertelsmann DirectGroup China in the past two years is providing a new sense of direction for the company to grow.

"When I first came to China, the company had a strong foundation," he says. "Questions revolved around how we could grow strategically in the next five years, how to expand the number of stores, how to increase online sales, how to expand target customer groups and how to leverage joint ventures."

Ellis jokes that he has had successes and failures, but has always been able to manage, thanks to his two secret weapons: his local management team, and his wife.

His wife was born in China and lived in the country for 11 years before she

left for New York. She also has a strong business background as an investment banker at Morgan Stanley, New York.

"My boss is lucky," says Ellis. "He hired me and got my wife for free."

JV Strategy

The history of Bertelsmann AG in China dates back to 1993, when former German Chancellor Helmut Kohl made a historic trip to the country. Representatives of Bertelsmann began to discuss with the relevant authorities in Shanghai the possibilities of co-operation in the media industry. In 1995, China's largest joint venture (JV) book club between Bertelsmann and China Science and Technology Book Company was set up.

For Bertelsmann DirectGroup China, its two JVs in 2003 and 2005 have been the most significant for the company's expansion into China's book retailing and distribution markets, Ellis says.

In May 2003, the Chinese Government announced that foreign companies could enter China's book retailing market as part of the latter's World Trade Organization (WTO) commitments. After that, Bertelsmann set up a JV with the 21st Century Book Chain Company by buying 40 percent of its shares. Through the JV, the 21st Century Book Chain Company could avail of Bertelsmann's consulting services, in marketing and sales for example, and Bertelsmann members could buy books shown in catalogues in chain stores.

By the end of July 2006, the chain stores available to Bertelsmann members around China were 38; that number is expected to increase to 58 in one year.

The partnership also helps Bertelsmann gain another key advantage in fending off competition from online book retailers like dangdang.com and joyo.com.

"We offer the most purchasing channels to customers," says Ellis. "We are the only company that can provide as many channels as possible including catalogues, Internet, short messages, hotline, fax and chain stores. We also offer many payment channels like credit card, debt card, cash on delivery and pre-payment."

But some still have difficulty with the more advanced systems.

"It's more convenient and much cheaper to buy books from bookstores," says Liu Jiaxing, a 19 year-old sophomore student from Beijing Youth Politics

College. "Many of my classmates joined the club when they were in middle school, but it always took them days to get the books they wanted and they had to pay postal or delivery fees."

Liu didn't join the club membership until 2005 when Bertelsmann opened a bookstore in Wangjing District, which is close to her college. Prior to that, she always ordered books from the Dangdang and Joyo websites. "They are efficient in delivery. If I order books in the morning, I can get them in the afternoon," she says.

The chain stores should be good news for Bertelsmann members in secondary cities, where people usually have to wait for a longer time and spend more to get the books they want.

"Among the new 20 stores, most will be in secondary cities like Hangzhou, Nanjing, Xi'an, Wuhan, Ningbo and Qingdao," says Ellis.

The secondary city strategy also comes from Bertelsmann's unsatisfactory business in major cities like Beijing. Before October 2005, there were 16 stores in Beijing, but since then 12 stores have closed down, and now only four exist in the capital. Insiders believe higher book prices are the major reason for this.

"Actually we did a trial in Beijing last year to test the result of opening many stores without a strong member file in a city," says Ellis. "The conclusion from the worthwhile trial again proved that our business model — including the store as one of the three key channels — should rely on members."

He explained that DirectGroup China practically doesn't compete, price-wise, with Dangdang and Joyo. "Other competitors rely on low prices, while we want to give premium services and more value to our members with more exclusive titles which are sold in the CLUB prior to the market."

Pricing is a weapon for business, but compared with European nations, prices and profit margins are lower in China. In Germany and France, the profit margin is 25 percent higher than in China, and the price of a book much greater. In China, the average price of a book is usually 1.6 euros ($1.9), but is 16 euros ($19) in the two European nations.

Another significant JV for the company was the one with Liaoning Publishing Group (LPG), a major publishing group in China. As part of its WTO commitments, China opened up the book wholesaling market in December 2004. In May 2005, Liaoning Bertelsmann Book Distribution Co was set up with a registered capital of 30 million yuan ($3.8 million), 51 percent of which was contributed by LPG and 49 percent by Bertelsmann DirectGroup. Liaoning Bertelsmann Book Distribution Co was granted a wholesaling license to distribute books in China.

Thanks to this venture, LPG entered the international market by gaining access to international distribution networks and the resources of Bertelsmann.

According to Ellis, Bertelsmann DirectGroup China was able to "introduce more excellent Western content and distribute them to China's Bertelsmann book clubs and readers through LPG's local networks".

New Markets

Bertelsmann DirectGroup China's core business is expected to grow by double digits in the next few years, Ellis says. At present, Bertelsmann has 1.5 million members in China.

"It is a stable number, and we expect to maintain the number at the moment to ensure business stability," he adds.

In the West, Bertelsmann's target members are women aged between 35 and 55, who have two kids, working husbands, and long for romance and excitement. In China, the target customers are different. Members are usually students from schools and universities, aged from 15 to 25.

"The problem now is to have more members joining," says a salesman at a store in the Wangjing District, on condition of anonymity.

From 2004, DirectGroup began to launch beauty mom clubs and issue catalogues six times a year. Now they are trying to introduce English language books aimed at mature Chinese readers and expatriates.

"We have been trying to win the hearts of those above 25," says Ellis, "and we will continue to do that."

By Ding Qingfen
(2006-10-16)

Star Platers

An Interview with Tim Bowen,
COO of Sony BMG

To a record label, its musicians are everything. It's no different for Sony BMG Music Entertainment, the world's second-largest record company.

"A record company is somewhat like a football club," says Tim Bowen, Chief Operating Officer (COO) of Sony BMG, during a recent trip to Beijing. "With a team of good players and a professional coach, a football club can lead the league. And with a group of excellent artists and an experienced executive, a record company can rank at the top of the list."

After taking up his post in March, the executive has been devoted to reorganizing the company, and has had, he says, a tough time.

"I have been trying to create a new type of company, a company which is leaner, smaller, and more artist-focused," he says.

The music behemoth has a history of big names including the likes of Elvis Presley, Celine Dion, Mariah Carey, and Beyonce. The reorganization comes at a time when the growth of the digital and online music business has been incredibly fast, recently dwarfing CD sales worldwide.

According to the International Federation of the Phonographic Industry, the digital music market was worth $330 million in 2004. That figure increased to $660 million in 2005, a 100 percent increase. Moreover, sales generated worldwide from the music sector decreased by two percent during the same period.

In the United States, whose music market accounts for 81 percent of the global market, sales of albums fell by 20 percent from 2001 to 2006. What's more, the digital music is just gaining steam. By 2008, its market size is expected to be $3.75 billion. Under such pressure, record companies are shifting their business to the digital sector. Sony BMG is no exception.

"For a long time, everyone has been blaming us for not investing in technology. We want to, but the procedures are complicated," says Bowen.

He says the company started investing in the digital music sector more than seven years ago. "The digital job is being done," he states. "Everybody is aware they don't have enough new or hit artists. This is a problem for Sony BMG as well."

Making trashy records and ignoring the consumers' concerns is no longer the way to make money, Bowen says. Consumers nowadays have more discerning tastes in music. Thanks to technology, they are in charge of the record industry — the opposite of the landscape 10 years ago, he says.

The measure of an artist is how many albums he releases, but how much money he earns.

"The transformation makes getting the best artists a top challenge," says Bowen. "But it's exciting for the industry as well."

The digital revolution has provided many ways for companies to sell music to consumers: mobile phones, the Internet, video and radio. These are also avenues through which companies can promote their business.

"The digital platform is a way to interact with consumers much more closely," says Swee Wong, Managing Director with Sony BMG Music Entertainment Inc.

"The digital business is huge," says Bowen.

At Sony BMG, 10 percent of its global sales come from the sector, and that figure will keep increasing. South Korea ranks first in the world for sales coming from mobile music and Internet download businesses, with 55 percent of the music market. In the United States and the United Kingdom, the figure ranges from 25 to 30 percent.

"The business can be profitable if you get hit artists," says Bowen.

The More, the Better

Despite the fact that South Korea is the second largest market for Sony

BMG in sales, the Asia-Pacific region is a small contributor to the company's business, and China much smaller.

"China needs our continuous efforts and that of all record companies," says Bowen.

China's ballooning digital music market particularly deserves the company's efforts, he says. According to a report by the research company InStat, China's digital music market will make up one third of the entire market by the end of 2006, and will reach $62 million by 2007.

"China is a big opportunity thanks to the digital music market," says Bowen.

China's digital music market, despite the existence of piracy, accounts for 30 percent of Sony BMG's business here, says Wong.

"It will grow a lot annually," he says, declining to give more details.

Wong was appointed MD of Sony BMG China last August (2005) after having served in the BMG Music Group Asia-Pacific for seven years. He is optimistic about future sales in China.

"There have been many ideas popping up in his mind, and the biggest is to get more Chinese artists and stars," says Miranda Yao, Project Manager with the company.

Wong, for his part, says, "In each country, we have committed ourselves to developing local artists. China is no different. Our focus here is developing Chinese artists, but it will take time. We will do whatever it takes to have a good reservoir of Chinese artists."

Before Wong joined the company, it signed agreements with five popular local artists, including Chen Kun, Liu Yifei, Yu Quan, and Han Xue.

"It's hard to be specific on how many more we will have, but what I can say is we will have 20 to 30 by 2011," says Wong.

For Sony BMG, the criterion for choosing artists seems simple. "We need those with star quality, and it doesn't matter where they are from or how old they are," says Wong.

When asked about the five recent additions to the company's roster, Wong smiles. "They are the right ones. They have the star quality we need."

China Focus

The main purpose of Bowen's recent visit to China was to attend the board meeting and announce the opening of Star Bright (in Beijing) whose task is to explore the digital music sector.

"It is exciting, everyone is very enthusiastic about the business and wants to do business with each other," says Bowen.

Compared with the online music business in China, where they have been defeated by piracy, record companies are attracted to mobile music businesses such as selling ring tones. But even in this sector piracy has been an issue.

A report from InStat shows there are 7,000 online music download service providers in China, but few are legitimate.

"Piracy is obviously a major problem. Although the Chinese Government has taken a lot of steps to crack down on it, relatively speaking, it's still around. It's not easy to promote artists through the Internet," says Wong.

Few, however, can resist the growing, enticing mobile music market here, thanks to China's position as the world's top mobile phone consuming nation. In 2005, China's mobile phone subscribers totaled 393 million, and according to an estimate from the Ministry of Information Industry, the nation will have an additional 48 million mobile phone users by the end of 2006, which pushes the volume up to 440 million.

It's the same story in Japan, which has one of the largest mobile phone user populations in the world. There, the mobile music sector is the dominant profit source for Sony BMG.

About a year ago, Sony BMG started a partnership with China Mobile and China Unicom, along with sohu.com and sina.com, to provide music content.

But the effectiveness of that cooperation will eventually boil down to how to obtain as many star musicians as possible, especially from the domestic scene.

"We have to realize the potential of the artists," says Wong.

By Ding Qingfen
(2006-11-06)

Super Link

1. Bertelsmann to Drive Further into China

Bertelsmann, one of the world's top five media companies, sees huge potential in China's media and publishing markets and hopes to generate about 10 percent of its global sales revenue in China in the next few years. China, the fastest-growing major economy in the world, now only accounts for roughly one percent of the company's global sales revenue.

Gunter Thielen, Bertelsmann AG Chairman and CEO, introduced the group's China development strategy in Beijing in the morning.

"Bertelsmann expects to establish 10-15 joint ventures in China in the next few years through cooperation with local partners," said Thielen.

Four divisions of the group, Gruner + Jahr, BMG, Arvato and Direct Group, have operations in China and employ about 1,600 people. The other two arms of the German group, RTL Group, Europe's No. 1 broadcaster, and Random House, the world's largest trade book publishing group, are considering establishing operations in China, according to the chairman.

By Rong Xiandong
(2007-06-21)

2. Booksellers Join Hands

Germany-based media conglomerate Bertelsmann AG launched a joint venture company yesterday by acquiring a 40 percent share in a Beijing-based private retail bookstore chain.

The new company is the first nationwide joint venture retail bookstore chain in China, following the State Press and Publication Administration's release of a provision this May (2003) giving the green light to Sino-foreign joint ventures in the retail and wholesale book business, in compliance with China's commitment to the World Trade Organization.

The remaining 60 percent is owned by the Chinese partner — the 21st Century Book Chain Co — China's first private national bookstore chain, which owns 18 outlets in 10 major cities, including Beijing, Nanjing, Shenzhen and Xiamen.

The move is seen as a win-win success, but neither side would reveal the total amount involved in the transaction. The new company will offer a full range of products and services nationwide, from a wide selection of books, audio and video products, to greeting cards and gifts, according to Christina Fang, General Manager of the 21st Century Book Chain Co. But in its beginning stage, the joint venture will concentrate its business in Beijing and Shanghai and neighboring regions.

"We are going to launch three new stores in downtown Beijing, and one or two new stores in Shanghai before the end of the year," said Fang.

"According to the deal, six to seven of the 18 outlets owned by the 21st Century Book Chain Co will join the new joint venture following a restructuring, and a number of the remaining outlets will be shut down and some of them will be sold off to rivals," said Luo Ruiren, Chairman of the 21st Century Book Chain Co.

Bertelsmann refuted the widely-speculated rumor that the company is in talks with Chinese partners for a joint venture publishing house. Bertelsmann is going to focus on the success of the joint venture, said Christian Unger, President in China of DirectGroup Bertelsmann.

By Huo Yongzhe
(2003-12-04)

3. Joint Book Venture for Bertelsmann

German media group Bertelsmann will further expand its business in China's book wholesale market, through a new joint venture called Liaoning Bertelsmann Book Distribution Co Ltd.

The venture, a partnership between Bertelsmann's DirectGroup and Liaoning Publishing Group, was established after receiving government approval, the two sides announced in Beijing yesterday.

DirectGroup holds a 49 percent stake in the joint venture, which has registered capital of 30 million yuan ($3.6 million). Liaoning Publishing Group holds the majority 51 percent share.

"The new company will initially focus its business on the wholesale and marketing of books from publishing houses in China, though its licence allows the nationwide distribution of newspapers, books and periodicals," said Pan Yan, the new venture's General Manager.

The two investors aim to build a powerhouse book distributor, by combining talent and experience from both sides.

"The group will exploit Bertelsmann's expertise and international connections as well as the Liaoning Publishing Group's publishing resources and national distribution networks," added Pan.

As a bridge between publishers and retailers, the company will provide value-added services, design tailor-made promotion plans for individual products and promote book sales.

"Cooperation with Bertelsmann will help Liaoning Publishing Group — which is preparing for a market listing — improve its competitiveness and expand its business in the domestic and international market," said Yu Xiaoqun, Deputy General Manager of Liaoning Publishing Group.

"It is a significant step for Bertelsmann's future growth in China," said Holm Keller, President of Bertelsmann Corporate Development Asia and board member of the new venture.

China lifted the ban on foreign investment in the book distribution sector last December (2004) in line with its World Trade Organization commitment.

In April 2005, another publishing distribution joint venture was founded between Xinhua Bookstore's Head Office, British company PAC-Poly Investments Ltd and other domestic publishers and private investment companies.

Foreign investors are not yet allowed to operate alone in China's publications distribution market.

"Bertelsmann, in any case, does not want to," said Keller. "We lack the ability to fully comprehend the Chinese market. We have learned globally that it is essential for the success of a media company to cooperate with the best local partners."

The German media group has ten years' experience in the Chinese book distribution market through a joint venture with China Science and Technology Book Company and a shared acquisition of Beijing's 21st Century Book Chain Co.

It sells books through catalogues, an online store and club centers, and has more than 1.5 million members throughout the country.

By Zhang Lu
(2005-05-25)

BCG Sees China AS a Top Market in Five Years

An Interview with Hans-Paul Bürkner,
President and CEO of Boston Consulting Group

The Boston Consulting Group (BCG), one of the world's leading management consultancies, has been active in the Chinese market since the early 1980s, and set up its first office in Shanghai in 1993. China is now one of BCG's fastest-growing markets; small wonder then that its current President and CEO Hans-Paul Bürkner pays the country five to six visits a year.

During his latest visit to China on August 9, 2007, Bürkner talked to this reporter in Shanghai about his company's goal and strategy in China, his observations of the Chinese consulting industry, the knowledge-based economy and his thoughts on the scientific decision making process.

Q: As the global CEO of BCG, what are your goals and expectations in the Chinese market?

A: We will certainly grow significantly in China. In the last several years, BCG China has grown much faster than BCG as a whole. In 2006, we grew 20 percent worldwide, and in China we grew more than 30 percent. I also expect (BCG) China to grow faster than our worldwide average (growth) in the next several years. Today China is still a midsized market (for us) but we would expect this to change over the next few years. I am sure that in five to ten years' time, China will be among the top five markets in the world (for us).

Q: What strategy or specific measures are you going to take in order to achieve the goal?

A: I think the key element is to build a strong group of people here, both domestic Chinese and international consultants. Another key lever is to serve both international companies who want to establish themselves and expand their business in China, and Chinese companies who have strong ambitions both in the domestic and international markets. Their needs are different from those of European or American companies, given that they are in a different stage of their development and that they have relatively less experience with consulting firms.

Q: How do you plan to convince them of the value BCG offers?

A: Well, the best proof of the cooking is the eating. You really have to work with them, often starting with smaller assignments, demonstrating the value that we can help them generate and then expanding the relationship.

Q: Servicing international companies and Chinese companies, as you said, is a part of your strategy in China. Do you have any preference for either of the two groups of target customers?

A: No. They are on the same footing. We will undertake big efforts to help Chinese companies here and abroad, knowing that they have to get to know consulting more and knowing that it will take time. At the same time, we already have many international companies as good clients in China.

Q: As a veteran executive in the consulting industry and one who visits China regularly, what are your observations of the Chinese consulting industry?

A: The consulting industry in China is growing very strongly in all kinds of fields — strategy, corporate development, organization, operations and IT and … essentially in all industry sectors. Regarding Chinese companies: I think they increasingly value the services they get from consulting firms, learn through projects and see the value they are getting from the firms.

Q: The consulting sector is fairly fragmented in China for the time being, do you think there will be any significant consolidation in the industry in the future?

A: The consulting industry is very fragmented around the world and is also fragmented here in China. I don't think this is going to change in a major way. Yes, there are some mergers and acquisitions in the industry, but at the same time new companies are being established: I am sure there are hundreds (of consulting firms) here in China and tens of thousands around the world. There are some large ones and lots of smaller ones and countless one-person consulting firms. This I believe will continue to be true, both in China and globally. But only two to three handfuls of companies are able to provide truly global services.

Q: Do you think there will be any Chinese consulting firms growing into global players such as BCG in the coming years?

A: I am sure that Chinese consulting companies are very ambitious, and I am also sure that, in 10 or 20 years' time — it just takes a long time — there will be Chinese consulting companies who are operating globally. There are already very strong Indian companies such as Infosys, Wipro and Tata Systems. They have built a strong franchise, starting initially with technology, and then expanding into organization, operations and other fields. Infosys has established a consulting unit in the US, for example. I think one needs to be well aware of the ambitions of companies from India and China, and, as I said, I assume that there will be some global players from both countries over the next 10 to 15 years.

Q: What are your suggestions on how they can grow into global players?

A: First of all, they have to provide very good services here in China. If you don't have a strong home base, you cannot be a viable global player. Second, they have to clearly differentiate themselves through the type and quality of services they offer. And thirdly, they have to become able to deliver uniform quality around the world.

Q: Many people are skeptical about consulting services and whether they deliver value for money. As CEO of one of world's leading management consulting firms, what's your view on this issue?

A: Yes, many companies do not understand the value of consulting. But many others have worked with consulting firms and got very positive experiences. The firms have also invested a lot in order to demonstrate what they can achieve together with their clients. So we have a large and growing number of clients who have seen the value of consulting first hand, and are now using more and more consulting services. It's a matter of time: It takes 10, 15 or — in some markets — even 20 years (for consulting services) to really get accepted. And this is true for any country. It was true in Japan. When we started in middle of the 1960s, Japanese companies were very skeptical. In Germany, initially companies would use consulting services only when they were doing very badly. Today the best companies are using consulting firms regularly.

Q: How long do you think it will be before consulting is widely accepted in the Chinese market?

A: As I said before, Chinese companies have to gain experience (with consulting firms). I guess it will take another 10 years for the market to reach maturity.

Knowledge-based Economy

Q: Are you particularly interested in the knowledge-based economy, which usually has a closer relationship with consulting companies?

A: It is knowledge-based and innovation-based companies that not only relate to consulting companies but also all kinds of companies around the world. It is about putting new ideas into reality, ranging from new products, new services, new manufacturing approaches, new institutions, new business models, etc. It is also about generating ideas. The knowledge-based society or knowledge-based economy means that everybody tries to continuously look for new opportunities and seek development. The key element of the knowledge-based economy is experience, willingness to experiment, to move forward and to change and improve, but not to stand still.

Q: How do you structure the company to achieve its goals?

A: I think one of the key elements is that you must ensure decision-making is not just a top-down process but that there are a lot of decentralized decision-makings. People not only have the right but also the duty to develop new things. Allowing people to make mistakes is to encourage experimentation and stimulate activity to challenge the old things and create new things. If you punish every mistake that happens, then people will not try new things. Knowledge-based innovation means trying out things and accepting that some of these things will not be successful.

Q: For Chinese companies, this will be a sort of revolutionary approach as well. Are there any companies in China interested in this?

A: Over the last several years, China has built a very strong manufacturing base. A low cost manufacturing base was the key to success. More and more R & D centers are being set up, not only for foreign companies but also for Chinese companies. And as Chinese companies also move to foreign markets, we have to understand that you cannot drive anything centrally. So you cannot make the decision out of Shanghai, Beijing, or wherever. But you have to adapt to the new chances. That is to say, entrepreneurs have to decentralize decision making, which will become a natural part of the evolution of Chinese companies. If you try to always do things in the same way everywhere, and try to ensure that everything is happening top down, you will fail. You will have to mobilize for people the creativeness of the organization by granting people freedom to try out new things through experimentation. It comes not by forcing creativity everywhere but by allowing openness in creativity, because you can no longer decree this from the top.

Q: In the course of evolution, what's the common pitfall companies face?

A: The problem is probably that you would like to be in control. So you will not provide openness for a long time. And only when you really fail, you open up, but it may be too late. Some companies have for too long focused on their particular business model, which doesn't work any longer. A very centralized business model will lead to nowhere but bankruptcy. There is no systematic approach to getting everything right. Usually change is a process and there must be some ups and downs.

Q: What benchmark do you use to judge the changing process?

A: You are looking at a 5 to 10 year period, rather than just looking from one year to the next. Because sometimes you make some changes, and the first 6 to 12 months after the change looks like it's going badly. So you cannot judge whether it is right or wrong in the initial stage. More time is needed to get more experience.

Q: Would you say that the service-oriented economy puts a higher demand on knowledge than a manufacturing-based economy?

A: I don't think so. Speaking of manufacturing, there is other supportive work like logistics, designing and engineering of the new products, marketing, selling, insurance and banking. Chinese companies are not only producing goods but also have to find these additional processes to maintain all-round development. This is why the knowledge-based economy is required both for the service sector and in the manufacturing sector. And manufacturing also needs stimulus to accelerate its continuous growth. Therefore, creating new ideas, improving how we do things and what we do is also a great concern for the manufacturing sector.

By Zheng Lifei and Wang Lan
(2007-08-21)

Red-Hot Passion

An Interview with Hideki Ozawa,
President and CEO of Canon China

The Italians and the French have long been romanticized for their passionate approach to life, but the Japanese are more commonly stereotyped for their strong work ethic than anything else.

Yet, just four months after Hideki Ozawa took the reins as President and Chief Executive Officer (CEO) of Canon China Co Ltd, he launched his ambitious Passion Day scheme. The unconventional idea certainly raised a few eyebrows, but Ozawa was dead serious about injecting a dash of European "joie de vivre" into the workplace.

Every Monday, Canon China provides all staff, including the CEO himself, with red ties or scarves to wear in the office. Some employees have even punctuated the unique look with personalized accouterments such as red handbags, red shoes, and red watchbands. The central motif here, of course, is red, red, and red.

"A good week starts with a happy Monday," says Ozawa of his unusual idea. "Eye-catching colors contribute to a more dynamic and passionate work environment."

Sounds a little strange? Hold on, it gets even weirder. Ozawa has come up with a slew of employee morale boosting schemes, such as the Greeting Activity, and the Canon Open Day. Staff members are encouraged to greet everyone when they meet throughout the day, whether in English, Chinese or Japanese. A special team even circulates throughout the building, endlessly repeating the phrase "good morning" to remind everyone to greet each other.

"These are trivial things, but they could open the door to more effective communication," says Ozawa. "Asian people can sometimes be introverted, shy and reluctant to openly express their ideas. We have a tendency to bury ourselves in work rather than speak out."

Ozawa wants to inject emotion and creativity into Canon's corporate culture. He was born in Japan, but has spent much of his career in the United States. He also worked for Canon in his home country, Singapore and Hong Kong before coming to the Chinese mainland.

The Passion Day concept has been well received throughout the company's Asia regional offices. His unconventional approach has contributed to strong sales growth, and has given Ozawa a reputation as a marketing guru.

The CEO began his career at Canon as a salesman 32 years ago, and he knows what it takes to be an effective salesperson. Passion and flair are everything, but customer relations require a modicum of restraint and modesty as well. It's a delicate balance, but it all boils down to communication.

"It starts with effective communication between people, the sales team and the customers," says Ozawa. "You can have innovative products and a progressive corporate culture, but you can't sell anything if you don't build a solid rapport with the customer."

It's not only about fancy scarves and jovial greetings. Employees are expected to dress informally on Casual Fridays as well. Ozawa's goal is to turn every employee into an effective salesperson.

The company's China operations are becoming increasingly sales-oriented. Canon secured government approval to directly import and sell its products in China just last year (2004). All of the company's products were previously required to be imported via Hong Kong, and its manufacturing facilities in China were solely focused on exports.

The Canon brand is popular throughout Europe, the United States and Asia, but a third party survey showed that the company's brand profile was not as powerful as in China, particularly in second-tier cities.

"It is probably because we don't have much of a presence in those places," says Ozawa.

Ozawa realized that Canon needed to launch a substantial marketing campaign

to promote its brand throughout the country. If every
employee is a salesperson,
he says, the company can
market its products and brand
image more effectively.

"Canon China is a sales
company, and all employees,
regardless of which department they work in, should be
acutely aware of customer
service," he adds.

The CEO summarized
his extensive sales experience in the Constitution of
Seventeen Articles on Sales,
a document which has been
distributed to every employee
throughout Asia via e-mail
and internal publications.
Canon China now employs
more than 800 people, three
times as many as in 2002.

"I hope that my Chinese colleagues can develop their skills rapidly and
bring a sense of passion to the workplace," says Ozawa.

Canon will gradually reduce its Japanese staff in China and put more locals
into managerial positions.

"Ideally, the CEO of Canon China should be a Chinese person," he says. "The
entire company will be completely run and managed by locals in the future."

Ozawa wants to more than double Canon's current annual sales in China to
$1 billion by 2007. The country accounts for a quarter of the company's sales in
Asia, excluding Japan and South Korea.

"I expect Canon China's sales will beat all other Asian countries in the near
future," says Ozawa, who is also President of Canon Asia Marketing Group.

The company wants to become the top player across every digital product category, including cameras and digital video cameras. Ozawa hopes the expanded marketing initiative and unconventional approach to customer service will push the company's brand profile past its competitors by 2008.

The neon Canon logo now graces the skylines of the 15 cities the company has its subsidiaries in. It has also actively sponsored several sports programs, such as football and baseball leagues.

"Statistics show that most people who regularly watch football on TV are either customers or potential customers," says Ozawa. "We are shifting from customer satisfaction to customer delight. The idea is to make customers happy, by entertaining and moving them."

"Customer delight" is about providing better products, more convenient and diversified purchasing channels, faster delivery and more effective after-sales service.

Canon has established product exhibition centers — known as Canon Imaging Plazas - in Beijing and Guangzhou, to give consumers the opportunity to try products before they buy them. It is now also capable of delivering products nationwide within 48 hours. The company recently opened a quick service center in Beijing, the first of its kind in Asia outside of Japan, capable of fixing Canon's full domestic consumer imaging product line. Some inkjet printers and digital cameras can be repaired within an hour.

In 2004, the company even began offering mainland consumers warranties for products purchased in Hong Kong and Macao.

"Providing differentiated service will help us realize our market goals," says Ozawa.

By Li Weitao
(2005-11-07)

Canon China's
Road Map to Success

A Follow-Up Interview with Hideki Ozawa

"Speak less, do more," is gospel among Asian business leaders. Hideki Ozawa,,President and CEO of Canon China Co Ltd, however, is an obvious exception.

When Ozawa took the helm of Canon China in 2005, he vowed to help the company achieve a 30-percent sales growth per year and increase sales volume to $1 billion in 2007, up from $451 million in 2004.

Ozawa's ambitious plan reinvigorated the Japanese company. In the past two years, Canon China has gone through several restructurings, including establishing an independent division for printer products and adjusting its distribution channel. Moreover, the company has tried to add more Chinese characteristics to its brand to appeal to a larger percentage of the population.

Ozawa recently spoke with the reporter about his road map to success in China.

Q: Before coming to the Chinese mainland, you worked in Hong Kong, Singapore and the US. What's the difference between the mainland and other markets?

A: Before coming to the mainland, I got the impression that the market was different from other markets. Actually, the basics for running a successful business are the same, whether it's the mainland, Hong Kong or the US. For example, consumers always want products with lower prices but higher quality. And distributors want to have higher profit margins everywhere. For Canon, the key is to delight our consumers through our services and products, which is a basic principle for us.

Q: When you first became Canon China's CEO in 2005, you said you would lead the company to $1 billion in sales in 2007. How far have you progressed, and what measures will you take to achieve that goal?

A: We set up that goal when I arrived in China. Thanks to the huge growth potential of the market, we were able to grow as planned. And I believe we will get even better in the coming year.

Q: Canon has been making great efforts to expand into second- and third-tier cities. What is your strategy for building a strong brand in these markets?

A: China is a market of tremendous potential, thanks to its population of 1.3 billion and 10 percent annual GDP growth. Also, the nation is going to hold the 2008 Olympics and the 2010 World Expo. Those factors are quite positive for the growth of companies. In the past two years, most of our consumers — who number about one or two million so far — have come from first - tier cities like Beijing and Shanghai. But now, as the income level in other parts of China rises, we are trying to reach out to another two or three million new clients. We hope to beef up our localization efforts, make the Canon brand and products friendlier with Chinese consumers and turn Canon (China) into China's Canon.

Q: Can you give us an example of how you plan to do that?

A: For example, we have just introduced a printer, belonging to the PIXMA series, in the Chinese market. PIXMA is a difficult English word for the Chinese, so we gave it a Chinese name — Tengcai, which means fast and colorful. Adding more Chinese characteristics to our products is one way to enhance brand recognition in China.

Q: Canon China has restructured itself in the past two years. In the coming years, will Canon undergo further restructuring?

A: We have established different business divisions for key products to better meet the market demand. It has proved to be quite successful, and we will continue that approach in the coming years.

Q: Canon has an extremely long product line globally. What products will you introduce into the Chinese market in 2007?

A: Currently, Canon's global sales revenue is around $34.9 billion, and we plan to reach $50 billion in 2010. Introducing more products is an important way to realize the target. We will launch the SED (surface-conduction electron-emitter display) television soon. Moreover, we will further expand into the printer segment. We have introduced our projectors to the Chinese market recently and we expect major growth in the market in coming years.

By Wang Xu
(2007-05-22)

Super Link

1. Snap Happy

In the 1990s, Tang Xiao, a Beijing resident, was proud to have relatives who traveled abroad. And the cachet of having a family that traveled was increased by the goods they brought back.

Fashionable clothes and electronic goods of all kinds were always top of Tang's wish list when relatives asked if he wanted anything from abroad, but with his passion for photography, something he was particularly keen to get his hands on was a camera.

Why did he ask his jet-setting family to bring him a camera from overseas instead of buying one in China?

At the time, trade rules meant imported cameras were extremely hard to come by and, once located, tariffs made them prohibitively expensive. Things changed dramatically when China joined the World Trade Organization (WTO) in December 2001. In January 2003, China, in accordance with its commitments to the WTO, scratched its quotas on imported cameras. This resulted in a flood of imports.

The subsequent growth of the digital camera market has been astounding. In the first five months of 2003, digital camera imports through South China's Guangdong Province, surged 32 times year-on-year to 666,000 units. In Shanghai and Beijing, imports climbed even higher, up 53 and 66 times respectively.

Tang was just one of millions to benefit from the opening-up of the market. He was able to buy a foreign-brand digital camera at a fair price. Another benefit brought about by China's entry into the WTO is that foreign makers were allowed to directly sell products made in China.

Most big names in the global digital camera market had already set up manufacturing facilities in China few years ago. But prior to the country's accession to the WTO, foreign companies usually had to form joint ventures to sell the products made in their Chinese factories. A solely foreign-invested company was not allowed to directly sell products made in its China plants. Foreign digital camera makers' factories in China mainly produced goods for export.

Japan's Canon established a plant in Zhuhai in South China's Guangdong Province as long ago as 1990. The plant mainly produces digital cameras, color Laserjet printers, scanners and electronics components. According to Hirosuke Asano, President of Canon Zhuhai Inc, the annual business turnover of the plant surged to $973 million in 2004, as compared to $21 million in 1991.

Because of the way the market was previously restricted, products made at the plant on the mainland "had to be exported to Hong Kong and then reimported to the Chinese mainland," says Asano. And due to the complex rules governing imports and exports, Canon was not allowed to conduct business itself — it had to appoint agencies to deal with the imports.

Canon has a number of manufacturing facilities in China. A plant in Suzhou, a city neighboring Shanghai, is much larger than the Zhuhai plant. Asano expects the turnover of Canon Zhuhai Inc to hit $1 billion in 2005.

In stark contrast, Canon's annual sales in China are much smaller. China accounts for a quarter of Canon's sales in Asia, excluding Japan and South Korea, with last year's (2004) figure reaching $460 million, says Hideki Ozawa, President and CEO of Canon China Co Ltd.

Canon secured government approval to directly import and sell its products in China last year, which gave a major boost to its business growth in the country. Ozawa hopes Canon's annual sales in China will hit $1 billion by 2007.

China's entry to the WTO has apparently greatly benefited foreign businesses such as Canon, enabling them to sell more digital cameras at competitive prices. With the country throwing the market wide open to foreign competition, the price of digital cameras has dramatically fallen. Cameras used to be a luxury for most households in the country, but now 6.3 percent of the Chinese have digital cameras and another 3.4 percent plan to buy them, according to industry statistics.

Tang, however, expects even more benefits from China's WTO membership.

On January 1, 2005, in line with its commitments to the WTO, China started imposing zero tariffs on digital cameras and their parts and components, as well as on a number of information technology (IT) products. In 2004, tariffs on digital cameras and their parts/components were 10 percent and 12 percent respectively.

"Zero tariffs mean the full opening of the domestic (digital camera) market," says Zhang Guobin in a research note. Zhang is an analyst with Global Sources.

The market opening has not only brought rapid market access for foreign companies, but also a wider range of choices and better value for Chinese consumers. Zhang says there are up to 30 players in China's digital camera market.

Thanks to the country's low labor costs, big names such as Fuji, Canon and Sony, as well as US giants Kodak and Hewlett-Packard, have all built plants in the country. Digital camera production in China hit 25.96 million units last year, accounting for 45 percent of the global output.

"China will remain the global manufacturing center for digital cameras," says Zhang.

Such localization has resulted in cheaper products for Chinese consumers. Due to the previous high tariffs, there was a huge market for smuggled digital cameras. A great number of digital cameras from Hong Kong were illegally brought to the Chinese mainland without tariffs being paid. People who bought the smuggled cameras were unable to get guarantees or warranties. Analysts believe the dropping of tariffs will help curb the smuggling of digital cameras.

And the fall in the prices of digital cameras and their components, largely a result of the dropping of tariffs, is helping spur the country's digital camera boom, says Guo Chang, an analyst with Beijing-based research house CCW Research.

In 2004, China saw sales of 26.48 million units, a year-on-year increase of 196.9 percent, according to CCW Research. More than 60 percent of digital cameras were bought by consumers in big cities, but an increasing number of consumers in third- and fourth-tier cities are also dipping into their wallets.

By Li Weitao
(2005-12-12)

2. Local Vendors Hurt

Despite the enormous benefits brought about by China's WTO entry, local manufacturers have suffered under the tidal wave of competition and some even face going under.

In 2002, Chinese manufacturers, led by Lenovo, Founder Technology and Tsinghua Unisplendor, were estimated to have a 10-12 percent share of the digital camera market. Their market share has been dropping as foreign competitors have taken over. In 2004, Founder Technology was forced to cut investment in its digital camera business, a sign that it will gradually pull out of the market. Some small homegrown brands have already pulled the plug on their digital camera operations.

"Obviously we (Chinese makers) are not competitive in the market as most core technologies are owned by foreign rivals," says Founder Technology President Qi Dongfeng. "Domestic makers have been long relying on price cuts. But now it's hard to survive as foreign makers are taking the initiative to cut prices."

The price wars are so intense that Chinese consumers can now buy a 4-megapixel digital camera for less than 2,000 yuan ($250). Guo expects more and more players, mostly local vendors, to be forced to pull out of the digital market.

Some foreign makers are also suffering under the intense competition on price. HP has already pulled out of China's digital camera market.

"Price wars will continue since Chinese consumers are very price-sensitive," says Guo.

By Li Weitao
(2005-12-12)

Carrefour Keeps Pace with Expansion

An Interview with Jose Luis Duran,
CEO of Carrefour Group

Customers at China's Carrefour hypermarkets spend an average of 110 yuan ($13.8) each visit; a significant figure when multiplied by the country's consumer base. And the world's second-largest retailer said it plans to keep pace with the rapidly expanding domestic market.

Jose Luis Duran, CEO of Carrefour Group, said the company would open 20 hypermarkets this year (2006), compared with 14 in 2005.

The new stores represent one-fifth of Carrefour's expansion worldwide for 2006, Duran said. In total, the company plans to open 45 hypermarkets in Asia, 30 in Europe and 25 in Latin America.

"That pace will continue through 2008 at least," said the CEO.

Carrefour currently operates 76 supermarkets in China. In 2006, Carrefour has already opened seven new stores in the country and will introduce another 13 this year, he said.

Carrefour has also opened 230 Dia outlets (its discount stores) in China, and plans to open 70 more this year (2006).

With the national economy growing at more than 9 percent a year, China's retail market is expected to expand by 8 to 10 percent a year to $2.4 trillion by 2020.

To grab a bigger part of the huge domestic retail market, foreign retailers are opening more stores, even as China is relaxing its industry policies.

Wal-Mart, Carrefour's global rival, intends to open 18 to 20 new stores throughout the country in 2006.

This quick expansion is also part of the French retailer's global strategy; its rate of new store openings will increase sharply during the 2006-2008 period in its key market, Duran said.

The company intends to open about 100 new hypermarkets in 2006 — its largest number of openings in a single year and double the average for each year between 2001 and 2004.

In total, taking into account other formats, supermarkets, and discount and convenience stores, Carrefour plans to open 1,000 new outlets in 2006. These figures are equivalent to 1.5 million square meters of retail space.

"In short, we will be opening more square meters in fewer countries, in order to increase the impact of each euro invested," said Duran.

Carrefour has withdrawn from countries such as South Korea that are not sufficiently profitable, and decided to focus its efforts and investments on key markets in which it can lead.

"It will still take some time for China to become truly significant, but we have opened more stores in China in 10 years than we opened in Spain and Brazil in 30 years," said Duran.

Carrefour made revenues of 2 billion euros in 2005 in China, only about 2 percent of the group's total worldwide revenue.

Besides the expansion, Carrefour will have more debuts in the market, said Luc Vandevelde, Chairman of Carrefour's Supervisory Board.

The retailer will open its first environment friendly supermarket in the world here.

The "green" supermarket will be built in Beijing and will use 30 percent less water and electricity than other Carrefour stores, said Vandevelde.

Plans for the store, which will open before 2008, include recyclable bags and special electric trams.

This is also the first time that Carrefour has bought real estate to open a store rather than renting an existing space.

Duran said Carrefour believed it would not have any difficulty finding the right locations and people for its expansion.

"We will stick to cooperation with local partners who are good at finding

the good sites," said Duran.

The company itself also has a group of 40 development managers to seek locations for hypermarkets.

The retailer recently signed an agreement with China Europe International Business School (CEIBS) to support the school over a 3-year period. In return, Carrefour will have priority to recruit elite masters from CEIBS.

More local people will take senior positions in the company, said Vandevelde. Eighty percent of the hypermarkets' general managers are Chinese and the share will continue to increase in the near future.

By Dai Yan
(2006-05-31)

Super Link

1. Carrefour Opens Flagship Store in Beijing

Carrefour opened its fifth store in Beijing on March 17, after three years of lying dormant in the national capital's market.

The new outlet, in the newly developed Zhongguancun west district, will be the French retailer's flagship store in Asia.

With a floor space of 11,600 square meters, much more than that of any other Carrefour store in the country, the latest outlet is comparable with Carrefour hypermarkets in Europe in terms of layout and other aspects such as food safety and environmental hygiene, according to company sources.

"The new store is very important for us, as it is located in a high-technology area that is gathering a large number of IT enterprises and white-collar workers, as well as college students," said Jean-Luc Chereau, President of Carrefour China. "And I hope it will be a good beginning for our growth in the area."

As an area that lacks big shopping centers and supermarkets, Zhongguancun is attracting more foreign retailers.

PriceSmart, one of Carrefour's major rivals, also plans to open its N-Mart supercenter in the area this year (2004).

In the wake of the Zhongguancun plaza store's opening, one or two more Carrefour stores will also be opened in Beijing this year.

And its store in Jinan, capital of east China's Shandong Province, will also open soon, according to the company.

The openings are an obvious sign that Carrefour has begun to speed up its expansion in the country, after two-and-a-half years of restructuring.

Entering the Chinese market in 1995, the retailer infringed upon foreign retail regulations about three years ago.

It was then ordered to sell its excessive shares upon the regulated 65 percent limit to local partners.

During the past two years, Carrefour has not been allowed to open a new store. It had to first restructure its existing outlets.

"After two-and-a-half years of effort, we have completed our revamp in China, and now we are heading into a fast-growing period for the country," said Chereau.

Company sources said Carrefour plans to open more than a dozen new stores around the country this year.

Last month, Carrefour opened two hypermarkets in Northwest China's Xinjiang Uygur Autonomous Region and East China's Shanghai Municipality.

As more foreign retailers are gaining a foothold in China and the country lifts the restrictions on the industry, Carrefour is eager to expand and accumulate a greater market share, say analysts.

China, in accordance with its commitments to the World Trade Organization, will lift regional limitations on foreign chain retail operators by the year's end.

All restrictions on foreign retailers will be removed by 2007, when China's chain retail market will be fully opened up.

But earlier in March, 2004, some 100 deputies submitted a proposal to the 10th National People's Congress, suggesting legislation on a hearing system for the opening of mega stores.

Industry experts say the proposal apparently targets the expansion plans of foreign-funded stores like Carrefour.

Chereau, however, is not concerned.

"We can deal with the international trade concept, but we are also able to deal with local ones, and I believe consumers will decide what they would want," he said confidently.

The French retailer ranked first among foreign supermarkets in 2003, with annual revenues of 13.4 billion yuan ($1.6 billion), according to statistics from the China General Chamber of Commerce.

By Zhang Lu
(2004-03-18)

2. Different Strokes

Although it's a French company, Carrefour has mastered the local touch in China.

In the upscale Gubei area of Shanghai's Changning District, Carrefour's mall offers more imported foods than any other stores in the city.

On the first floor, which has been leased out to sports brands such as Adidas AG and Nike Inc, cosmetics retailer Sephora set up its second Chinese store here a year ago, meaning steady rent payments for Carrefour.

These factors are believed to have made it Carrefour's most profitable outlet in the country.

Another store, in Quyang in the Hongkou District, has a totally different look.

It was the first supermarket Carrefour opened in China, and sells mostly low and medium-level goods. It almost resembles a vegetable market.

The store, surrounded by low-income neighborhoods, even offered free snacks once in a promotion that attracted many older people for breakfast, before they went on to shop.

Since it began operating in China in 1995, the French retailer has developed a string of stores to meet the varying tastes and demands of different areas.

It now has 79 malls in China, 10 of which specialize in selling fresh meats and live fish. In addition, the group also operates 200 discount stores around the nation, making it the largest foreign retailer in the country.

A recent survey by CTR Market Research, a Shanghai retailing research firm, shows Carrefour had secured at least 5 percent of the market share in the 15 major cities where its stores have a penetration rate of 47.2 percent.

Different Consumers, Different Stores

Yang Qingsong, Information Center Director of the China Chain Store and Franchise Association, attributes Carrefour's success to its special business models.

Each Carrefour store has its own autonomy, and is able to make direct local purchases to keep a minimum level of inventory. Carrefour attempted to create national purchasing and distribution channels two years ago, but failed because of the significant differences in customers' demands in different markets.

"This is largely related to the different consumption patterns of different cities," explains Yang.

Local purchasing has not only fueled Carrefour's growth in China, but helped it build a good relationship with local governments and suppliers.

These suppliers have contributed to a large part of Carrefour's profits in China.

To enter Carrefour stores, they have to pay miscellaneous fees for promotion, priority location and priority marketing.

It is said these fees make up 36 percent of Carrefour's annual turnover.

Carrefour's also has a policy to lease out a large part of the first floor of each store to garments, cosmetics and accessories sellers, all of which bring in steady rent.

Wal-Mart's Centralized System

While Carrefour has firmly established itself in China with a flexible and effective localization strategy, Wal-Mart, with its strong global strategy, is not doing as well, despite being the world's largest retailer.

Wal-Mart is known for its central control, cost controls, and powerful information and logistics systems.

It brings suppliers and logistics players under its system.

In China, however, its global purchasing and distribution system is greatly hindered by government policies and the outdated information systems of local suppliers.

Wal-Mart hasn't yet built a logistics center in China as effective as the one in the United States.

Expressways are much slower and more expensive in China than in the United States, which adds greatly to Wal-Mart's transportation costs.

As it operates on a smaller scale, Wal-Mart is also struggling to keep prices as low as in the United States; many of its stores in China have price tags not lower than its competitors.

However, although Carrefour excels with a flexible and local strategy, many regard Wal-Mart as the future of China's retailing industry.

Lang Xianping, a Hong Kong scholar, says domestic chain stores rely too much on entry fees for profits and that will eventually weaken the industry's operational capability.

In the long run, he says, Wal-Mart's advanced management and central control network will be what domestic retailers are looking for.

But for now, Wal-Mart is playing catch-up with its French rival.

Before Carrefour started to negotiate with Shanghai to open its first store, Wal-Mart had already made overtures without success.

Its insistence on locating its Chinese settlement center in Shenzhen in the south meant it had to put off its Shanghai ambitions for eight years.

To make things worse, authorities in Shanghai announced in 2003 that no new malls could open within its inner ring road, pushing any proposed Wal-Mart stores to the outskirts.

It was not until September 2005 that Wal-Mart opened its first outlet in the city, close to the inner ring road in Pudong.

Wal-Mart's unified settlement means that all of its taxation flows to Shenzhen, making the opening of new stores less appealing to local governments.

Wal-Mart's relations with suppliers are also tense.

A supplier in Jinan, East China's Shandong Province, set up a website for better communication as required by Wal-Mart, but could not stand the low prices Wal-Mart bid and eventually gave up any further attempt to do business with the US buyer.

In the meantime, Carrefour gets on well with the supplier, since the French retailer has turned discount requirements into promotion fees, rather than pushing too hard on prices.

Carrefour stood fifth in a ranking of the country's top 30 chain stores by the Ministry of Commerce in the first half of this year, with a turnover of 11.9 billion yuan ($1.5 billion) from its 79 stores.

Wal-Mart ranked 14th, with a turnover of 6.2 billion yuan ($775 million) from 60 stores.

The two retailing giants are now withdrawing from other countries and shifting their focus to the China market.

"Competition between the two foreign retailers will be more fierce in the future," says Yang.

By Yin Ping
(2006-09-11)

Coca-Cola Aims to Make China Its Largest Market

An Interview with Doug Jackson, President of Coca-Cola China

2007 marks the 80th anniversary of Coca-Cola's entry into China, now the company's fourth largest market after the US, Mexico and Brazil.

The world's largest beverage company, which recently launched an $80 million global research center and opened a new China headquarters in Shanghai, is planning to boost investment in sales infrastructure and product range in the country, a market that could become Coca-Cola's largest, the company says.

Doug Jackson, who became President of Coca-Cola China in April, spoke with the reporter about the company's goals and strategy in China.

Q: As the new head of China operations, what's your short-term goal and long-term vision for the Chinese market?

A: Our goal in the next few years is to sustain the current strong growth momentum. The non-alcoholic drink market grows by 14 to 15 percent a year in China, and we hope we can outdo the average market performance to increase our sales volume and market share. We are also planning to expand our product range and provide more choices for our customers.

We believe that China could become the largest market for Coca-Cola; however, it is hard to predict when it will happen, but it certainly will. Our long-term vision is to make China our largest market.

Q: What will be your priority in the coming years, especially in the next two? You said recently that you plan to invest significantly in infrastructure. Could you be more specific?

A: Yes. I think in the next few years we will continue to invest in the vendor equipment area. We'll continue to increase our cool drink equipment across China very aggressively. While we grow in those areas, our bottler is also going to invest in trucks, distribution facilities and salespeople. So we have a huge increase in the number of sales officers in some smaller towns and cities, as we open them up or increase their infrastructure. Of course, we will also invest in our R & D center. We will have about 200 people, up from the current 40. And we will make significant investments in the next two years in research and development. These are principally some of the areas where we will be aggressive.

Q: Coca-Cola has carried out some major acquisitions in America. Does the company have a similar plan for China, and will the recent dispute between the French food and beverage companies Danone and Wahaha have any impact on your acquisition plans in China?

A: Well, I think in terms of our acquisition plans, we will always continue to look at everything that happens in the marketplace. There are many companies involved in our business in China and the non-alcoholic drink business is very big in the country. But we are still growing organically. Our sales grew by 18 percent in the second quarter (in the Chinese market). This is huge in terms of volume, a big organic growth. If such growth slows then perhaps we would look at acquisitions more closely, and then see if the opportunities stay. We will certainly keep watching the developments between the companies you mentioned, Danone and Wahaha.

Q: What kind of companies will you target if you make such acquisitions? Will bottling companies or local beverage makers be your priority?

A: I think we will just make sure that we understand everything in the industry. We wouldn't specifically target anyone. I think currently we have wonderful partners, a strong partnership with COFCO, with which we have just opened, a new bottling factory in Jiangxi Province. And we have a very strong partnership with Swire, another longstanding partner. So we don't see any change in that partnership.

Q: What do you perceive as the major challenges for you to grow in the Chinese market?

A: I think there are quite a number of challenges. The first is trying to calculate the speed of our investments. The challenge is try to estimate how this growth will continue in the next three, five, ten years. So what will be required on our investment capabilities are factories, bottling lines, infrastructure and people. Secondly, it's a very competitive market. Everybody knows China is a huge potential market, and you have to compete fast and aggressively to win in the market. Thirdly, the pace of change in the Chinese market is very quick. Obviously if you are not on top of your consumers and competitors, and have the R & D capacities to launch new products, then you'll fall behind very quickly. You need to make sure you're running faster than others, or you will lag behind. So these, I think, are the major challenges.

By Zheng Lifei

(2007-08-07)

Super Link

1. China to Become Coke's Top Asian Market

Global beverage giant Coca-Cola expects its sales growth in China to exceed 16 percent in 2004, overtaking Japan as its biggest market in Asia in terms of volume.

To fuel its continuing expansion, the company will open more bottling factories after this summer's series of promotional campaigns comes to an end. It has announced plans to build three new bottling plants in China.

But according to Brenda Lee, the company's Director of External Affairs, Coke is also looking at other locations for new plants. Construction has begun at the $12 million Lanzhou plant in Gansu Province, where production will probably start by the end of 2004. Work on a $11 million plant in the southwestern municipality of Chongqing and a $5.6 million plant in Zhanjiang in southern Guangdong Province will start soon, Lee said.

Its summer campaign includes a series of new TV commercials, said John Cheung, Vice-President and Marketing Director of Coca-Cola (China) Beverages Ltd. This time, Coke will target China's teens, who are beginning to exert an influence on trends and lifestyle attitudes, Cheung said.

Coke is the No. 1 brand in China's carbonated soft drink market, with a national share of 23 percent during the first quarter. Together with allied brands — Sprite, the No. 2 brand Fanta, and local brand Smart — the company holds more than 50 percent of the Chinese market, double that of its global rival PepsiCo.

The competition in the non-carbonated market, especially the ready-to-drink tea sector, hots up during summer. Coke introduced a new tea drink called Modern Tea Workshop last week. It was launched in Shanghai and Hangzhou, and will be promoted by Hong Kong movie stars Tony Leung Chiu-wai and Shu Qi. The beverage forms part of a line of tea drinks that Coke is producing in cooperation with Nestle.

In May, Pepsi joined with Unilever to launch Lipton's Iced Tea in Guangzhou, capital city of South China's Guangdong Province. The US-British alliance is a 50-50 venture, in which Pepsi contributes its bottling facilities and distribution networks, and Unilever its famous tea brand and recipe.

China's growing bottled tea market is currently estimated to be worth 10 billion yuan ($1.2 billion). It used to be dominated by two Taiwanese brands — Master Kong and Uni-President.

By Dai Yan
(2004-06-22)

2. Coke: Making Corporate History in China

Coca-Cola, the world's largest beverage maker, is now making corporate history in China, 80 years after it first entered the country.

"The rapid growth we have achieved in China has been seen very rarely in Coca-Cola's past," said Paul Etchells, Deputy Group President of Coca-Cola's Pacific Group and the former President of Coca-Cola China.

The company set up its first bottling plant in Shanghai in 1927. By 1948, Shanghai had become Coca-Cola's largest market outside the United States, with annual sales exceeding more than 1 million unit cases.

"Our colleagues at the time had the farsightedness and vision that China would one day become a very important market for us," said Etchells.

Coca-Cola, among the first group of multinational companies to come to the country, reentered the China market in 1979.

"We have seen our business steadily growing since then, and encountered our golden development stage in 1990s when we set up more than a dozen bottling plants, laying the foundation for our later expansion," said Etchells.

Coca-Cola's sales volume in China, according to Etchells, has doubled in the past five years; at the same time the beverage company has also expanded its product offerings to drive business and cater to diverse customer tastes.

"The huge, rapidly expanding market, in which consumers' taste are also changing dynamically, is a big challenge for us and we have to learn to cope with the changes in the market," said Etchells.

Coca-Cola saw its sales volume in China increasing 18 percent in the second quarter of 2007, with consistent growth across all product categories.

The impressive results, Etchells said, further bolstered China's status as a powerful growth engine for Coca-Cola.

"We believe such strong momentum will be maintained in the coming years," he stated. "And we hope to see rapid growth in every product category in future, and not only in sparkling beverage segment."

The beverage giant, which has just celebrated its 80th China anniversary in July 2007, will still grow "strongly" in the country in the future, Etchells maintained.

China overtook Japan as Coca-Cola's fourth largest market in 2005. The country is expected to overtake Brazil in two years to become the third largest market, said Douglas Jackson, the incumbent President of Coca-Cola China. China, Jackson said, would outpace Mexico to become the second largest within five years; after that, it could only take "a couple of years" for China to become Coca-Cola's biggest market.

In addition to increasing its capacity to meet the soaring demand in China, the beverage giant is also planning to beef up its investment in sales infrastructure and broaden its product range, Jackson said.

"Coca-Cola is going to add more bottling facilities in areas that "are not well represented," he added.

The company inaugurated a 100-million-yuan bottling plant in Nanchang, capital city of East China's Jiangxi Province, on July 18. This is its 30th bottling facility in China. The Atlanta-based soft-drink giant is also planning to put "a significant amount of investment" in sales infrastructure such as increase of sales force and vending machines. Coca-Cola has expanded its products beyond its iconic sparkling beverage to encompass fruit juice, tea, water, coffee, energy drinks and other offerings.

With more than 50 product offerings in China at present, the company will further expand the product range "to provide more choices for customers," according to Jackson.

"Eighty years ago, it would have been beyond our wildest imagination that China could one day become one of the world's most important markets for us," he said. "We are now operating in one of the most dynamic and fast-growing markets in the 21st century, and we are honored to witness the miraculous growth of China's economy and be a part of this success."

By Zheng Lifei
(2007-08-10)

Magic
Middle Kingdom

An Interview with Bill Ernest,
Executive Vice-President and Managing
Director of Hong Kong Disneyland Resort

Their intentions are crystal clear. Simplified Chinese characters are everywhere, and regional products such as Inner Mongolian milk are on sale at food and beverage stands. Travel agents offer customized promotional packages, and special tickets were issued for the Golden Week peak travel period in May.

Hong Kong Disneyland has been doing everything it can to attract more visitors from the Chinese mainland, says Bill Ernest, Executive Vice-President and Managing Director of Hong Kong Disneyland Resort.

The scripts, written in simplified Chinese characters and available at two shows — Golden Mickey and the Lion King — help mainlanders understand the storylines, Ernest tells the reporter. In the past, says Ernest, all the shows at the theme park were in English, and Chinese-language scripts were simply unavailable.

Visitors can also opt for familiar Mengniu dairy products, providing a welcome alternative to other famous beverages such as Coca-Cola. Ernest says Hong Kong Disneyland signed an agreement in April, 2006 with domestic milk producer Mengniu, making it the theme park's official dairy supplier.

The executive vice-president says Disneyland has been actively seeking co-operative opportunities with other mainland companies.

"It is always nice to have our visitors see brands from their own region," he says.

He adds that offering familiar food and beverages is very important, since visitors will immediately feel comfortable in the park. "Mainland visitors enjoy our food, especially the noodles, dim sum and barbecue."

Mainland visitors also tend to take a lot of pictures when they travel, so Disneyland has set up five locations throughout Fantasyland where visitors can meet characters and take pictures with them at any time of day.

"We set these locations aside, because we know our Asian guests, especially mainlanders, love to take pictures," says Ernest. "This only happens at the park in Hong Kong, but not at other Disneyland parks. Guests from the Chinese mainland are wonderful. They are curious about what our park looks like and what the attractions are. And they love to take photos."

The park has also launched a special promotion, "Extra Magic", which is exclusively targeted at mainland visitors. Visitors can choose their own "Extra Magic" when they book a trip to Hong Kong Disneyland through a travel agent. The offer includes a photo on Space Mountain or the Many Adventures of Winnie the Pooh, a 2-for-1 meal deal, or a Disney-themed souvenir. The promotion is available until the end of September (2006).

Ernest mentions another promotion, "Double the Magic", that provides

Hong Kong citizens with a second free trip to the theme park.

"Our friends from the mainland can't visit Hong Kong as frequently, so we offer them something else," says Ernest.

More and more mainland visitors have been coming to the theme park since it opened in 2005. Ernest says word-of-mouth has been a huge help. "Our visitors always tell their friends about their great experiences here."

He states that between 85 and 90 percent of visitors have provided positive feedback, and that Disneyland offers guests a unique experience.

"We spend a lot of time thinking about the storytelling, costume design, the parades, the attractions and the different theme products. We want our visitors to really immerse themselves in the whole experience," he says.

With two Broadway-style shows, unique Disney attractions, a nightly fireworks display, and two spectacular hotels, there's always something for everybody in the family, Ernest tells the reporter.

The park was swamped with visitors during the Chinese New Year in 2006, and it had to shut its gates after hundreds of mainland ticket-holders tried to force their way in after being turned away when the park reached full capacity. But Ernest says they managed to successfully cope with the crowds during the May Day holiday.

The park sold special entry tickets from April 30 to May 6, in order to guarantee that guests came to the park on specific days, he says.

Mainland travelers currently account for one-third of the park's visitors, with another third from Hong Kong. Most other park-goers are from elsewhere in Southeast Asia.

The Hong Kong Disneyland Resort is a joint venture between Walt Disney Co and the Hong Kong Special Administrative Region (SAR) Government. It employs 5,000 people. The SAR Government estimates the first phase of the project will bring up to HK$148 billion (US$19.0 billion) to Hong Kong over the next 40 years. Earlier reports have quoted Shanghai Mayor Han Zheng as having confirmed that the city is preparing to build its own Disney theme park. It is currently waiting for permission from the State Council.

Hong Kong Disneyland, however, declines to comment on the possibility of competition from the mainland's most developed city.

By Jiang Jingjing
(2006-05-29)

Super Link

1. Disney: Cash Cow for Dairy Firm

A Chinese dairy giant has teamed up with Hong Kong Disneyland to become the official supplier for the theme park, the Hong Kong Disneyland Hotel and Disney's Hollywood Hotel.

Inner Mongolia firm Mengniu Dairy Industry (Group) Co Ltd and Hong Kong Disneyland yesterday announced the launch of the new alliance.

Mengniu, established in 1999, has already become one of the world's largest liquid milk suppliers. It will supply Mengniu milk, the Ai He yogurt drink and Future Star milk to visitors at Hong Kong Disneyland. It will also sponsor some of the food and beverage wagons found throughout the park.

Bill Ernest, Executive Vice-President and Managing Director of Hong Kong Disneyland Resort, said: "The family is at the heart of both brands — Hong Kong Disneyland as the No. 1 family vacation destination in the region and Mengniu as the provider of healthy drink products for everyone to enjoy."

Yang Wenjun, President of Mengniu, said the alliance could bring about more chances to cash in overseas.

"The cooperation will offer international guests a chance to taste Chinese dairy products, and therefore open up more overseas markets for the firm," Yang said.

Mengniu currently has more than 20 production bases in 15 provinces. It has developed more than 100 kinds of different products, including liquid milk, ice cream, milk powder and milk tablets.

In 2005, Mengniu saw revenue grow by 50.1 percent to reach 10.8 billion yuan ($1.35 billion). Its net profit grew by 43.7 percent.

"Selecting Mengniu is a natural decision for Hong Kong Disneyland, because of its top quality and widely accepted brand image," said Disneyland's Ernest. "It is always nice to have our visitors see some brands from their own region."

He said the theme park had been actively seeking cooperation opportunities with other mainland companies.

By Jiang Jingjing
(2006-04-25)

2. Disney Theme Park Awaiting Government Nod

Disney's boss has confirmed that the firm is awaiting approval from the Chinese Government to build a theme park in Shanghai after successful talks with city leaders.

Group Chairman George Mitchell said the company had been in discussions with Shanghai officials for "a long period of time" to build a new Disneyland in the metropolis.

He added that talks were now under way between the Shanghai municipal government and the State Council, which has the final say over the project.

"Our discussions have been with Shanghai officials, and now they are engaging in talks with the national officials," said Mitchell. "We have an interest in proceeding and we hope that satisfactory terms can be worked out."

Mitchell made the comments to China Daily while in Beijing to attend the official opening of a branch of DLA Piper, a global law firm of which he is also the chairman.

Speculation over Disney's plan to open a theme park in Shanghai intensified after the opening of Disneyland Hong Kong last September.

Mitchell insisted there was a market for both attractions, and that a new park in Shanghai would not be detrimental to the long-term success of the Hong Kong site.

"There has been very careful analysis from us and Chinese Government officials," he said. "There are a very large number of people in the Shanghai area and we don't think that this (a new park) will have any more of a negative effect on Hong Kong than say having a park both in California and Orlando,

Florida.

"We are looking forward to a long and what we hope will be a productive relationship in Hong Kong and Shanghai."

While Mitchell said he was "very pleased" with the operation in Hong Kong, he admitted there had been some problems.

During the Chinese New Year holidays in 2006, the park had to close its gates to hundreds of visitors holding pre-purchased tickets after it reached maximum capacity soon after opening.

"These kinds of issues always occur at every new park in different contexts, but we try to work them out and we try to be sensitive to what local people want," said Mitchell. "We always make very careful plans regarding how we are going to operate, but things can never turn out exactly as you predict. There is always a period of adaptation."

As previously reported, it is believed an area of land in Pudong's Chuansha area has already been earmarked for the Shanghai park.

Mitchell said it was impossible to put a timeframe on the project.

"We try to proceed as quickly as possible after the execution of the contract, but until we execute a contract we don't get into when we are going to start," he said.

By Jamie Thomson
(2006-06-24)

Changes in Store

An Interview with Joseph Tucci,
Chairman and CEO of EMC

More than 30 years ago, Joseph Tucci was a beach lifeguard in the United States, professionally trained and ready to rescue swimmers in peril.

Tucci's heroic background seems to have done wonders for his career; he has already rescued two fallen high-tech giants from the brink of disaster.

He first displayed his miraculous touch in 1990, when he joined Wang Global. He promptly saved the once-high-flying tech firm from bankruptcy and sold it to the Netherlands-based Getronicis in 1999.

A year after that, Tucci joined data storage firm EMC Corp and restored its leadership in the global industry by breathing new life into sales and profit growth, at a time when technology companies were dealing with an industry-wide meltdown.

"In fact, I much prefer to grow companies," says Tucci, Chairman and Chief Executive Officer of EMC, now the world's largest provider of data storage and information management solutions.

And China happens to be a major market for Tucci to take EMC's business to an even higher level. As a leading executive at several major global technology firms, Tucci has paid visits to China two to three times every year.

"China is a major place where EMC can make a big difference," says Tucci.

"And China can make a big difference for EMC."

The country's information technology (IT) market will likely grow at a compound average growth rate (CAGR) of 18.5 percent between 2005 and 2009, according to Beijing-based CCW Research. And IT spending throughout this period will reach 2 trillion yuan ($250 billion), which will generate enormous demand for data storage and information management.

Data storage and backup solutions are now believed to be one of the most valuable businesses in the IT market, due to the information explosion. On June 23, 2006, Tucci announced that EMC would pour $500 million into China within five years, to cash in on these new opportunities.

It's a huge jump in the firm's investment plan; between 2001 and 2005, it only invested about $150 million on the mainland. Tucci says EMC has been planning to invest $500 million for a long time, and believes it will pay off in the future. He also announced last week that EMC would double its investment in India to $500 million by 2010.

The investment in China could be more strategic, however. As part of its investment plan, EMC will set up a research and development (R & D) center in Shanghai, the first of its kind in China. Globally, the company has more than 20 R & D centers, with four in India. The increased R & D effort in China marks a big step forward for EMC, which had previously partnered with local software maker Neusoft for such activities.

Betting on India is a natural choice for the company, now one of the top 10 most valued technology enterprises in the world. And EMC is becoming more software-focused, generating 37 percent of its global revenues from software in 2005.

Unlike China, India is already a global software powerhouse, with a huge number of skilled software engineers. China's fledgling software sector still has a far way to go. And EMC is ready to grow with the local market through this aggressive investment, says Tucci.

EMC will spend "a large portion" of the $500 million investment on R & D activities in China. The Shanghai centre will recruit about 100 local engineers, and 500 by 2008. EMC also started manufacturing data storage gears in China early 2005. Localized manufacturing, R & D centers, and significant investments in the coming years will be key to expanding EMC's business in China.

Despite its global dominance, EMC has been lagging behind IBM in China. And the country still only accounts for a small portion of EMC's global sales; totals for the entire Asia-Pacific accounted for only 11 percent of its worldwide revenue of $9.7 billion in 2005.

"We want more people to sell our products and serve our customers (in China)," says Tucci. "Over the next several years, EMC will recruit more people, and set up more solution centers, centers of excellence. We'll partner with more local universities in key research projects and improve support capabilities. I'm a simple person and I bet on people. We always start with people."

In China, EMC has been focusing on big corporate clients that tend to buy storage gears and software. Smaller businesses have also been starting to place orders in recent years, but insiders say EMC is facing a shortage of salespeople. So in most cases, the company has to rely on its partners to sell products to small businesses and provide services, which has hurt its competitiveness.

But there are other concerns. EMC's major rival Hitachi Data Storage (HDS) has said it plans to grab a 50 percent share of China's data storage market by expanding its service centers and marketing campaigns.

And anti-virus specialist Symantec has acquired Veritas Software, a provider of enterprise storage and backup solutions, for $13.5 billion. This is expected to further intensify the battle for control of the data storage market, both globally and in China.

By Li Weitao
(2006-07-03)

Hardsell for Software

An Interview with Denis Yip,
President of EMC Greater China

It is *de rigeur* for company executives to set internal sales targets each year and work towards achieving them. These targets are often ambitious to help boost morale.

Denis Yip's goal, however, seems impossibly high to attain.

"We aim to double our software sales in China each year over the coming five years," says the President of EMC Greater China.

That means Yip must work to multiply software sales by 32 times within the five-year period — unimaginable to many of his peers.

But he has a point: the starting base is low, since US-based EMC, one of the world's top data storage companies, generates most of its revenues in China from hardware sales. And now Chinese companies' information technology (IT) spending is shifting to software from hardware.

"We have not done a good job in (boosting) software sales in China (in the past few years)," says Yip, who joined EMC in 2006 after working at IBM for 15 years.

In 2006 EMC generated global revenue of $11.2 billion, with software and service revenues accounting for 54 percent.

However, according to him, "the proportion in China is much smaller." EMC has traditionally been a hardware vendor, but now its software sales alone have helped the firm squeeze into the ranks of the top six software makers in the world, trailing behemoths such as Microsoft and Oracle.

Unlike Western companies, Chinese businesses usually put a premium on hardware when mapping out their IT budgets. "There is truly a gap between Chinese and Western companies (in placing orders for software products and services)," says Yip. "But things are changing. Chinese businesses are gradually embracing software and services. You can see the rapid growth of Microsoft and SAP in China."

EMC has also started benefiting from the trend. In 2006, its software sales in China doubled, which encouraged Yip to release a five-year blueprint that sets a lofty target to double the figure each year. The company president now hopes software sales could account for one-third of EMC's total revenue in China by 2011.

He has good reasons: storage is now one of the fastest-growing segments in the IT industry and few businesses can survive without information storage and management.

A recent White Paper by research house IDC found that the amount of digital information created, captured and replicated worldwide was 161 billion gigabytes in 2006. Information storage is crucial for many businesses and organizations. Immigration officials need to take and store photos of travelers entering a country. Banks need to store customer account information; telephone banking requires voice recording, which in turn requires expensive equipment packed with disk drives.

"Typically, a two-megabyte e-mail requires a storage and backup capacity of 1.2 gigabytes," says Yip.

For EMC, information is not just about storage on servers, tape drives and disk drives. The firm is now refashioning itself as an information management company rather than a corporate data storage firm.

"Information is now the most valuable asset for businesses. And it needs to be protected, stored, leveraged and optimized," says Yip. "Businesses need a total solution for information management that requires extensive software and services."

IDC forecasts that the amount of digital information could grow six-fold to hit 988 billion gigabytes by 2010. The forecast for the China market is not yet available, but IT growth in the country is usually 30 percent greater than mature markets such as the US.

"We see more than half of our opportunities coming from Chinese banks and financial institutions," says Yip. Three of China's top-four banks have adopted

EMC's solutions.

Telecom and Internet companies could also be major buyers. Analysys International, a Beijing-based research house, expects fast-growing video sharing websites to give a strong boost to the storage market. Analysys forecasts that the whole storage market could be worth 9.74 billion yuan by 2010, almost double that of 2006.

Expansion Drive

To capitalize on the information boom, EMC is now on an expansion spree, which Yip expects will help him attain his target. The firm has expanded its software sales force and allocated a marketing fund of $15 million to tap into the local market together with partners.

EMC has about 500 partners in China and plans to increase the number to 2,000 within one or two years. This year EMC will open four offices in China and plans to increase the number to 20 within five years to improve geographic coverage. That could help the company sell its hardware, software and services to small- and medium-sized businesses, which have begun placing orders for storage solutions.

In 2006 EMC Chairman and CEO Joe Tucci announced an additional investment of $500 million in China within five years, which could lay the cornerstone for EMC's future in the country. Most of that investment will be spent on research and development (R & D). EMC has opened a R & D center in Shanghai that now employs 135 people. Yip says the headcount could increase to 500 by the end of next year.

"We are also planning to open another R & D center in Beijing in June or July," he reveals.

Such R & D facilities could help EMC develop localized products and solutions to better meet the demands of Chinese customers.

But the challenge remains for Chinese companies to gain greater awareness of the importance of information management. EMC plans to start its first courses on information infrastructure in Chinese universities this summer.

The firm plans to partner with 20 universities by the end of this year and 50 schools by 2010.

By Li Weitao
(2007-04-09)

Networks Remain Key to Growth

An Interview with Carl-Henric Svanberg, CEO of Ericsson

Ericsson may not be as well known to average consumers as rivals such as Motorola or Nokia, but the Swedish giant has long been the leading firm in the telecom equipment market, a more lucrative sector than mobile phones.

Boosting Ericsson's share of an increasingly consolidated market may not be an easy task for Chief Executive Officer Carl-Henric Svanberg. In the past months, the industry has seen Lucent merge with Alcatel, and Nokia and Siemens combine their network businesses, partly triggered by Ericsson's decision to acquire Britain's Marconi in 2005. Such mergers could put the heat on Ericsson.

However, Svanberg said he was confident that Ericsson would continue to hold on to its leading position in the telecom equipment market as well as the top spot in China, which has been coveted by rivals such as Alcatel, Nokia and Siemens.

That's because Ericsson, since spinning off its handset business to form a joint venture with Sony, has been focusing on the telecom equipment market and investing more than any of its rivals in related technologies and research and development (R & D), Svanberg explained. And as Alcatel, Lucent, Nokia and Siemens are busy integrating their businesses, that might open a door for Ericsson to grab new business opportunities and expand its market share.

Svanberg said the network business will remain the key to Ericsson's future growth. But the firm is also pinning its hopes on professional services and the multimedia business, which are fueling Ericsson's business growth.

Ericsson is now the world's largest provider of professional telecom services, such as network design, planning, optimization, software development and managed services where mobile telecom equipment manufacturers take over and run networks for operators.

In the third quarter of 2006, Ericsson's sales from professional services surged 31 percent year-on-year. Multimedia businesses, such as mobile TV, have also been witnessing robust growth in recent years. Svanberg expects multimedia to be a major force in the global telecoms industry. To accelerate its multimedia growth, Ericsson recently restructured its global operations and established a new business division, the Multimedia Unit.

Ericsson's China operations are now also being restructured in line with its global realignment. Svanberg said Ericsson was open to acquisitions in the multimedia sector, including China. He added that Ericsson was in a position to

exploit business growth and maintain or even expand its leadership in China's future 3G (third generation) market, given the firm's strong technological know-how and marketing capabilities.

Extracts from an interview with Svanberg detailing how Ericsson will explore merger and acquisition (M & As) opportunities and contribute to the growth of China's telecom market:

Q: You have said Ericsson will continue to explore opportunities for mergers and acquisitions (M & As) if necessary. Could you hint at the direction of future M & A activities? Ericsson recently restructured its business and formed a new division, the Multimedia Unit. Will future M & As occur in that area? And given the continuing consolidation of the global telecoms market, will Ericsson consider buying some companies in China?

A: First of all, it's always a better alternative if you have the capability to realize organic growth and conduct R & D yourself, because when you acquire a company there is always the integration issue. On the other hand, if you acquire a company, it gives you the chance to leapfrog a bit. When you have some bolt-on acquisitions, you go faster. That could be an advantage, which is bigger than the regulation challenges. With that background, mobile infrastructure is an area where we have all the necessary competences and products. So we are not likely to conduct acquisitions (in that area). For example, in terms of IP technology, we are seeing more convergence of next-generation networks. Those are technologies of competences that we are in the process of developing, but we are also studying if we can accelerate that work by acquiring companies.

Multimedia is also an area where we always believe we can accelerate (business growth) if we can find the right companies and acquire them. Finally, in (professional) services, it could also be an opportunity for us to get quicker access to more skills, such as in system integration. From a general point of view, acquisitions are not more likely to occur in China. But neither are they less likely to happen elsewhere. There are always interesting opportunities in China.

Q: Nokia recently secured a network contract from Guangdong Mobile, which could be a breakthrough for Nokia (since Guangdong, the largest single provincial mobile telecoms market in China, used to be an area dominated by Ericsson). What do you think of Ericsson's current competitive edge, especially after a slew of M & As in the industry, such as the Alcatel-Lucent and Nokia-Siemens tie-ups?

A: If you have been following Ericsson's sales, you would have seen that they fluctuate a little bit between quarters. But overall they are very stable and showing strong momentum. So we defend our market positions quite well. We have a stable position. In certain provinces, we are bigger than anyone else. Overall, we have been in China for about 114 years. We probably have the strongest position of all the vendors. We have one-third of the market. I don't really see how that will change. I'm sure that (mergers) will help our rivals in certain situations, but they may also open up opportunities for us (to grow).

Q: What are your expectations for Ericsson's China operations? What is your long-term goal for the Chinese market?

A: On average, we estimate that we have a 33-35 percent share of the GSM market in China. Our ambition is to secure that market share also through the transition to 3G. That is definitely difficult to say as we even don't know when 3G will happen. But we do have that prediction. We do understand that Chinese vendors will get a much bigger role in the 3G network business than they had in the 2G network business. But on the other hand, there are several international 2G vendors that now are not providing equipment to 3G. We will try to hold on to our market share.

By Li Weitao
(2006-11-28)

In for the Long Haul

An Interview with Mats H Olsson,
President of Ericsson China

It's not the sunny forecast that industry players had hoped for, and certainly not the typical prelude to the introduction of a groundbreaking technology.

It is a dire situation, and telecoms equipment manufacturers are in trouble. Chinese telecoms operators are cutting back spending, and the government has yet to distribute 3G (third generation) mobile technology. The market is becoming crowded, and orders are dwindling for virtually every company that sells mobile technology in China.

Even Ericsson, the world's largest telecoms equipment manufacturer, has felt the squeeze.

"We did not actually see any (revenue) growth in China last year (2004)," says Mats H Olsson, President of Ericsson China.

The company is nonetheless still the top industry performer in both the Chinese and world markets. Ericsson received an order in South China's Guangdong Province in 2004 worth $805 million for the expansion of China Mobile's network. In October, 2005, the firm secured two orders worth approximately $290 million. Ericsson is generating revenues from new services for operators, such as consulting.

In contrast, many other mobile technology developers are struggling. They have announced few new contracts in the past months. High profile deals in particular have been virtually non-existent.

A planned, long-term approach to the Chinese market has been helping

Ericsson score big in the country and pull through. Consumer spending is down, but Olsson says that the company refuses to cut back. Ericsson is one of the most aggressive investors in China's telecoms sector. As early as 2000, the firm announced that it would double its investment in research and development (R & D) and operations by 2005.

Olsson claims that the company has delivered on about 97 percent of that promise, but says that even that is not enough.

"I hope it reaches 100 percent or even higher," he avers.

In September, Ericsson announced its plans to invest $1 billion in China within five years. The decision came during a lean period for telecoms equipment makers. Ericsson's aggressive R & D investments support its planned, long-term approach to the Chinese market. Between 2000-2004, Ericsson increased its R & D investment in China by 30 percent annually.

"We are proud of it and plan to increase the headcount by 50 percent this year," says Olsson.

R & D recruiting is difficult because it requires companies to heavily invest in training, says the company president. Ericsson's expansion into impoverished regions of China also underscores its long-term commitment. The firm recently opened a representative office in Guizhou, one of the poorest provinces in China. It is the first multinational telecoms enterprise to establish an office there.

"We will not leave a single city until we have established a presence there," says Olsson.

Many of Ericsson's competitors, by contrast, choose to hastily jump into local markets when they see business opportunities, he adds. They often quickly leave when they determine that potential has dried up.

"That is the major distinction between Ericsson and its competitors," says Olsson.

Over the coming five years, a significant amount of Ericsson's $1 billion investment budget will be directed at China's underdeveloped regions.

3G Gamble

The upcoming launch of 3G services in China is set to solidify Ericsson's dominant position in the country's telecoms market, just as it did throughout the 2G era. Chinese regulators have been delaying the release of 3G licences over the past several years. Media and industry speculation about the licensing schedule have consistently fallen short.

A number of discussions regarding the maturity of 3G technology and the selection of standards have dramatized the key issues, Olsson says.

"There was less speculation about 2G. The new technology should be introduced in China at the right time, just as 2G once was," he adds.

Some observers have even suggested that China not introduce 3G, partly because it has overshadowed the industry for so long.

"That is very bad advice. The question should be when and how to introduce," says Olsson. "I'm confident the government will make the right decision at the right time."

The current spending cuts by Chinese mobile operators should be temporary, and orders for 3G will be significant. Operators will continue to expand their existing 2G networks throughout the 3G era. This could also continue to offer opportunities for Ericsson.

The company controls about 35 percent of the country's 2G GSM/GPRS equipment market, and 15 percent of the CDMA gear market. Olsson believes Ericsson will maintain its market share throughout the 3G period, thanks to its established commitment to the country.

It has built a solid relationship with mobile operators China Mobile and China Unicom throughout the 2G era, says Olsson, and the company's association with fixed-line operators China Telecom and China Netcom goes back even longer.

China Telecom and China Netcom are widely expected to secure 3G licences in the future, which is likely to help them move into the cellular market. Ericsson has agreed to buy British telecoms firm Marconi for approximately $2.1 billion, which could help plug up some of the holes in Ericsson's product portfolio. Marconi primarily focuses on equipment for fixed-line networks. The acquisition is expected to make Ericsson even more attractive to fixed-line carriers such as China Telecom and China Netcom.

Local companies will play an increasingly important role in China's 3G market, but the country's competitive sector will not change significantly once the technology is introduced, and Ericsson will maintain its leading role, Olsson says.

"We have been growing steadily, especially in the 3G market over the past few years. And this momentum will continue," he declares.

Localization

Ericsson's history in China stretches back to 1892. This has contributed greatly to its understanding of the local market, Olsson says.

China is now one of the company's top three global supply hubs and a core R & D base. It is also the second largest single country market for Ericsson, after the United States. More than 97 percent of its employees in China are locals.

Olsson is one of the few top executives heading the China operations of a multinational telecoms company.

"I understand my Chinese colleagues a lot better than my Swedish colleagues," says Olsson. "In terms of mindset, I'm quite Chinese, or at least Asian."

He has spent much of his life and career in the region since joining Ericsson 23 years ago.

"My advantage is that I come from the top management team at our Swedish headquarters," says Olsson. "I have an outstanding network there."

This ensures that headquarters responds quickly to the Chinese market. Olsson also says he has "international exposure", something most locals lack. He has worked in a number of countries.

A number of local companies are going global due to China's strong economic growth.

"It is difficult to understand foreign cultures without some international exposure," Olsson says.

That will be a major challenge for Chinese firms entering the foreign market.

"It is difficult to manage operations across a number of countries," he says. "Perseverance, a common characteristic of Swedes and others who live in the colder parts of the planet, is part of Ericsson's corporate culture. It can help the firm pull through difficult situations.

"We don't change our strategy when the numbers don't come out as expected, and we won't do it if we have a bad quarter in China. We have a very warm culture, and we value our customers highly. We are not just selling commodities to them," he concludes.

By Li Weitao
(2005-11-21)

Super Link

Western Expansion

When Ericsson showcased a small radio base station at the 3GSM World Congress 2006 in Barcelona, the world's premier mobile event, the Swedish mobile telecom equipment maker found the market reception "overwhelming".

The radio base station, developed in China and branded as the "Flamingo", is the world's most advanced and smallest of its kind based on the second-generation (2G) telephony standard GSM, says Mats H Olsson, President of Ericsson Greater China.

The great interest showed by visitors, especially global telecom operators, has resulted in all of Ericsson's factories in the world manufacturing the Flamingo base station, which is responsible for handling traffic and signaling between a mobile phone and the cellular network.

"That was not our initial plan," says Olsson.

Ericsson has so far shipped "tens of thousands" of Flamingo stations that were developed at its research and development (R & D) center in Chengdu in Southwest China's Sichuan Province. It's not surprising that a product developed in China is gaining the global spotlight, given multinationals' increasingly localized R & D in the country. But Chengdu might be off the radar screen for many.

Ericsson has 10 R & D facilities in China, with the Chengdu center the only one staffed with "100 percent" local people, says Olsson. The Flamingo base station could be crucial for Ericsson to maintain its No. 1 position in the world's telecom equipment market. In addition to its strength in technology, size matters for the Flamingo at a time when it could be costly for a telecom operator to rent space to install base stations when building mobile telecom networks.

In December 2004, Chinese telecom equipment maker Huawei Technologies was selected by a Dutch mobile operator to deliver and install a nationwide 3G WCDMA network in the Netherlands. One of the major reasons why Huawei outbid its foreign rivals is that the Chinese firm developed a small-sized base station, which could save up to 30 percent of the total cost of operation, according to Huawei.

A large number of operators around the world are upgrading their mobile phone networks to 3G. To ensure a smooth upgrade, the GSM and WCDMA networks usually co-exist for a long time. That means both GSM and WCDMA base stations would be placed in the same space.

"A small-sized base station is really very attractive," says Liu Lu, head of the Chengdu center.

But for Olsson, it's more about how a "Go West" strategy in China is paying off. Ericsson opened an office in Chengdu in 1995 and established an R & D center in June, 2004. Five years later it located its western China head-quarters to the city. The success of the Flamingo is encouraging the firm to increase investment and staffing in Chengdu center by 25 percent and 30 percent respectively in 2007.

"The headcount increase would be higher than the average national growth (of the company)," says Olsson.

China mapped out a "Develop the West" policy in the late 1990s to boost the economically lagging western provinces. But due to less advanced infrastructure, big companies, especially multinationals, have been slow in heading for the wild west.

However, after Ericsson opened its R & D center in Chengdu, its major competitors — Nokia, Alcatel and Siemens — have been rushing to catch the same boat.

"We are happy to be ahead of our competitors," says Olsson, adding that an increasing number of multinationals will gradually transfer some R & D activities from the eastern part of China to the west.

"Bigger cities like Beijing and Shanghai are usually the top choices for inexperienced multinationals (when seeking to establish R & D facilities)," he says. "Ericsson's first R & D center in China is also located in Shanghai. But we are wiser now. Personally I don't see any reason why Shanghai and Beijing are more attractive than Chengdu now."

In less affluent cities like Chengdu, multinationals can enjoy labor cost advantages. Also, the University of Electronic Science and Technology of China and a number of government-run, top-notch electronics research institutes are based in Chengdu, producing a large talent pool.

For Olsson, there is another major factor. In Chengdu, he can frequently meet with senior government officials. "I don't recall any meeting with top officials in bigger cities (than Chengdu)," he says, adding that some R & D activities are being "hampered by bureaucracy".

Geographically, Chengdu is a gateway to Southwest China, and the city is now quite aggressive in attracting foreign investment. According to Jiao Weixia, director of the Sichuan Provincial Investment Promotion Bureau, more than 120 of the world's top 500 corporations have invested or set up representative offices in Sichuan.

In China's bureaucratic culture, government officials seldom leave mobile phone numbers on their business cards.

"It's impossible that there will be no mobile phone number on my card as well as those of my colleagues," says Jiao. "You can always reach us."

In 2002, when Ericsson planned to increase its activities in Chengdu, Sichuan Vice-Governor Huang Xiaoxiang made a suggestion that local manufacturers get involved in Ericsson's sourcing activities.

The Zhongguang High-tech Industrial Development Group then became one of the suppliers. It developed eight products for Ericsson, with five already shipped by the company on a large scale. A product developed by Zhongguang was recently submitted to Ericsson's headquarters in Sweden and it beat out a French rival that has long been a supplier of Ericsson.

"That is a big breakthrough, since it means that Zhongguan's products will be used in each of Ericsson's R & D facilities around the world, whether it's in the United States, Germany, France or Sweden," says Liu.

In 2006, Ericsson's indirect procurement in China for products developed by the Chengdu R & D center totaled 86 million yuan. This year (2007) it could hit 700 million yuan, says Graeme McCusker, Executive Vice-President of Ericsson Greater China, and General Manager of its western China operations.

Chengdu is not the only western Chinese city of importance to Ericsson. In September 2005, it became the first multinational telecom vendor to open an office in Guiyang, capital of Southwest China's Guizhou Province. Olsson played a major role in deciding to open the office.

"From the market standpoint, Guizhou is not one of the attractive markets; little investment has been made in telecom infrastructure as it is one of the poorest provinces in China," he says.

McCusker still sees lots of opportunities in western China as domestic operators are now turning to the emerging markets — from the steppes of Inner Mongolia to the rugged peaks of Tibet — to build up user bases as telephone penetration in cities becomes saturated.

"Operators' business models continue to change on a daily basis," says McCusker, adding that Ericsson's western expansion is in line with the business transformation of operators.

By Li Weitao
(2007-06-18)

Talent Crunch

An Interview with James S Turley,
Chairman and CEO
of Ernst & Young Global

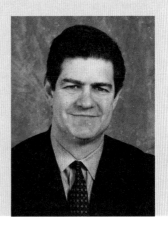

Modern market economies have their own systems of checks and balances. Enthusiasm among investors is typically followed by increased demand for financial integrity and expertise.

Companies from developed economies continue to launch new projects in China, and Chinese enterprises have already begun looking for new assets overseas. This is where Ernst & Young, one of the world's largest accounting and consulting firms, comes in. Demand for financial advisory services has reached the point that the company is now planning to significantly and enthusiastically expand its presence in China.

James S Turley, Chairman and Chief Executive Officer (CEO) of Ernst & Young Global, says that the company's development in China is "limited only by the outstanding people we can get."

Ernst & Young already has 8,000 employees at its China operations, but Turley says he would like to increase staff levels to as many as 20,000 professionals. This would mean bringing in more than 1,500 recruits per year.

He says he has even thought about moving some Putonghua-speaking accountants from the United States, Malaysia, Singapore, the Philippines, and other countries to compensate for the shortage of manpower in China.

This is not yet a clearly defined or articulated goal, but there is already compelling evidence of the direction that the company is quickly heading in.

The company boasts a staff of over 2,031 people in Beijing alone. At the Ernst & Young China head office in Hong Kong, there are over 2,000 people, and the Shanghai office employs about 2,282.

With 10 offices already established throughout China, Turley expects to add even more geographical coverage to the company's mainland operations, especially in the country's interior. Ernst & Young China currently has only two offices outside of the country's more industrial eastern coastal regions, in Wuhan, in Central China's Hubei Province and in Chengdu, in Southwest China's Sichuan Province.

The company's knowledge management program helps it cope with the rapidly growing demand and expansion of manpower, Turley says.

This program is not strictly for internal training, although the company is firmly committed to investing in staff potential; it runs a range of training plans, both online and offline, from professional knowledge skills to English language courses.

It is focused on making the company a global leader in knowledge-based services. Knowledge management in China is used to promote corporate governance and financial responsibility in the developing economy, and it reinforces Ernst & Young's ties with the government and other corporate entities.

Turley says that is meant to create a business environment that can benefit everybody, where China can be better prepared to adopt global business practices, such as international financial reporting standards (IFRS).

This is a set of accounting standards governing how particular types of transactions and other functions should be reported in financial statements. Many publicly listed companies throughout the world are adopting IFRS.

Ernst & Young's thriving business is increasingly based on its ability to reach out to an audience that finds its expertise useful and valuable.

This of course refers to corporate executives, but in China it often includes economic officials as well.

The organization often brings in its experts from the United States, Europe, Australia and other Asian economies to share their experiences and ideas with interest in China.

Turley says Ernst & Young is particularly proud of its successful corporate governance programs that it developed with several of the Central Government's financial agencies.

He is thus quite familiar with officials from the People's Bank of China (PBOC), the country's central bank, the State-owned Assets Supervision and Administration Commission (SASAC), and the China Securities Regulatory Commission (CSRC).

"China is on a journey," says Turley. From his conversations with government officials and corporate executives, he is convinced that the country is committed to IFRS. The results of this will be positive, he adds.

The government is attempting to lower the banks' non-performing loans (NPLs) and merge non-tradable shares in the A-share market with traded ones.

These are all signs that Beijing is not trying to hide the issues, and that it is willing to listen to expert opinions.

"Positive things will happen whenever one lays the issues out on the table," says Turley.

He says that Ernst & Young's mainland business has been growing rapidly, despite the fact that its China operations are hampered by a shortage of solid talent. China is actually one of the company's strongest growth sources, he adds.

Chinese employees might lack English proficiency, but there is otherwise very little difference in overall quality between the company's Chinese and Indian recruits.

"One of the beauties of these growing economies," says Turley, "is that their education systems are very good."

Ernst & Young employs 114,000 people throughout the world. In the fiscal year ending June 30, 2006, it reported a worldwide revenue of $18.4 billion. This represents a year-on-year revenue increase of $1.5 billion and a growth rate of 10% in local currency terms.

It also reported satisfactory performance in several future growth markets that it had identified as strategic investments, such as China and India. In each of the important "BRIC" countries — Brazil, Russia, India and China — revenue increased by at least 25%.

By Zhang Xiaogang
(2007-09)

ERNST & YOUNG

New Ernst & Young Chairman Focuses on "People First"

An Interview with David Sun, Chairman & Managing Partner for the Far East Area & China

May the moment come when David Sun is quietly confident his firm's "people first" philosophy is being put to good use in China, despite staff shortages.

Indeed, Sun, the Chairman & Managing Partner for the Far East Area & China at Ernst & Young, is finding it a big challenge to locate enough quality manpower to serve the accounting firm's rapidly expanding business in the country. It's a big test of his leadership.

In fact, it is arguably the biggest hurdle for the whole professional services industry in China in recent years.

As the Chinese economy continues to grow, it creates great demand for large volumes of professional services in complicated accounting, taxation and legal issues, and it especially needs individuals familiar with both domestic and international regulations. Finding enough professionals who have the skills and experience in such areas has been a challenge for Ernst & Young, as well as other large professional services firms.

"In America, there are 350,000 CPAs to serve the country," said Sun. "Considering its 300 million population, there is one Certified Public Accountant (CPA) out of a thousand. China has around 130,000 Chinese Institute Certified Public Accountants, which means there's an average of one CPA for every 10,000 people."

And even in 10 years, China will probably not reach the same CPA ratio as the US. But with the continuing developing economy, there will be a significant need for qualified CPAs.

"Only when the firm has enough qualified people can it provide the best quality service to maintain continuing growth," said Sun.

People, quality, and growth have been the three pillars that have supported the professional accounting firm's growth into a global giant, but Sun deems the first as the foundation stone.

That is why all four of the major international professional accounting firms have launched major recruitment campaigns throughout China.

In 2004, KPMG recruited 400 graduates fresh out of Chinese universities. In 2005, PricewaterhouseCoopers (PwC) and Ernst & Young recruited 1,000 throughout China. Both PWC and Deloitte plan to recruit around 10,000 new people in the next five years in China. And so does Ernst & Young.

Ernst & Young established its tenth office in Chengdu of Sichuan Province in April 2007, and one of the firm's criteria for choosing the location was whether it was near top-level universities, apparently to supply it with recent graduates.

Sun believes that fresh graduates are easier to be trained, as they are energetic and eager to learn.

Based on this concept, a graduate's major is not a focal point during the recruitment. Rather, integrated ability and learning capacity are the key elements in this knowledge-intensive industry.

The recruitment procedures at Ernst & Young are tough. First, students are screened according to their majors, standard of English, professional qualifications and academic results. Selected candidates then take a written test. A handful of applicants are invited to meet managers for an interview, and the finalists meet with a partner.

Within limited time, applicants have to try their best to leave a good impression, demonstrating their communication and leadership skills, analytical strengths, as well as their ability to work with others.

The firm values and expects integrity as a very important quality in its employees, as well as a precise and prudent working style.

However, it takes years to become a professional.

Sun defined professionals as those who understand the difference between good and bad results, have gained abundant experience from work, and are familiar with management practices. He added that a person could only learn these on the job.

In fact, the firm has launched a series of on-the-job training programs aimed at different levels to update employees' knowledge and skills, starting from the orientation training to pre-promotion training, management skill training and overseas exchange programs.

Moreover, the way to becoming a professional is not easy. Heavy workloads can leave little time for staff to prepare for the exams that are necessary to acquire a CPA. A large number of employees choose to leave giant firms due to high pressure and overtime.

"Overtime work is very popular during peak season. Sometimes you even work 18 hours a day," said an employee from Ernst & Young.

To tackle the problem, Sun is going to advise managers to say no to impossible engagement deadlines, sparing staff more time to prepare for the exams.

"It is not a 100-meter dash. It is a marathon, and they should keep the strength to win a lifelong run," said Sun.

But even Sun put in plenty of overtime early in his career.

Sun believes corporate culture is crucial in managing the firm. Sun says maintaining a good corporate culture does work in encouraging people to stay, rather than just raising wages.

With about 30 years professional service experience, Sun also applies his culture theory to the solution of corporate governance issues the firm has been committed to.

"Corporate governance is a worldwide problem. Even in a well-developed market like the US, scandals like Enron still happen," said Sun. "In China, the pay to directors is relatively low, so the chance for scandals doubles."

"You can certainly set some rules and regulations or some professional guidelines, and it is really necessary to establish rules in a developing country. But regulators such as the China Securities Regulatory Commission, and the State-owned Assets Supervision and Administration Commission of the State Council can only do so much."

"The companies need to create a good corporate culture to attract people," he adds.

In China, few directors are aware that they are there to serve the investors, not themselves. Only when a service culture is established from top to bottom, alongside a transparent information disclosure system, can corporate governance be improved.

In the coming year, Sun will lead Ernst & Young China to continue serving large state-owned enterprises clients such as the Industrial and Commercial Bank of China, Air China, Ping An of China, the People's Insurance Company of China, Dong Feng and Bao Steel, and help privately owned enterprises to develop better corporate governance and provide a training service for them under the WTO concept.

In his spare time, the chairman likes to take long runs, believing the exercise also strengthens him mentally and helps him cultivate endurance and a strong will.

Before taking the helm as chairman of Ernst & Young China in 2006 from his predecessor Anthony Wu, Sun worked with the firm for 29 years. He is chairman of Audit Practice, a member of the Management Committee of Ernst & Young on the Chinese mainland and Hong Kong, and a member of Ernst & Young's Global Audit Executive Committee. Sun is active in serving the accounting profession and the community in Hong Kong. He is a Council Member and a past president of the Hong Kong Institute of Certified Public Accountants and also a member of the American Institute of Certified Public Accountant and the Illinois Society of CPAs.

By Zhang Ran
(2006-09)

Super Link

Eleven Business Leaders Honored

Ernst & Young announced the 11 winners of its Entrepreneur of the Year award for China at a ceremony in Beijing on February 2, 2007.

Sometimes referred to as the Oscars for the global business community, the awards were given for the first time in the country.

"China's rise as a global economic powerhouse is one of the most significant transformative events of our time. Many Chinese entrepreneurs are showing the world their capabilities, leadership, and achievements," said David Sun, Chairman of Ernst & Young China.

"The 11 winners selected by the independent judging panel demonstrate that more and more Chinese entrepreneurs are making significant contributions towards the economic growth and prosperity of China," said Sun.

Winners selected from four categories — media, IT, retail, and industry and commerce — included Liu Changle, Chairman and CEO of Phoenix Satellite Television Holdings Ltd; John Deng, Chairman Vimicro Corporation and Jiang Nanchun, Chairman and CEO of Focus Media (China) Holding Ltd.

Nominations for the awards opened in September 2006. The nominees were assessed according to entrepreneurial spirit, the company's financial performance, strategic direction, national and global impact, innovation, and personal integrity and influence.

"We want to honor the leader of a business who has strong curiosity, perseverance, dreams and the personal integrity to mobilize other people to realize their dreams together," said Raymond Woo, Chairman of the China Operating Committee, Ernst & Young China.

"We will make the awards a long-term program in China," said Woo.

The program was established in the United States 20 years ago and has been expanded to more than 35 countries.

By Lu Haoting
(2007-02-03)

Fujitsu Chief
Takes on Rivals

An Interview with Naoyuki Akikusa,
Chairman of Fujitsu

Naoyuki Akikusa, Fujitsu's Chairman, might be Japanese, but he frequently turns to traditional Chinese wisdom to improve his company's business practice.

"I'm always ready to absorb Asian management philosophy, especially from China," says Akikusa.

And it seems to be working. Since he took over Fujitsu in 2003, the loss-making domestic business of the world's No. 3 IT service provider (after IBM and EDS) has turned a corner. Its China market has been growing at an annual average of 27 percent.

Akikusa says he applied to the business world some of the ideas he had read in the works of Chinese military strategist Sun Tzu and late Chairman Mao Zedong.

"I got a lot of inspiration from the *Art of War* by Sun Tzu and Mao Zedong's work," says Akikusa.

IBM, which generated more than $47 billion from services in 2005, is a formidable opponent. But Akikusa adopted "guerrilla tactics", as used by Chairman Mao. His flexible tactics have jolted IBM even as Fujitsu sought ways to exploit the US giant's weaknesses.

Akikusa spends much time learning from Fujitsu's rivals. He says he follows Sun Tzu's idea that "one who knows his own strength and that of the enemy is invincible in battle".

And the outspoken CEO does not conceal his bias against US corporate management culture.

"The American corporate culture is largely based on MBA courses, text-books and figures," he says. In 2000, at a time when the Internet bubble was bursting, Akikusa was overseeing Fujitsu's semiconductor business in the United States. With many technology businesses going bust, Fujitsu's chip orders dropped. The slumping figures led to calls for Fujitsu to close its chip business.

But Akikusa held firm and the chip unit has now become a major driver for Fujitsu's business.

"Such an experience has taught me to always take a long-term view in business operations — which is in line with Asian and Chinese cultures — instead of the US philosophy," he says.

The CEO says modern US corporate culture leads executives to bow to revenue figures, analysts and investors, and take a short-term perspective to bolster sales.

He believes business leaders can learn much from Asian and Chinese cultures to shift to a long-term tactical perspective.

Revamping Fujitsu

Since he took over Fujitsu, Akikusa has been trying to reshape its corporate culture and inject new blood into the 72-year-old company. This change is crucial to its business in China, which is an increasingly strategic market.

In June 2006, Fujitsu launched a "chief representative" mechanism. It divided its global markets into four regions, with China being the only single country market.

Regional chief representatives were given greater power than previous regional heads. All of them were members of Fujitsu boards and had the right to restructure their regional businesses.

This is a dramatic change for Japanese companies, which usually keep decision-making within Japan.

Haruhito Takeda, President of Fujitsu (China) Co Ltd, has been given larger authority and has successfully consolidated the firm's sprawling businesses, ranging from services and semiconductors to electronic devices.

"Our aim is very clear: We want our businesses to rapidly expand," says Akikusa. "And the consolidation must be decided and implemented by Chinese management teams and employees."

The CEO says all Japanese firms, including Fujitsu, need to adopt a mindset change that allows them to better compete in China.

"Previously, they sat down in Japan and mapped out strategies for the China market," he says. "In the early days of their entry to China, this practice seemed to work well as there were few local rivals.

"But now there have been dramatic changes to the market landscape. We need to think locally and partner with local companies to align with China's industrial policies and economic growth."

In previous years, a slew of underperforming Japanese companies, including Panasonic, Mitsubishi and NEC, were forced to pull out of some industries such as the mobile phone market, where competition had intensified.

In many cases this was blamed on slow decision-making processes at the firms' Japanese headquarters.

"In the rapidly changing information and communications technology sector, we need to have an even faster decision-making process. The traditional Japanese practice is now largely obsolete," says Akikusa.

The consolidation of Fujitsu's businesses — including 39 subsidiaries in China — has been going well, especially in the communications sector. Subsidiaries previously reported to different departments at the Tokyo headquarters, which largely undermined the firm's competitiveness in the local market.

The consolidation is already starting to pay off. Since 2003, Fujitsu has consolidated its semiconductor businesses in China.

Nantong Fujitsu Microelectronics Co is a joint venture formed by Fujitsu in East China's Jiangsu Province. The company, which focuses mainly on semiconductor assembly and testing, in 2006 generated a profit of $100 million, up 80 percent year-on-year. It was the best performer out of Fujitsu's 39 subsidiaries in China.

Akikusa says a software integration firm in Fujian Province owned by Fujitsu also saw a major business uptake, helped by its alignment strategy in China.

By Li Weitao
(2007-01-30)

High Stakes Chips

An Interview with Haruhito Takeda,
General Manager of Fujitsu China

To seek the truth from facts: this is the core philosophy of the Communist Party of China, developed by Mao Zedong 70 years ago. But now this has become a catchphrase for Haruhito Takeda, General Manager of Fujitsu China, and other top executives.

While many Japanese companies in China are criticized as slow to localize their operations to adapt to the world's fastest-growing economy, Takeda, using that philosophy, thinks his company has found the key to success. Nantong Fujitsu Microelectronics Co Ltd, in which Fujitsu has a stake of almost 39 percent, gives testament to the effectiveness of the theory.

When Nantong Fujitsu, a semiconductor packaging and testing factory, opened in 1997 in Nantong, a city beside the Yangtze River in East China's Jiangsu Province, it had only two foreign customers. These were Fujitsu, and Siemens, a strategic partner with the Japanese firm.

A decade later, nine of the top-10 largest semiconductor makers in the world are its customers, and the firm has become the largest domestic chip packaging and testing company in the world's biggest semiconductor market.

Nantong Fujitsu processed 3.46 billion chips and generated sales of 2.18 billion yuan in 2006, compared to 181 million pieces and 99.8 million yuan in 1998.

"When Japanese companies first came to China, they wanted to combine Japanese technological strength with the manufacturing capability in China, so

Japanese businesses usually wanted to control their joint ventures," says Takeda.

But after a comprehensive review of the strategy, Takeda, who has led Fujitsu China for 10 years, says that the strategy did not prove successful and it became imperative for Fujitsu to adapt different business models to fit different operations.

While many Japanese companies choose to have a Japanese manager lead their subsidiaries or joint ventures, Fujitsu decided to let Chinese partners run Nantong Fujitsu, taking advantage of the Chinese desire for high growth and knowledge of the local market.

Takeda says letting Chinese take the lead also stimulates local management to run the business better and gives more room for local talent.

From 2006, the Japanese electronics and information services firm even stopped assigning a deputy general manager to Nantong Fujitsu, positioning itself instead as a tutor in technology and management. Now there are just six Japanese employees at the joint venture, in positions such as production management and technical supervision.

Fujitsu still keeps three seats on Nantong Fujitsu's 11-member board; the other eight include four from Chinese investors and four independent directors, so that the company can guide the development of the joint business in line with its own strategic needs.

At the same time, both the Chinese and Japanese sides are working together to drive the growth of the joint venture.

Shi Mingda, Chairman and General Manager of Nantong Fujitsu, says that while Chinese management sees the bigger picture when it comes to strategy, the famous Japanese fastidiousness for detail reminds Nantong Fujitsu not to pursue high growth at the cost of quality.

"Our core competence is Japanese quality at Chinese costs, an almost invincible combination in the market," says Shi.

He reveals that his company is expected to make an initial public offering (IPO) on a domestic stock market to raise over 400 million yuan in 2007.

Instead of worrying about the dilution of Fujitsu's interests, Takeda believes the IPO adds another guaranty of his company's control over the firm.

"With the IPO, a better corporate governance will create a more transparent structure of Nantong Fujitsu, which is good for us too," says Takeda.

He adds that giving more authority to the local management team does not mean the role of Nantong Fujtsu will be weakened; instead, he thinks, it will be strengthened.

In 2006, the Japanese firm aimed to increase contribution from its overseas business to 50 percent by 2010, with China alone contributing 10 percent.

It began restructuring its Chinese operations to form a united Fujitsu, by concentrating all resources on key markets such as semiconductors, telecom solutions and information technology.

As Fujitsu streamlines its businesses, its Tokyo headquarters will give more responsibility to the Chinese venture to reduce costs and increase global competitiveness. The Japanese company will also consolidate its 39 subsidiaries and joint ventures in China to generate synergy.

Fujitsu's wholly-owned semiconductor design house in Shanghai will also bring more customers to Nantong Fujitsu. The company will build a joint design house close to Nantong Fujitsu, so both businesses can increase competitiveness by providing value-added services.

"With joint efforts from Chinese and Japanese investors, we have become the largest domestic semiconductor packaging and testing company, and our goal for the next three to five years is to become one of the top-10 companies in the world," says Shi, adding his firm currently ranks about fifteenth globally.

According to Shi, Nantong Fujitsu will invest more than 200 million yuan over the next four years, to more than double its production capacity to 8 billion chips a year and sales to 5 billion yuan by 2010.

By Liu Baijia
(2007-04-09)

Super Link

Fujitsu Eyes Expansion in China Market

Fujitsu Ltd hopes to more than double its sales in five years in China, through a consolidation of its 39 operations in its most important overseas market, said a top executive with the Japanese technology giant.

Hiroaki Kurokawa, President and Representative Director of Fujitsu, said sales from China will rise from the current 24 billion yuan ($3 billion) to 60 billion yuan ($7.6 billion) in 2010.

The key to that growth won't be more offices or staff, but uniting the many subsidiaries the company has scattered around the country.

"This year is the beginning of our reform," said Kurokawa in an interview in Nanjing.

Since taking over the world's third largest technology service provider in 2003, Kurokawa's first job was to bring Fujitsu's loss-making businesses in Japan into profitability.

In Fujitsu's first fiscal half ending in September, the company booked operating income of $469 million in Japan, an increase of 14 percent year-on-year, according to its financial results released on October 26.

But the firm is still struggling with a slowdown in its home market, meaning that the focus of its new wave of reform is overseas expansion.

In the first fiscal half, Fujitsu's net sales from overseas operations rose by 18.5 percent. Net sales in Japan grew by just 4.4 percent over the same period.

In June, Fujitsu decided to set up overseas groups in China, the Americas, Europe, and Asia, in an attempt to grow sales of the four regions, from the current 30 percent to 50 percent in 2010.

Haruhito Takeda, President of Fujitsu China, said his company had maintained an annual average growth rate of 25 percent since 2001. With China's increasing demand for technology services, he said, keeping a similar growth rate was possible.

However, he added, severe challenges were still ahead for the biggest

Japanese technology service provider.

One such challenge is intense competition. Almost all of the top-10 technology consulting and service providers in the world, including IBM, EDS, HP Services, and Accenture, are targeting China as a growth market, meaning Fujitsu will have its work cut out for it to stay on top.

Another issue is the highly fragmented system of subsidiaries the company has in China.

Currently, the firm has more than 18,000 employees, most of whom work at its semiconductor or electronic device factories, employed at 39 different subsidiaries and reporting to different departments in the Tokyo headquarters.

What is even more challenging is that Fujitsu China has about 1,500 technology service engineers scattered in different locations in Beijing, Shanghai, Fuzhou, Nanjing and Xi'an.

These separate companies make consolidation a pressing issue for Fujitsu.

"Now we have guidelines, but to execute (the plan) is much more difficult," said Takeda.

He said Fujitsu China was working on a three-year plan (2007 to 2009) to integrate the staff and resources of its subsidiaries.

"Everybody knows we can compete against IBM for large clients," said Takeda. "But we are weak and scattered, so we must unite."

Fujitsu China now has only one legal professional, but it will soon establish a legal affairs department, with experts from Japan and China, to discuss how to combine resources from different subsidiaries.

By Liu Baijia
(2006-11-14)

A Sustained Growth

An Interview with Steve Bertamini, Chairman and CEO of GE Northeast Asia

I f you happened to have visited the website of General Electric in August 2007, what you would have seen on the homepage is not the usual conches, apples, turbines or windmills, but a Countdown to Beijing page, with images of Beijing and the Olympic Games to be held in the Chinese capital.

It is a rare move for the US industrial giant to change its homepage to feature a special, but it does highlight GE's commitment to the Chinese market.

All this comes with a change of attitude towards the world's fastest growing economy. Steve Bertamini, Chairman and CEO of GE Northeast Asia and President of GE Capital Asia, said the significant shift started about five years ago, when China began to be seen not just as a cheap manufacturing base and a market for exports.

Since then, GE has turned to create a China-oriented business.

"We are still in the early stages of that, but fast-forwarding five years from now, it will really help to transform our business here to make sure we continue to grow at a healthy speed for many years to come," said Bertamini, in an interview.

Global markets have become increasingly important for the US giant, which makes half its revenues, and has more than 50 percent non-American employees.

In 2006, GE China's revenue grew by almost 30 percent year-on-year to $5.4

billion.

In the first half, due to a large revenue base in 2006 and the spin-off of GE Plastics from the industrial conglomerate, the growth rate was slower, at about 12 percent.

However, Bertamini expected that full-year growth could be between 15 to 20 percent, without taking the GE Plastics spin-off into account.

In terms of the company's long-term growth, Bertamini was even more optimistic.

"In 5 to 10 years, China can become one of the largest markets for GE, possibly the second or third after the United States," said Bertamini.

GE's infrastructures, industrial solutions, and healthcare units all showed good growth momentum. However, GE Commercial Finance, its consumer finance unit GE Money, and the media arm NBC Universal, still lag behind, except for a high-profile investment in Shenzhen Development Bank.

With the continuous opening-up of the country, the company can bring in more services from the other three business groups and tap the potentials from new trends in the fourth largest economy in the world.

"This is a long race and we do not worry too much about what it is now," said Bertamini.

The key to GE's success in the world's most populous nation is to align its development with the direction of the nation.

One of the first things that Bertamini did when he came to China was to read the nation's 11th Five-Year Plan for 2006 to 2010, which is believed to be the best source for understanding the country's strategies.

He believed one of the biggest trend in China is the shifting of people from rural regions to cities.

The latest figures from the National Bureau of Statistics show that by the end of 2006, 577 million Chinese lived in cities and towns, and the urbanization rate of the country was 43.9 percent, 4.8 percent higher than that at the end of 2002.

It is estimated that about 12 million people on an average will move from villages to cities and towns every year by 2050.

Urbanization means more demands for water, houses, power, transport, and healthcare — fields in which GE has a presence.

Another trend that GE reads from China's blueprint is its emphasis on sustainability. In 2005, GE launched an Ecomagination initiative, trying to increase investments in and sales from environment-friendly products and become a good corporate citizen in that regard. The move came accidentally at around the same time that China was drafting the 11th Five-Year Plan.

In May, 2006, GE Chairman and CEO Jeff Immelt came to Beijing and launched the campaign in China.

The company announced that it would spend $50 million on research and development of green technologies in the country in the next five years.

Bertamini said that one especially relevant research project deals with clean coal technology, which is under development in GE's Shanghai research lab with 15 top scientists in the field.

He hoped the Chinese Government could promote several big state-owned coal companies to apply GE technologies on a trial basis, because without pressure from the government, many companies do not have incentives to deploy new technology at high costs.

In September 2007, Immelt paid his second visit to China this year and witnessed the signing ceremony between GE and Wuhan Iron and Steel (Group) Corp. The power generation solutions from GE are expected to save 1.2 billion yuan in electricity bills and reduce 2 million tons of carbon dioxide emission annually for the country's third largest steel maker.

Bertamini said that thanks to strong pushes, GE China has already got about 10 percent of its revenue from green products, ahead of GE's global goal to get 10 percent of sales from Ecomagination products by 2010.

In the next three years, the ratio could increase to 20 percent, he added.

By Liu Baijia
(2007-10-30)

Rural Health

An Interview with Joe Hogan,
CEO of GE Healthcare

In most developed countries, a minimum amount of medical care is usually available to citizens, no matter how dire their circumstances are. But in China, which has the world's fastest growing economy, when a farmer or his family has a serious disease, his only hope of getting through the crisis is to have enough money saved.

There are news reports day after day detailing how rural families struggle to raise 200,000 yuan ($25,000) to seek cures for their dear, sick father or mother, while their annual income from growing rice is just 5,000 yuan ($625).

Developing health care facilities and medical systems for the nation's rural population have become pressing issues for the government.

General Electric (GE) Healthcare, the world's largest diagnostic equipment provider and information technology company, has a predominant market share in top-level hospitals in many of the nation's cities, and considers this the right time to expand to China's vast rural areas.

"We are committed to the effort that the Chinese Ministry of Health is making to focus more on rural health," says Joe Hogan, CEO of GE Healthcare.

During his visit to Beijing, Hogan speaks enthusiastically about the Chinese market, and says his firm is looking forward to a working partnership with healthcare clinicians and various key government officials, to try to support Chinese healthcare efforts.

The CEO tells the reporter that large-scale medical equipment does not imply costliness, and that GE Healthcare has many types of high-performance equipment that operate at low cost, perfectly suited to the country's rural areas.

"We produce portable, cost-effective equipment such as CT, X-ray and portable ultra-sound machines ," he explains. "These can be used in hospitals and clinics in the countryside."

Hogan has positive things to say of China's rural market potential.

"The strategy is to make sure there is proper infrastructure in place to help support the medical system," says Hogan. "What we have proposed to the government is the hub-and-spoke system in these areas."

This means creating larger regional centers, he says, tied together by primary care clinics that help get patients to more advanced facilities through effective channels. This is an efficient method to prevent the duplication of facilities, equipment and doctors.

"GE Healthcare, which has a long product line, has advantages in providing proper alignment for hospitals and clinics of all levels," emphasizes Hogan.

China Experience

The firm, a global leader in diagnostics, entered China in 1979. The company says that almost all top-level hospitals in China use GE-labelled CT, medical resonance imaging and X-ray systems.

"We are a pioneering company — we don't just export equipment to China, but have our own Chinese engineers and production facilities in China for China," says the CEO. "We have been thinking of China as one of our most important countries in global business."

Currently, GE Healthcare has more than 3,000 staff in China, a factor the firm claims has given it a unique understanding of what the market needs.

China is not a homogeneous country, and the distribution of large-scale medical equipment should be considered with regard to the local economic development level, states the CEO.

"We are mindful of working with Chinese health services to determine the most appropriate and cost-effective medical equipment for a given region," says Hogan.

Installing the necessary medical equipment in rural communities will help improve the accuracy of diagnoses and reduce costs eventually, he says.

To fulfill the basic medical demands of the public, the Chinese Government has carried out specific measures so as to establish medical systems in communities and to develop medical reforms in rural areas.

Inaccessibility and unaffordability of the healthcare system for the public are among the top issues to be solved in China, from the government's point of view. Officials now manage medicine pricing, examination expenses, and the acquisition of large-scale medical facilities.

China currently is seriously short of medical resources, however. Despite its huge population, accounting for 22 percent of the world's people, China's medical resources make up a mere 2 percent of the world total.

In addition, 80 percent of current medical resources are allocated to cities; moreover, two-thirds of these resources are centralized in large hospitals, while rural areas and urban communities are often deprived.

As for medical care insurance, about 44.8 percent of the urban population and 79.1 percent of rural people have no healthcare insurance.

Besides focusing on rural communities, the company is also eyeing the "early health" model, which means care focused on pre-symptomatic disease detection, early diagnosis and disease prevention.

"We are focusing on early health, not late disease," observes Hogan.

The firm says this trend is particularly important in China, since the country has dramatically increasing rates of strokes, cancer, diabetes and heart disease. If the nation fails to control the growth of these problems, it will face not only the loss of millions of lives but also the potential loss of $500 billion in national income over the next decade, according to the World Health Organization.

Early Treatment

GE Healthcare says it is enabling doctors to find diseases earlier and treat them when there is less of a burden on the healthcare system.

"Today, most healthcare systems in the world are based on therapy, and people are treated when they get sick. Our entire portfolio is centered on how to keep people healthy, or when people do need therapy, targeting the minimum-invasive therapy," says Hogan.

He says that about 70 percent of the world's medical resources are devoted to treating people for disease, but GE Healthcare believes that about 50 percent of the resources should be devoted to treating people for disease, and the other half for keeping people healthy. That means early diagnosis and early treatment are required.

Hogan cites the example of breast cancer, the early diagnosis and treatment of which will reduce chances of death and significantly lower the economic burden on society.

The company recently launched a survey on breast health, together with the web portal sohu.com and the People's Liberation Army 307 Hospital, who it hopes will increase public awareness of breast cancer.

GE Healthcare, headquartered in the United Kingdom, is a $15 billion unit of the General Electric Company. Worldwide, GE Healthcare employs more than 45,000 people committed to serving healthcare professionals and their patients in more than 100 countries.

In 1991, the company set up its first factory in Beijing. Today, three independent research and development centers have been established to produce state-of-the-art medical products, officials say. Of all the products made in China, 60 percent are exported.

This achievement has also qualified the company's Shanghai manufacturing site as the first one in China approved by the US Food and Drug Administration (FDA) for the production of terminally sterilized large-volume medical items and peripherals.

The firm's revenues in China stood at $700 million in 2005, accounting for more than 5 percent of the firm's global revenues.

By Jiang Jingjing
(2006-10-16)

Super Link

1. GE Pushes "Green" Business

General Electric brought its environmental program to China on May 29, 2006, a major initiative to help the US conglomerate double its business in the world's fastest-growing major economy.

Jeff Immelt, Chairman and CEO of the US giant, signed a memorandum of understanding with the National Development and Reform Commission (NDRC) to provide environmentally-friendly technology to China, and formally kicked off the company's Ecomagination program in the country.

"Today signifies the interface of two major internal themes at GE: Commitment to China and Ecomagination," said Immelt at the launch ceremony in Beijing.

China has become a significant emerging market for the world's largest industrial giant. Its sales in China reached the previous goal set by Immelt, which was to grow revenue in China to $5 billion in 2005, almost twice the 2003 figure.

He said he expected business to enjoy sustained growth in China in the next five years, and to double again in that period.

GE's Ecomagination plan ties in with China's emphasis on energy efficiency and its requirements for environment friendly solutions.

The company launched Ecomagination in 2005, aiming to achieve annual sales of $20 billion in 2010 from environment friendly products and solutions.

But the figures released two weeks ago showed that sales from its Ecomagination products have already reached $10.1 billion in 2005, up from $6.2 billion in 2004.

Steve Bertamini, Chairman and CEO of GE China, said his operations also received several hundred million dollars in revenue from Ecomagination products in 2005.

At the same time, China put energy efficiency first on its agenda, promising to cut energy consumption per unit of gross domestic product in 2010 by 20 percent from the end of 2005.

Zhang Guobao, Vice-Minister of NDRC, welcomed the efforts to help China's energy efficiency and environmental protection.

According to the memorandum between NDRC and GE, the US giant will provide technology such as coal gasification, wind energy solutions, regional jet development, advanced locomotive development, desalination, and energy-efficient lights.

In October 2005, GE signed a contract with the Ministry of Railway to provide 300 rail cars worth $450 million, which will cut gas exhaustion by 28 percent.

The US behemoth also signed a memorandum of understanding with Tsinghua University in May 2006 to jointly develop clean technology, and take advantage of the university's strength in developing green energy solutions and GE's experience in learning customers' demands and the local market environment.

By Liu Baijia
(2006-05-30)

2. Medical Checks

Propelled by expansion in the healthcare sector, China's medical equipment business is expected to increase more than seven-fold in the next four years.

But foreign equipment makers may not be able to fully partake in the prospects, as regulatory changes in 2005 have thrown some challenges their way.

The medical equipment business is predicted to grow to $1.7 billion this year from last year's $1.2 billion. The projection for 2010 is $12.5 billion.

With their advanced technologies, efficient service and powerful influence, foreign equipment makers were supposed to be among the big beneficiaries of the country's healthcare system.

But complaints in 2005 from patients and their families about over-prescription of medicines and clinical tests prompted some changes in the sector.

Angered by irregularities and vowing to provide affordable healthcare services to people, the Chinese government launched waves of efforts and regulations, trying to curb peoples' rising healthcare bills. The medical equipment market became a key area to regulate.

In March 2005, three ministries revised the approval process on procuring large medical equipment.

Hospitals buying equipment like CT and nuclear magnetic resonance spectroscopy CT (also known as MRI) need to apply to local health authorities and get approval from provincial authorities.

The National Development and Reform Commission in December also told local price regulators to closely monitor the prices of medical tests that involve large equipment.

The commission said hospitals were not allowed to make profits on tests.

Local authorities were encouraged to calculate the costs of these types of tests and publicize the results.

In China, the overwhelming majority of hospitals are state-owned, but their healthcare budgets are still quite low and are often just enough to pay staff salaries. Paying doctors and nurses for their services is not tradition in China, and the average diagnosis fee is 5 yuan (60 US cents) per patient. Hospitals often make up their losses by selling medicine and providing medical tests.

As a result, bribery and over-prescription of drugs and tests become common problems in hospitals.

Foreign companies could be impacted significantly if test prices were streamlined to combat these problems. Whether the equipment used during the test is made in China or imported, the price of the test would still be the same.

This means tests using imported equipment, which are often more advanced, could cost the same as tests performed with locally manufactured equipment, thus suppressing the demand for imported equipment.

Chih Chen, President of GE Healthcare China, the biggest provider of large medical equipment in the country, says his company understands and supports the actions that the government took and will take.

Chih poses a question: "Are the measures taken now reasonable? Should we just suppress the demand for large equipment or shall we allocate resources more scientifically?"

He adds that it is far too early to say whether Chinese hospitals had purchased too many medical machines, and the problem now is how to solve the resource disparity between big cities and rural areas.

Every four to five people out of a million in China — as opposed to 34 in a million in the United States — have access to a CT machine.

There were over 5,000 CT machines in Chinese hospitals at the end of 2004, but 80 percent of them were in developed eastern regions, according to the China Medical Equipment Association.

When it comes to trying to secure better healthcare for Chinese people, cutting back on medical equipment purchases is not the ultimate solution, says David Jin, President of Philips Medical Systems China.

The Chinese population accounts for 22 percent of the world's total, but its healthcare expenses are only 2 percent of the global total. Foreign equipment makers must figure out how to cope with the suspension of equipment procurements and the demand for cheaper equipment in small cities or rural areas.

GE Healthcare, which launched a worldwide Early Health campaign in 2005 in the United States, kicked off a similar one in China in June.

The concept encourages healthy people — those with no outward sign of disease — to take medical tests regularly to prevent cancer and heart disease.

Chen believes the healthcare model in the future will change from a treatment-focused one to a more preventative model geared towards early diagnosis. This change will be a major growth engine for hospitals.

David Chang, President of Philips China, also thinks this type of model is a good direction to take.

Zhong Nanshan, an academician with the Chinese Academy of Engineering, and a top respiratory disease scientist, says expensive healthcare bills are often accrued because patients usually go to doctors in the late stages of diseases.

However, if people can detect symptoms earlier and get treated accordingly, the fatality risk and expenses will both reduce dramatically.

According to research by GE Healthcare, the cost of treating breast cancer in the early stages is less than 10,000 yuan (US$1,200) and the survival rate is 95 percent for the next five years.

But for a late-stage patient, the survival rate is only 16 percent, and the treatment costs more than 100,000 yuan (US$12,000).

While the change benefits the country and patients, equipment providers like GE also win. More people will take a CT scan, for example, to get an early diagnosis. The utilization of equipment is higher and the demand for more equipment is also higher.

Making the medical diagnosis affordable to more people is another way to create a market demand in the midst of challenges.

Philips, which has a joint venture with Chinese medical equipment maker

Neusoft, regards partnership as a key in the medical equipment sector, both in China and globally.

Chang says that since the joint venture was established in 2004, it has already designed three models of economy equipment.

"While some competitors may suffer from the regulatory challenges with products focused on high-end segments, our economy products can help us benefit from demands in small cities and rural areas," says Jin.

GE Healthcare also reveals it is learning about the demands in those markets, and needs to promote the development of economy products.

By Liu Baijia
(2006-07-17)

Fashion Forward

An Interview with Leo Lui,
President of Hermes China

This year Hermes has three anniversaries: its 170th birthday as a French luxury brand, the 70th year since it made its first scarf, and its first decade in Chinese mainland market.

Although it usually takes a low-profile marketing approach, Hermes kicked off campaigns in Shanghai late in May 2007, enlarging its Shanghai boutique at Plaza 66, its biggest on the mainland, and opening a month-long Hermes scarf exhibition at the Shanghai Art Museum.

The company plans to open four stores in 2007 and beginning 2008 will develop three to four outlets annually, says Leo Lui, President of Hermes China.

Lui was appointed to the position in September 2006 after joining the firm in Paris in May 2006. The Hong Kong-born Chinese, who graduated with an MBA from the HEC School of Management in Paris, has 24 years of professional experience in the fashion and luxury industries, working with L'Oreal, Moet Hennessy and Louis Vuitton in France, Hong Kong, Taiwan and on the Chinese mainland.

Lui says Hermes has been expanding in stages in China through "very strong double-digit growth" in the past two years. He declined to reveal exact figures.

"China is still small for Hermes," says Lui. "The sector is under development. In five years time, it will be one of the top-five for us." Japan, France and the United States are currently its main markets.

Hermes has over 280 outlets in nearly 40 countries. Since opening its first boutique on the mainland at Beijing's Peninsula Palace Hotel in 1997, it now has eight stores in Beijing, Shanghai, Guangzhou, Tianjin, Dalian of Northeast China's Liaoning Province and Hangzhou, capital of East China's Zhejiang Province.

The Tianjin store is a shop-in-a-shop opened in February 2007, in partnership with department store Isetan. In Japan, the Paris-based firm has had a long-term relationship with Isetan, and it chose the same approach in that mainland city.

"If it works, we are open to such partnerships in the near future," says Lui.

Other than the Tianjin shop, Hermes wholly owns its other seven stores.

"We make the direct investment here since it enables us to better control management and customer service in particular," says Lui .

In addition to expansion, Lui also focuses on creating a good environment for employees. He proudly notes that in the first four months of the year, the company had zero turnover in its staff. He believes human resources are the most important asset for a company.

In China's luxury sector, staff turnover in sales and marketing is frequent. As more new brands arrive and more new shopping malls are opened, companies want to recruit experienced people.

Hermes has 14 types of products, including ready-to-wear, leather goods, and silk scarves and ties. China is different from mature markets where leather goods normally sell the best.

This could be due to the development of the Chinese luxury market, which started mostly with men about 10 years ago who wanted to demonstrate their success by wearing expensive suits and watches, Lui explains.

But Hermes has seen leather goods and silk scarves and ties catching up, as an increasing number of women have started to buy Hermes products like Kelly and Birkin handbags.

"We want to communicate with the local customers the richness of our 14 departments of products," emphasizes Lui.

Lui says Hermes does not consider itself a luxury brand, but rather offers products made by craftsmen using the best natural material, the most skillful craftsmanship and the best methods of production to create a useful item that can

last for generations.

With that philosophy, the company targets two types of customers — entrepreneurs who own their own businesses and look for high quality, and young professionals working for multinational companies, who want to show that they have good taste.

To meet customer demand, Hermes offers products across a wide price range, from a 1,000 yuan perfume to a diamond leather bag priced at 1.6 million yuan.

In 2007, the company worked with the Chinese contemporary artist Ding Yi, who designed a scarf called the Rhythm of China that is printed with a number of small colorful checks.

Hermes' Artistic Director Pierre-Alexis Dumas says he was dumbfounded when he received the design, and that it will be central to the Hermes scarf exhibition in Shanghai.

By Jiang Jingjing
(2007-07-02)

Watching China

An Interview with Guillaume de Seynes,
Chairman of La Montre Hermes and
the Executive Vice-President of
Hermes International

Luxury brand Hermes is using a number of tactics to try and expand in China, one of which is touting its new mechanical offerings.

For the first time in its long history, Hermes has started offering mechanical watches to its customers, a tactic that Guillaume de Seynes, Chairman of La Montre Hermes and the Executive Vice-President of Hermes International, hopes will bring more sale in a country where consumers prefer mechanical watches.

For Hermes, the development of China's watch market is paramount. Among the French giant's 14 categories of products in China, its watch business accounts for over 10 percent of the firm's total revenues, higher than in most European markets, says de Seynes.

Hermes currently distributes from 30 points of sale in China, including more than 20 spots in watch retailer shops, two shop-in-shops, and six Hermes Boutiques in China.

Hermes is looking to further develop the Chinese market through these three channels, as it plans to expand its distribution network in 2007.

"We aim to open two to three Hermes boutiques in China each year, which can benefit the visibility and credibility of our watch collections," the chairman says. "In addition, we will open one to two shop-in-shops (Hermes watch boutique in department stores and watch retailer shops) this year (2007), and also seek competent professional local dealers."

China Openings

Following the opening of two Hermes' watch shop-in-shops in Paris in the Galeries Lafayette and Printemps department stores, Hermes opened its first watch boutiques in Asia in Kunming, in Southwest China's Yunnan Province and in Anshan, in Northeast China's Liaoning Province, in 2005 and 2006 respectively.

Watches are one of the few products that are sold outside Hermes boutiques, since the brand believes that working through watch dealerships in various cities can quicken the pace of product exposure across the country.

Distributing such pieces is a job for professionals, de Seynes says.

"It is a tough job for our sales people in the boutique who sell scarves and ties," he continues. "So in each boutique, we have appointed a watch ambassador who can provide professional services to customers to explain the uniqueness of our watches. We offer a lot of in-depth professional training to our staff."

Hermes takes a very discreet attitude in selecting dealers. Instead of going for retailers who carry 30 or even 50 brands, Hermes prefers to work with watch dealers that are family owned.

"We have to be very selective with our partners," says de Seynes.

Nevertheless, the firm is strict on one thing with their dealers: No discounts. Hermes always says no to offering discounts to their VIPs, since it believes that playing with prices can only do harm to the brand.

"Even Sharon Stone came to us twice, asking for a discount, and we turned her down," says de Seynes. "However, she still remains our loyal customer."

Since launching its first quartz watch in 1978, Hermes has attracted numerous wealthy and famous women with its watch designs. At the end of last year, it finally launched mechanical pieces, with the aim of drawing more male customers, who were originally the major target group of the brand.

Vaucher Acquisition

The Hermes Group recently announced it had taken a significant new step in its strategy to expand its watch business, by forging a partnership with the Sandoz Family Foundation.

According to de Seynes: "We are indeed stepping into the next chapter for Hermes with the new collaboration with the Sandoz Family Foundation, embodied through the recent acquisition of a 25 percent stake in Vaucher Manufacture Fleurier."

"With two independent families sharing the same vision in the development of luxurious watches, we are confident about our ability to deliver beautiful products to our customers with a commitment to the highest level of quality," he says.

The partnership will also help Hermes obtain technology in making mechanical watches.

De Seynes says the luxury mechanical timepiece targets watch lovers and watch collectors with its prestigious movement, superb craftsmanship, and its high value and scarcity of production.

For example, the recently launched Cape Cod Eight Days Jumping Hours watch sells for 266,350 yuan.

At the moment, mechanical watches only account for 4-5 percent of the unit's total output, a ratio that will grow as it plans to produce women's mechanical watches this year.

Unlike France, where customers do not mind wearing quartz watches, Chinese watch lovers usually prefer mechanical offerings.

Hermes sold 127,000 watches for a revenue of 1.4 billion euros in 2005, accounting for 7 percent of the group's total turnover. Hermes watches have over 1,000 points of sale, including 249 Hermes boutiques.

The Hermes Group, founded in 1837, designs, develops and markets high-quality products in 14 segments, including leather goods, silk scarves and ties, tableware, jewelry, and perfumes.

By Jiang Jingjing
(2007-01-08)

The Art of Life

An Interview with Segolene Audras,
Managing Director of Hermes China

Watches, jewelry, bags and clothing are among the top choices for Chinese consumers when they make their first luxury purchases, simply because they can wear them every day and show them off all the time.

This only represents the initial stages of luxury consumption, however. The real luxury lies in the lifestyle associated with these products.

With this in mind, how far away could Chinese consumers be from stepping into the real world of luxury products, which includes everything from brand name bedding to teacups and even ashtrays?

French luxury brand Hermes has been patiently anticipating the arrival of these kinds of trends, and believes there is still a lot of room for these products to develop a consumer base.

"Our Chinese customers have already bought the "Art of Living" line in our stores," says Segolene Audras, Managing Director of Hermes' China operations. "Some buy items for use at home and in the office, but some buy the items for their friends and relatives."

Audras says Hermes' customers have been eagerly buying the brand's traditional products such as silk ties and leather bags, but they have also started showing interest in the company's "Art of Living" line. They buy Hermes towels for their summer holiday trips, for example, or table sets for family gatherings.

"We have seen a growing number of these customers here, who want to either treat themselves or share something nice with their family and friends," says Audras.

Hermes is one of a handful of farsighted brands that have already launched home and leisure-oriented products in China, even though the market is still developing.

The company's "Art of Living" collection was introduced to the nation during the opening of the brand's first boutique here in 1997.

"We believe every Hermes boutique should display products from all of our 14 departments," says Audras. "We are now creating more room to display all of these lines, including the Art of Living line. This means we've had to further expand our existing boutiques."

Hermes' 14 product categories include leather products, silk, ties, menswear, ladieswear, perfume, watches, agendas and small leather products, shoes, accessories, riding equipment, home and leisure products, tableware and jewelry.

The "Art of Living" collection is incredibly diverse, but is organized around three main themes designed for the individual customer and those close to them, or for friends and colleagues as gifts.

The line also includes a number of different categories, including household linens, bathroom textile products, bedsheets and baby blankets, beach linens, leisure and travel items, home decor products, glass and crystal, silverware, and furniture.

Audras tells the reporter that Hermes plans to introduce its Pippa collection, a folding furniture series, to China later this year (2006).

"Upon introducing this line, which includes wooden armchairs, desks and tables, we plan to enlarge one of our five boutiques," she says, but declines to reveal the location of the store.

Hermes has two stores in Beijing, and one each in Shanghai, Guangzhou and Dalian. It will open its sixth boutique in Hangzhou in June, Audras says.

All Hermes products are sold through its boutiques, except for perfume, watches and tableware, which can be sold by select dealers in certain stores.

Audras says Hermes has a very wide range of products, and all of them are developing rapidly in China. She says the "Art of Living" items are less known in China than the silk and leather products, but that all of these product categories are important to Hermes.

"All departments have to gather together to represent the brand, its value and the story behind it."

She says that although the "Art of Living" line is growing rapidly in China, there is still room for the collection to grow, and that Hermes tries to bring the creativity, elegance and craftsmanship of its "Art of Living" line to its other 13 categories.

"When a customer looks around in our shops, they can always find something for themselves from this line," she says, adding that customers can also find something for friends and family.

Chaton Saconay, the department's Artistic Director, says, "'The Art of Living' is the art of surrounding oneself with beautiful and useful things."

"When we create an item, we aim to make it last," says Audras. "We use the best materials, from textiles to wood, leather, glass and crystal. The company provides a wide range of products in different price brackets, so that customers can always find something affordable.

"You can see the quality materials and the elegant, simple designs. All this enhances one's lifestyle, and the company will bring more products and designs to the Chinese market."

In order to strengthen communication between the company and its Chinese customers, Hermes launched a simplified Chinese version of its company magazine, *Hermes World*, in March 2005. The magazine, first published in 1973, comes out twice a year in eight languages.

Hermes was established in 1837 as a maker of riding equipment, and the first "Art of Living" article was created in 1929. It was a crystal ashtray for automobiles. The department for "Art of Living" products was created in 1974.

By Jiang Jingjing
(2006-06-05)

Super Link

Second Choice

Not Beijing, but Shanxi. That's the strategy Beijing's Scitech Plaza, one of the city's oldest high-end department stores, employed when it celebrated its 14th anniversary in 2006.

In promoting its 25 percent anniversary discount, the store skipped Beijing altogether and concentrated its ad blitz on Shanxi, an interior province in North China once mostly known for its dry hills and grim coal mines.

As the management correctly gauged, there's more juice in Shanxi's nouveau riche than the salaried of Beijing. Hundreds of Scitech faithful from Shanxi flocked to Beijing, many flying in for the yearly bash. They stayed at an adjacent luxury hotel, also owned by Scitech, and splurged on 14,000-yuan La Mer cosmetics, 20,000-yuan fur coats and 7,000-yuan shoes.

Together with an army of fellow moneybags from Hebei, Inner Mongolia and Tianjin, the shoppers from Shanxi sent Scitech's sales figures soaring to 20 million yuan on the anniversary day, the store's highest-ever single-day revenue.

Scitech's anniversary strategy reflects a larger trend of wealth spreading from a handful of traditional urban centers such as Beijing, Shanghai and Guangzhou to the so-called second-tier cities, and even obscure small towns.

Pick any weekend and check the license plates at the parking lot of Yansha Outlets on Beijing's 4th Ring Road. You will be surprised how many of those shiny sedans are from out of town, mostly from neighboring Hebei Province. Clearly, for the have-money-will-spend class in second-tier cities, driving to Beijing to shop for luxury brands has become the new Sunday morning sport.

Follow the Money

Residents in smaller cities, boasting rapidly growing purchasing power and appetite for high-end products, have drawn the attention of top international luxury lines, which are increasingly gravitating to these second-tier cities.

Louis Vuitton, which entered China 15 years ago and has 16 boutiques spread across 13 cities, has opened shops in three new cities in the last two years — Wenzhou, Kunming and Shenyang. The company's next targets are Chongqing, Harbin, Sanya, Suzhou, Ningbo, Nanjing and Urumqi, according to the company's CEO Yves Carcelle.

French luxury giant Hermes chose Kunming, capital of Southwest China's Yunnan Province, to open its first watch boutique in China two years ago, selling timepieces for up to 260,000 yuan each. The following year it expanded to Anshan, a steel manufacturing base in Northeast China's Liaoning Province.

In 2006 writing instrument giant Montblanc took over all its outlets from local partners and started operating directly in first- and second-tier cities.

Hugo Boss' strategy in secondary cities is simple, according to Lars Larsen, Managing Director of Hugo Boss Hong Kong Ltd: Be the first. At the end of March 2007, Hugo Boss had 75 points of sale in nearly 40 cities.

The huge population base in small cities is the main attraction for the luxury segment. China's second-tier cities are huge compared to those in Europe or the United States. Luxury brand executives point out that China has over 100 cities with populations of over one million each, opening up immense possibilities.

Economic liberalization has spawned tens of thousands of private entrepreneurs in the Zhejiang, Jiangsu, Fujian and Guangdong provinces. In Northeast China's Liaoning, Jilin and Heilongjiang provinces, there is a long tradition of ostentatious consumption. In Shanxi the ultra rich, mainly mine owners, are known to flaunt their Ferraris and flash their Omegas.

The demand for luxury products has been growing so rapidly in secondary cities that it exceeded the level of demand in first-tier cities 10 years ago. If high-end brands were eager to enter the main cities a decade ago, it's thus hardly a surprise to see them flock to small cities now, says Liu Wei, Chief Analyst with Shanghai-based Integration Strategy Consulting Co Ltd.

Social Marker

Liu says a new affluent class has emerged in small cities. They have a strong desire for social recognition and want to stand out in a crowd.

"What they care about is not necessarily the intrinsic value of the products," he says. "All they need is something that's seen as expensive by others, such as Rolex watches and BMW cars."

Chen Zhan, a Research Director at TNS, a leading international market research firm, agrees.

Although the rich in both first- and second-tier cities have similar desires for luxury goods, Chen says, those in smaller cities have a vaguer perception of brands than those in large cities, with less knowledge about their origins, history and characteristics. What's known and understood, however, is their effectiveness as an immediate social marker.

Still, first-tier cities are far from saturation. Trend trackers report the emergence of a new breed of big-city consumers they call "understaters" or individuals who prefer more low-profile brands such as Anna Sui and Mac Jacob.

Thus, it remains imperative for brands to spread out. One strong factor is rising operating costs, with rentals and wages skyrocketing in cities like Beijing and Shanghai in recent years. It can take several million yuan just to set up a boutique on a Beijing main road.

Finding new growth areas with low costs tops every brand's agenda, especially for late comers who have already lost the first round to market pioneers from a decade ago.

It's relatively easy to set up shop in emerging cities, says Liu; after operating for over 10 years in the main cities, most brands have developed solid networks in distribution, logistics, hiring and staff training, so they can expand to smaller markets more easily.

Local governments are game, too. They like to have luxury brands open outlets in their areas as their arrival shows that these cities have arrived.

Fighting piracy is another important factor propelling fashion brands towards small cities. Fakes, typically, are more rampant in these cities than the top ones. Entering these markets is thus seen as an effective strategy to tackle the problem.

Industry observers say it's hard to tell whether big cities or the second-tier ones are more important for business. In big cities, sales growth may be slower as the largest group of consumers is the middle-class office workers. In second-tier cities entrepreneurs are the main patrons and sales growth can be much faster, they say.

Yet in terms of management, human resources, market environment, infrastructure and logistics, big cities are still miles ahead.

Xiao Mingchao, General Manager of marketing research firm called Shengshi Indexes, says customers in the main cities are indispensable. "They still set the trends that their counterparts in second-tier cities follow."

Different Strokes

Different market situations should result in different operational methods, says Xiao. "The focus in main cities should be to develop brand loyalty, improve customer relationship management and encourage more purchases from regular customers."

In smaller cities, reaching out to new customers should be the main thrust. Thus luxury sellers should concentrate on raising brand awareness, carry out more public relations campaigns and improve the distribution channels in these cities.

Nigel Luk, Managing Director of Cartier Greater China, was recently quoted by *Fashion Times* as saying that jewelry giant Cartier opened new boutiques in small cities mainly as a means of cultivating the market, rather than seeking profit. Reuters reports that the company aims to launch 22 to 24 boutiques in China by 2008, almost double the existing network.

But some analysts say there is a gap between service quality in first-tier and second-tier cities.

Declining to name the brand, Dirk Jehmlich, General Manager of Trendbuero Asia-Pacific region, says that attendants at some of this brand's boutiques in Taiyuan, the capital city in Shanxi Province, are "pushy" and pester visitors to buy its products. But in the large cities, the same brand's outlets let customers be.

Jehmlich says such practices are dangerous. "Small-city customers may one day find out the difference when visiting Beijing or Shanghai. That may completely ruin the brand image."

By Jiang Jingjing
(2007-05-21)

Reductive Reasoning

An Interview with Shane Tedjarati,
Vice-President of Honeywell International Inc and
CEO of Honeywell China

When some American commentators said that the developed world should put more pressure on large developing nations like China and India to set a timetable for the reduction of greenhouse gas emissions, they had not yet heard the harsh words of Ma Kai.

Ma, minister of the all-powerful National Development and Reform Commission, said on June 4, 2007 that local officials who failed to achieve emission reduction goals would be held accountable and could lose their jobs, a severe punishment usually only given in cases such as failure to properly handle large disasters.

The Most Important Thing

For Shane Tedjarati, it is a good signal that China is stepping back from purely pursuing economic growth, and is now paying serious attention to energy efficiency and environmental protection. This is also good news for his company, Honeywell.

"The most important thing we can do in China is contributing to energy efficiency and the environment," says Tedjarati in the interview.

China has set itself a goal — that by 2020 it will reduce its energy consumption per 10,000 yuan of gross domestic product by 20 percent, from 2005 onwards. Because the country is still in an accelerated industrialization stage and energy demands will remain strong, this is quite a challenging task.

Multinationals attempting to get away from price wars launched by local competitors regard energy efficiency as a realm where they can fully play to their strengths.

Jean-Pascal Tricoire, CEO of the French Industrial Company Schneider Electric, visited the country twice in the past year to promote its intelligent home and energy efficiency concepts to Chinese real estate developers. In May 2006, Jeffrey Immelt, Chairman and CEO of General Electric, kicked off the company's Ecomagination initiative in Beijing, committing to spend $50 million on developing environmentally friendly products in China. For Honeywell, nearly 50 percent of the product portfolio company-wide is linked to energy efficiency. It is estimated that the global economy can operate on 10 to 25 percent less energy just by using today's Honeywell technologies.

Tedjarati says that because of long product lines across the globe, business units in China are important, so the company is able to handle multiple tasks at the same time.

Local innovations in energy-saving technologies are also being developed at Honeywell China. For one product, Honeywell turbochargers allow an engine that is about a third smaller to provide the same power as a full-size engine. That means about 20 to 25 percent less fuel usage and emissions while still providing consumers with cars that go when they hit the accelerator, a valuable contribution, indeed, in today's energy conscious world.

Tedjarati says that making cars more efficient would be a significant contribution to help China, the world's second-largest automobile market, achieve its goal of energy reduction.

Honeywell, a world leader in energy performance contracting management, which has saved customers more than $3 billion in energy and operating costs, also wants to extend its leadership into China.

The company signed up its first Chinese client in August, 2006 — Shenzhen Tsingtao Beer Asahi Co Ltd — for which Honeywell guaranteed to cut factory energy use through its management techniques by 17 percent a year over a five-year contract.

Tedjarati says his company now expects to sign more contracts for energy management.

Honeywell is also working on an "intelligent home", which uses advanced technologies and products to save 30 to 40 percent of energy consumption at home.

With the prospects of a growing energy efficiency market, more Chinese companies have also joined the field, and some have introduced solutions and technologies that made them targets for mergers and acquisitions (M & As).

Yet Honeywell, which has a strong track record in M&As during its 120-year history, has to date kept a low profile in China, unlike competitors such as Schneider Electric, Siemens and GE, which bought or invested in local companies.

Tedjarati says that in the early stage of his leadership, Honeywell China was focused on adjusting its strategies in the nation and building a strong organization.

"M & As are one of the things that we did not do in China, but now it is at a tipping point," says Tedjarati.

He adds there are many good domestic companies that can add their solutions and understanding of the local market to Honeywell, making the company more relevant to the Chinese market.

The East-West Way

The way that can be told of is not an unvarying way.

This is the opening sentence of the classic Taoist philosophy *Dao De Jing*, and also a catchword for Tedjarati, a fan of Chinese tradition.

Tedjarati thinks his company has found a way to its future in the world's fastest-growing major economy, taking an East to West approach.

"If we agree that China is part of our global theater, it is not just another market," says Tedjarati. "China is revolutionizing the world market in a unique way."

The traditional way for many multinationals of doing business in China is a West to East one: they invent a product, which becomes successful in the US and Europe, and so they bring the product to China.

Soon, the companies find their sales reach $10 million in a short period of time and the product has a good growth. Then the company makes some adaptations at home or in China and releases the product to the market.

Then, two consequences occur: the sales reach a bottleneck, as the product is mainly designed according to Western demands and fits into high-end segments of the Chinese market; and hundreds of Chinese manufacturers also find a way to make similar products, but at one-tenth of the price of their Western counterpart.

"You have just given birth to your competitors with the West to East approach," says Tedjarati, who has been doing business in China since 1992 and took on his current role at the US industrial giant in 2004.

What the company, based in Morris Township, New Jersey, has been focusing on is adjusting the conventional way of doing business in China, and building up capabilities to develop technology and products in China for the China market, moving from simple localization to local innovation. The capabilities acquired through the process of meeting the diverse needs in a market of China's scale and scope would be highly valuable to Honeywell's global success, Tedjarati believes.

While many multinationals think there are two Chinas, a developed one as seen in Shanghai and a developing country, Honeywell believes China is a microcosm of the world. It has all the features of the developed, developing and desolate worlds, as in the US, India or some least developed countries in Africa, but it also has money, so companies can experiment with their products and solutions in all segments of the market and different developmental levels.

"If we are smart and if we use China right, it will make us more relevant to the rest of humanity and make us a real global company," says Tedjarati, previously Managing Director for the consulting firm Deloitte in China.

The change to East to West would not be possible without support from the top management of Honeywell, Tedjarati points out.

When David Cote took over the position of Chairman and CEO of Honeywell in 2002, non-US markets were regarded as a key driver for growth, and China was one of the priorities.

Two years later, Tedjarati was recruited to head the China business and became the only country head directly reporting to Cote. Even today, few China heads can talk directly with the CEOs.

Resistance from headquarters is another difficulty to be overcome when multinationals want to put more resources into a single country.

The East to West approach, consistent with Honeywell's overall emphasis on listening to customers and providing products and solutions that meet their diverse needs, also convinced the chiefs of the company's four business units and won their support.

From 2003 to 2007, global revenues of the industrial giant have been growing at an annual average of 10 percent, and earnings per share grew at 19 percent a year on average. In China, its organic sales growth was even higher, above 20 percent in 2006. Tedjarati believes the momentum will continue in 2007.

In the past three years, the number of Honeywell employees in its fastest growing major country market almost doubled to 5,000.

Tedjarati says that with the ongoing execution of the East to West strategy, his company will continue to add more hands in research and development, as well as sales and marketing.

By Liu Baijia
(2007-06-16)

Up to the Challenge

An Interview with George Ko,
General Manager of Honeywell
Building Solutions in China

To double a business in three years may be deemed a desirable result for many companies, but for the US industrial giant Honeywell International Inc, that kind of growth rate in the Chinese energy performance contracting (EPC) market just isn't enough.

When George Ko, General Manager of Honeywell Building Solutions in China and Chief of the EPC business, proposed doubling the EPC business to his chiefs, he was told the goal should be even higher and that he could ask for all the support necessary for even more aggressive growth.

"This is a very challenging task, but it is also the best time to develop this business," Ko says in his office near Shanghai Hongqiao Airport on a rainy summer afternoon.

Energy efficiency and emissions control have become a pressing task for the Chinese Government, which lists sustained and eco-friendly economic growth as a top priority.

In the 11th Five-Year Plan (2006-2010), the world's second largest energy user aims to cut energy consumption per unit of GDP by 20 percent, although it is still expected to maintain an annual growth rate of 8 percent.

However, the reduction of energy use per unit of GDP in 2006 was 1.33

percent, lower than the planned five-year average of 4 percent.

This year, the central government has allocated 21.3 billion yuan on energy efficiency and emission control projects, 30 times the 2006 investment.

Zhan Shuzhong, Deputy Director of the Energy Management Contracting Association of China, estimated that to save 300 million tons of standard coal as needed to achieve 20 percent energy reduction, the country needs to spend 300 billion yuan over five years.

Honeywell, which commands over 30 percent of the EPC market in the US, received its first contract in August 2006 from Tsingtao Beer Asahi Co Ltd in Shenzhen, a South China economic hub neighboring Hong Kong.

In the five-year contract worth over 10 million yuan, Honeywell guarantees that it will cut the beer maker's energy consumption by 17 percent. That works out to 5.47 million yuan off energy bills per year.

Ko said his company had now inked about 10 contracts in just one year, and that he had visited over 100 potential customers in more than 10 Chinese provinces.

Zhou Minjie, the Shanghai Economic Committee's spokesperson, said 23 million yuan has been invested into 11 projects in the first half of the year and 12,000 tons of standard coal is expected to be saved.

In the past five years, over 600 million yuan was invested in more than 300 EPC projects in Shanghai.

In Zhejiang Province, more than 120 EPC projects were launched in 2006 and 48.70 million yuan has been invested.

Industries such as those of steel, paper-making and cement, and public organizations such as hospitals, airports and railway stations, which require power suppliers 24 hours a day, have an especially strong interest in EPC.

Ko claimed the Tsingtao deal was the first true EPC contract in China, in which a service company guaranteed energy reduction and provided financing.

"This not only reduces electricity bills, but quite often transforms clients' processes, so profound industrial knowledge is needed here," said Ko, who was born in Hong Kong and attended university in Guangzhou.

EPC projects in Western markets usually require thorough understanding of customers' business processes, strong financing capabilities and comprehensive technologies.

Many local firms have special expertise in one or several areas, like lighting or air conditioning, but many of them focus primarily on selling equipment while lacking total technological solutions or financial strength.

Ko said Honeywell's 30 years in the industry and its 2,000-plus projects provided Chinese customers with the benefits of experience.

At the same time, Ko's EPC team has doubled to 30 people, with professionals in energy efficiency, sales, laws and accounting.

Too much competition is a concern for many business executives, but Ko is in a very different situation: he needs more competitors in his area.

"This is still a young business in China and the market needs more players," said Ko.

Shanghai has announced that it will grow 120 local energy management service companies this year and provide several banks in the city with over 100 million yuan in credit lines.

Ko said many companies realized the need for higher energy efficiency, but EPC was still not an option, because the rate of energy consumption was not high enough to encourage companies to act now.

"The prices of resources like coal, oil, water and electricity have risen a lot, but they are still quite cheap for companies," said Ko.

Another question concerns the lack of standard measurement of effects.

There are many different metric measures in the market, so clients are often confused by differences and do not have an accurate analysis of return on assets.

By Liu Baijia
(2007-09-24)

Focus on "Premier" Service

An Interview with Richard Yorke,
President and CEO of HSBC Bank (China) Company Ltd

F our foreign banks, including HSBC, Europe's largest lender, have recently removed the last obstacles to provide RMB services to local residents in China. Richard Yorke, HSBC Bank (China) Company Ltd's President and CEO recently spoke to the reporter in Shanghai, outlining the bank's strategy.

Q: HSBC has begun to offer retail RMB services to local residents. What type of customers are you targeting?

A: Because of our limited network, we will not be targeting the broad retail market. The initial focus of our retail operations will be on expanding our Premier banking service, which is HSBC's global wealth management brand. A Premier customer, one who maintains an account balance of 500,000 yuan or above, will enjoy a number of value-added benefits.

Q: Will your lack of a large network in China be a challenge for the retail business?

A: While HSBC has the largest network of any foreign bank in China, we admittedly are very small in relation to our domestic peers. Moreover, we accept that we cannot realistically catch up with our domestic peers at any point in the near future.

As you know, for our organic banking business we are concentrating our efforts on HSBC premier service, and our retail outlets will concentrate on the key cities of Shanghai, Beijing, Shenzhen and Guangzhou.

Q: How do you view the emerging competition between domestic and foreign banks?

A: Overall, we don't believe that the situation between foreign and local banks is one of competition. Foreign and domestic banks have their own strengths and can complement each other's businesses in the overall market. This is a very dynamic and fast growing market, and I believe there is ample room for all market participants to prosper.

Q: What is HSBC China's financial position? Is the bank sufficiently strong to compete in the mainland market?

A: HSBC China has a registered capital of 8 billion yuan, which is one of the largest of the four foreign banks that have so far been locally incorporated in China. It is sufficient to meet the capital requirements of our existing and planned businesses.

Q: How is HSBC positioned in terms of profitability within the China market?

A: HSBC's organic bank business was already profitable prior to local incorporation, recording one billion yuan in pre-tax profit in 2006.

For the HSBC Group, the Chinese mainland is already the single-largest contributor of revenue in the Asia-Pacific market outside of Hong Kong, when the income from both our own business and our strategic investments is combined.

Q: What are HSBC's main advantages in the local market compared to other foreign banks?

A: As well as having the largest network, a solid financial position, and a very strong product suite, I believe HSBC's best assets in the China market are our brand and reputation. HSBC China has a 142-year unbroken history in China and with that we have exceptionally strong name-recognition and a high standing among local customers.

Q: You have been widely reported saying that staffing will be your biggest short-term challenge. Can you elaborate?

A: Finding experienced staff is indeed a challenge for HSBC, though it is not a unique one. All of our compatriots in the financial sector — both bank and non-bank, domestic and foreign — are faced with the same challenge.

The difficulty is not in finding fresh graduates and I continue to be highly impressed by the quality of young talents emerging from China's universities. However, it is a challenge to find talents with significant experience in banking and management, say four to six years of working experience.

This means we dedicate significant resources to staff training. For more than 15 years, HSBC's intensive "PRC Banker Development Programme" has helped provide local talents with international experience, grooming them into banking experts and enabling them to acquire international management experience.

By Wang Zhenghua and Zhang Lu
(2007-05-15)

Super Link

1. HSBC Gets Rural Nod

HSBC said it has received regulatory approval to open a wholly owned banking subsidiary in rural China. It is the first overseas bank to get the go-ahead from the China Banking Regulatory Commission (CBRC) to offer rural services.

The subsidiary, HSBC Rural Bank, will be based in Cengdu County of the city of Suizhou in Central China's Hubei Province, said Hong Kong and Shanghai Bank, a unit of HSBC Holdings, one of the world's largest banking groups.

HSBC rural's operation is expected to cover an area of 6,900 square kilometers, with a total population of 2 million. This area has a significant agricultural sector and a rapidly developing rural economy, the bank said.

Stephen Green, HSBC's Group Chairman, said: "We very much support China's policy priority to develop its rural economy and intend to play a full part in these ambitions."

The CBRC has introduced new rules to expand market access for financial institutions seeking to provide banking services in rural areas.

HSBC has extensive experience in rural finance in Brazil, India, Indonesia, the Philippines and Mexico, Green said.

Vincent Cheng, Chairman of HSBC, said his bank saw great potential for economic development in China's rural areas.

"Our rural bank will serve the needs of China's agricultural sector, which is undergoing rapid development, aiming to provide tailored financial services to rural communities and companies."

By Wang Zhenghua
(2007-08-10)

2. Local Incorporation Boosts Banks

HSBC Holdings plc, one of the world's largest banking and financial services organizations, said its first-half earnings surged by nearly 70 percent on the mainland after the bank gained almost unlimited access to RMB retail business earlier this year (2007).

The lender, among the first batch of banks to kick off their local incorporation business in April, reported a jump of 69 percent in pre-tax profit to $473 million on the mainland, compared with an average 13 percent climb around the globe between January and June.

Hong Kong-based Hang Seng Bank, which started as a local entity in late May, also reported an 86 percent surge in operating income on the mainland in the first half, along with a 21.3 percent increase in loans and 42.7 percent rise in deposits.

Local-entity status is expected to help other overseas banks to generate satisfactory growth on the mainland.

"We have reinforced HSBC's position as the leading international bank on the mainland," Stephen Green, Group Chairman, said yesterday in a statement.

"Our operations on the mainland following local incorporation grew strongly, with deposit and asset growth of over 50 percent and 26 percent respectively over the same period last year," he said.

The bank, the largest in Europe by asset value, added seven outlets on the mainland in the first half and recruited more than 800 new staff members.

"As a result of its leading position in wealth management, our business there was well positioned to benefit from the buoyant stock market and the steady flow of mainland companies listing on the Hong Kong stock exchange," said Green.

Increased overseas investment through Hong Kong into the mainland boosted the city's services and property sectors and provided further opportunities for HSBC to generate revenue growth, he added.

By Wang Zhenghua

(2007-07-31)

3. HSBC Plans Continued Expansion

HSBC, Europe's largest bank, plans to open more outlets in China in the years ahead now that its banking sector is fully opened. The bank rolled out a new branch in Xi'an, capital of Northwest China's Shaanxi Province, at the end of 2006, becoming the first foreign bank to expand its presence in western China following the country's deregulation of the banking sector on December 11.

"We are pleased to extend our network in western China and support the Go West campaign with our international banking services," said Richard Yorke, Chief Executive Officer of HSBC China.

The Xi'an branch, Yorke said, would strengthen his bank's position to meet the growing demand for international banking services in this regional economic center. HSBC, which opened a sub-branch in Guangzhou earlier December 2006, has now expanded its outlets to 29, including 14 branches and 15 sub-branches, making it the largest presence of any foreign bank in China.

"We will continually expand our network on the Chinese mainland in the coming years," Yorke said at a press briefing.

HSBC is planning to open more outlets in the country next year 2007, he said, but declined to reveal specific figures, saying it would depend on regulatory approval and the bank's "own ability to hire adequate people to manage them".

The opening of the Xi'an branch also made HSBC the second overseas bank to set up shop in the province, after Hong Kong's Bank of East Asia.

In a bid to support the Go West strategy, the China Banking Regulatory Commission said that as a measure of encouragement it had set up "a speedy and simplified" approval mechanism for foreign banks applying to expand to western China.

The commission also said it was studying and considering the idea of granting many more preferential policies for foreign banks to conduct local currency business in western China.

The statement did not elaborate.

HSBC, which owns 19.9 percent of China's fifth-largest lender, the Bank of Communications, already has two branches in western China, one in Southwest China's Chongqing and the other in Chengdu, capital of Sichuan Province.

By Zheng Lifei
(2006-12-23)

4. HSBC to Buy Chinese Bank Share

Britain's Hong Kong and Shanghai Banking Corp (HSBC) will pay $1.75 billion to buy a 19.9 percent share of China's Bank of Communications (BoCom), the two announced in August 2004 in Beijing after an agreement-signing ceremony.

On the sidelines of the ceremony, BoCom Chairman Jiang Chaoliang said his bank plans to be listed in Hong Kong in the first half of 2005. BoCom is China's fifth biggest bank and the largest shareholding one.

The deal between BoCom and HSBC, subject to regulatory approval, will be the largest foreign investment in the country's financial industry. The investment will help HSBC gain a big foothold in a promising market coveted by many foreign banks.

"But the investment will be HSBC's final one in China's banking industry," said John Bond, Chairman of HSBC Holdings at a joint press conference of the two banks' leading officials.

"We will concentrate on it to make it a success," he said.

HSBC now owns part of the Bank of Shanghai and 15.98 percent of China's Industrial Bank through its Hang Seng Bank subsidiary.

Bond said HSBC will benefit from BoCom's large branch networks in the country. BoCom has 2,700 branches and outlets in 137 cities in China. The two will set up a joint venture credit card company to issue a co-branded card, Bond said. The credit card business in China, which is still very small by international standards, is believed to have great potential.

Introducing strategic foreign investors is part of a strategy that China's commercial banks are employing to meet looming challenges from foreign rivals, who will enjoy a fully open Chinese banking market by the end of 2006. The other part of the strategy comprises the selling of non-performing loans and public listing.

By forging a strategic alliance with HSBC, BoCom aims to make good use of HSBC's advanced experience, particularly in corporate governance, new product development and risk control, said BoCom President Zhang Jianguo.

Jiang said that by signing the agreement with HSBC, his bank was finalizing the second stage of its three-episode reform plan, the first one being financial restructuring and the third one, going public.

BoCom said that it consolidated its capital base by accepting capital injection from the State, other shareholders and the social security fund. It also issued subordinate bonds worth 12 billion yuan ($1.4 billion) and sold bad loans with a face value of 41 billion yuan ($4.9 billion).

After all this, the non-performing loan rate of the bank is 3.34 percent and capital adequacy ratio is at 8.82 percent.

Jiang said his bank would try to get listed before China Construction Bank and Bank of China, which are also preparing for overseas listings. The listings of the two, both of which are bigger, would certainly have an impact on BoCom, if they went first, he said.

But he hinted it would be too much of a rush if his bank tried to achieve a listing in 2004.

"We want to avoid the Western holiday season because lots of foreign bankers will be on vacation and many funds are running out of their budget at year's end," said Jiang.

By buying into BoCom, HSBC has outpaced its main international competitors in China, such as US-based Citigroup and British company Standard

Chartered. Citigroup is reported to be interested in the equity shares of one of the biggest four State commercial banks — the Industrial and Commercial Bank of China, China Construction Bank, Bank of China, and the Agricultural Bank of China.

Citigroup now owns nearly 5 percent of the Shanghai Pudong Development Bank, and the two launched a credit card venture in February.

Standard Chartered, which makes two-thirds of its profit in Asia, was reportedly in talks with several potential partners on the mainland but had no timetable for a deal, according to Reuters.

By Xu Binglan
(2004-08-07)

Global Integration

An Interview with D.C. Chien, CEO of IBM China

In the past years, IBM underwent a transformation in order to become a globally integrated company. China, together with India, became a key element in its strategy.

The results are rewarding: in the second quarter, IBM's China revenues grew by about 30 percent year-on-year, compared with a global average of 9 percent.

In an exclusive interview, D.C. Chien, CEO of IBM Greater China Group, talks with reporters You Nuo and Liu Baijia about the role of China in the company's transformation and IBM China's strategies.

Q: IBM announced last year (2006) to move its global procurement center to Shenzhen, showing the increasing importance of the Chinese market to the company. In your transformation towards a globally integrated company, how does IBM define the role of China?

A: Please allow me first to share our global strategy. In the early 1990s, Lou Gerstner, former Chairman and CEO of IBM, started a transformation inside IBM. Many people have paid a lot of attention to that process.

In fact, our internal consensus is that the transformation we are undergoing now is even more significant than the one in the 1990s.

The reason is that in the early 1990s, IBM faced many difficulties.

But in the past two or three years, IBM actually did quite well. So when your business is smooth, it is more challenging to make significant changes. If you take a look at global integration, knowledge workforces in countries like China and India are changing the industry.

When IBM was founded, it did what many Chinese companies are doing now. Although IBM was called a multinational, its primary base was in the US, doing manufacturing and researches there, and then selling products to international market. This is phase one.

After the Second World War, many countries increased protection for their domestic markets. So in IBM Japan, you would see a mini-IBM. Different from phase one, there were also research and development, manufacturing, sales, and supports functions.

In the third wave, the changes are very big. Now if you go to IBM Japan, you will see that human resource function is done in Manila, finance and accounting in Kuala Lumpur, and hardware procurement in Shenzhen.

In this context, what is the role of China? I think this includes two aspects.

Firstly, it is whether we can continue to deliver better value to customers. Thanks to China's economic growth, it is regarded as a center for innovations and services in IBM. So we were the first foreign company to establish a research center in 1993 and then a development center, where we have 3,000 people, one of the largest in IBM. This targets at high-end services, and is not just for the purpose of cheap labor.

As a global integration company, we also support foreign customers from here with the talent resources in China. Half of our people in China serve domestic customers and the other at half work for global missions.

Q: What are your plans towards this process?

A: When we sold our PC business to Lenovo in 2005, many people began watching how IMB made its own transformation, and wanted to learn from that. I think IBM can help Chinese companies in their own transformations. One typical example is Chinese enterprises such as Huawei and Lenovo, who have grown big and strong in China and now want to go overseas. We can also contribute our share towards their development: we helped Huawei define its global financial system and helped Lenovo with its global IT system.

Another area where we can add value: after China's opening-up, subsequent to its WTO accession in 2001, many domestic companies accelerated their pace of development to fend off international competitors entering China.

Even in the government sector, IT plays a role. For example, in Xuanwu District of Nanjing, different government agencies ran different computer systems. Now, with service-oriented architecture technology, different platforms are combined together in a simple way. An application that took six days before now just needs one day.

Energy is a very hot topic in China now. IBM has a very large data center network in the world, and the 3,900 servers in it cover a space as large as tens of soccer fields. Recently we launched a green data center initiative and used energy efficient and virtualization technologies, so at present, we just have some 30 such servers, and manage to save electricity bills worth as much as those in a large US city. If a similar plan is executed in China, the savings can be huge.

I went to Dalian two weeks ago and IBM South Korea brought 150 of their customers to the city too. When multinationals come to China, IBM also hopes to play a role in their development in this country and provide know-how to them.

Q: IBM is transforming itself into a globally integrated company. Is IBM also aiming to become a nationally integrated company, so that its resources go to locations with the best workforces, instead of establishing many mini-IBMs everywhere?

A: In China, we look at the issue from several perspectives. First, we must get as close to our customers as possible. Large cities like Beijing, Shanghai, Guangzhou, and Shenzhen account for 45 percent of the total IT spending of the country, but what I often ask myself and my colleagues is: do we have 55 percent of our business from regions outside those large cities? So, besides increasing our presence in industrial sectors, IBM China is also trying to extend its reach. This year (2007), we have established four new branch companies, bringing the total to 26.

The second aspect is where we set up different functions — such as our application centers in Dalian and Chengdu — depending on the advantages of talents in certain regions.

Another area we are looking at is how to bring our image and products to 300 cities outside the 26 branches. Last year (2006), we launched a BlueSkye initiative to build a partnership with system integrators and independent software vendors. This year, we also opened a channel university, because we found many of our partners need management know-how, like how to control employee turnover, how to manage expansion when their organizations become bigger. So the channel university not only trains them in IBM products and services, but also management skills.

By Liu Baijia
(2007-10-10)

Deal in Line with IBM's Strategy

An Interview with Henry Chow, Chairman and
CEO of IBM China

When 39-year-old Henry Chow became head of IBM operations in Hong Kong in 1985, International Business Machines was affectionately called "Big Blue," a pet name signifying the size and solidity of the company, not to mention its famous huge mainframe computers.

Now Chairman and CEO of IBM China, Chow loves hearing his company being called "Deep Blue".

For Chow, being "deep" means professional and focused.

And, being deep means having the courage to let something go.

IBM, the first company to introduce personal computers to the world and make them popular and essential, is selling that business to concentrate on what it really does best.

No choice but success

On December 8, when the world's biggest IT company announced — after 13 months of negotiations and market speculation — that it would sell its PC unit to Chinese computer maker Lenovo, at a total value of $1.75 billion, some analysts said IBM had finally gotten rid of its money-losing PC hardware business.

But Chow does not think so.

"This is a perfect match. We compliment each other very well," said Chow, at IBM China's first official interview on the deal with Chinese media last week.

The deal is in line with IBM's strategy to focus on industry solutions.

IBM wants to focus its money and personnel on high-end enterprise solutions — rather than on price wars — offering effective solutions and services.

After contacting several potential buyers, IBM focused on Lenovo.

"When almost all of the world was looking at China, we knew it was right to co-operate with a Chinese company," said Chow.

He believed the new Lenovo Group had excellent complimentary strengths for the two companies: the rapid economic growth and strong manufacturing power of China, and a changing PC industry. Success is dependent only on the hardworking people of the new Lenovo, according to him.

The US giant cannot afford to lose its reputation, entrenched in PCs since their inception. Neither can the Chinese computer maker afford failure.

The company, with an unsuccessful handset-manufacturing operation and IT services sector, is courting global expansion, and has met a number of bottlenecks in achieving significant growth in the Chinese market; it has bet all that it has on a lucrative deal.

While Lenovo is strong on cost control, IBM's global branding, sales network, and finance will also be crucial for the new Lenovo, now the third largest computer maker in the world.

Chow ascertains that within a year, Lenovo products will be distributed to overseas markets through IBM's networks, with IBM providing financial aid to customers.

When the two companies announced the deal on December 8 in Beijing, Chow, the main player in concluding the deal, left the conference on his own. Back at his office, he called his key clients and listened to their concerns over the acquisition.

Their most fundamental concern was whether Lenovo would maintain the same quality of products and services as IBM.

Chow says there are always some employees who are uncertain about their future, but he also knows that they will only have more opportunities in the new Lenovo; the PC business in the company is still growing fast and has a bright future.

Not Only a Sale

For Chow, the deal means much more than selling IBM's PC business and utilizing the companies' respective strengths. It means a partnership not only with Lenovo, but also with China's IT industry.

Lenovo is a major player in distributing IBM's blueprint of its core businesses, with a contract signed to provide Lenovo with five years of IT service support.

As the "on-demand" strategy becomes a major part of IBM's trusted service support, the US giant can concentrate further on its expertise in the field. Companies do not need to have their own IT infrastructure, outsourcing the need to service providers like IBM, a common feature of business internationally.

IBM has won many large contracts around the world for its professionalism in service, but still needs to make some breakthroughs in IT services for local Chinese companies.

The deal with Lenovo will offer them that opportunity, thanks to Lenovo's influence with many Chinese companies.

Lenovo, one of the earliest customers of German software giant SAP's enterprise resource planning solutions, has helped SAP win more customers and deploy solutions.

Lenovo's advantage in costs also enables IBM to provide services at lower prices to customers all over the world, sometimes the last deciding factor in closing a deal.

IBM also has huge expectations of the Linux operating system — a UNIX open-source standard — and related software, in contrast to Microsoft's proprietary Windows operating system.

With IBM pushing and supporting Linux, the development of office software suites and other relevant applications are regarded as the most dangerous threats to Microsoft.

The world's biggest software company has admitted during internal meetings that IBM is a formidable adversary.

In another major move, IBM opened its China Software Development Lab in Beijing.

IBM's fifth global laboratory is expected to employ 2,000 researchers by the year end, 600 of them working on Linux-based software.

The company's cooperation with Lenovo will enable IBM to bundle its software with Lenovo's computers, and sell Lenovo computers with its proficient software solutions, potentially reducing Microsoft's stranglehold on the market.

With its history in semiconductors, IBM is also deploying a chip-production unit. "Deep Blue" launched its new website "Power.org," in Beijing on December 2, announcing a Power.org open standard alliance with 14 other companies.

Power.org provides the standards and specifications of Power processors, a chip architecture initiated by IBM and used in consumer electronics, networks, automotive applications, and IT devices.

International Systems Technology Co Ltd, a new 80-20 joint venture between IBM and China Great Wall Computer Group Corp, in Shenzhen, will produce IBM eServer P-series chips, based on the Power series.

"We still use Intel's chips in our PC products, but in high-end servers, we believed we should continue to invest in our own research and development," said Chow.

The Power.org alliance also includes a software developer and semiconductor manufacturer from China. If Lenovo participates, Power processors will go mainstream in products fully designed by a Chinese company.

By Liu Baijia
(2004-12-21)

Super Link

Technology Giant to Shift Focus to Service

IBM will shift its investment focus in China from manufacturing to technology services and innovation, said executives from the global technology giant in Beijing yesterday.

"Our business is changing, so our investment in China will also change," said Michael Cannon-Brookes, IBM's Vice-President of Business Development for China and India.

He said the technology firm's investments would go into areas such as IT service, business transformation, Linux operating systems, and people. IBM has already invested billions of US dollars in China.

In 2005, the tech firm procured hardware and services worth $1.89 billion in the world's fastest growing economy.

Samuel J. Palmisano, Chairman, President and CEO of IBM, said yesterday that technology service, the fastest growing segment in the technology industry, would be a top priority for his company in China, one of IBM's most dynamic markets.

IBM achieved year-on-year growth of 27 percent in China in the third quarter, compared with a corporate average of 5 percent.

While service is critical for IBM, it is also important for China, which is trying to move to the upper level of the value chain from its current position as a manufacturing powerhouse.

The Ministry of Education and IBM yesterday signed a memorandum of understanding to provide master and doctorate degrees in service science and management engineering in some 50 universities.

Henry Chow, Chairman and CEO of IBM Greater China Group, said his business had been working with the ministry for over a decade. The focus of this new cooperation is to train world-class talents and provide experience in business transformation to help China become an innovative nation.

In the past 12 years, the US giant has spent around $180 million in cooperation with education organizations, but it declined to reveal its latest spending.

By Liu Baijia
(2006-11-15)

Down to Earth

An Interview with Wolfgang Mayrhuber,
CEO and Chairman of Deutsche Lufthansa AG

He's not a spokesman for an entire continent, but Wolfgang Mayrhuber can certainly speak with authority on the global airline industry. The chairman of the Association of European Airlines sent out a clear message on his recent two-day stay in China: Europe takes the development of the Chinese airline industry very seriously.

It may have only been Mayrhuber's first business trip of the new year 2006, but the Chief Executive Officer (CEO) and Chairman of Deutsche Lufthansa AG says he visits China, the company's most important market, at least once a year. The country is both a revenue generator for Lufthansa's passenger airline business and a goldmine for the German carrier's other business arms, including cargo, aircraft MRO (maintenance, repair and overhaul), catering, leisure travel and aviation information technology (IT) services.

"Our aim is to grow all of them," says Mayrhuber. "All of our businesses have come to China. I hope all of them will be in a leading position in this country."

Lufthansa German Airlines is the top European carrier in China, and has the most weekly flights to and from Europe.

China has been the standout performer in the Asia-Pacific region for Lufthansa, with its number of passengers growing by an annual average rate of 20 to 25 percent over the past four years. China has replaced Japan as the airline's most important market in Asia; it accounts for 50 percent of its regional business.

When Lufthansa opened scheduled flights to the Chinese mainland in 1980, there were only three flights per week. It now has 31 weekly flights, primarily on B747s that can carry almost 400 passengers. (Editor's note: As of July 2007, Lufthansa has 38 weekly flights to the Chinese mainland.)

"It's visible how important this market is," says Mayrhuber.

With other European airlines fighting for a larger share of the Chinese market, Lufthansa plans to maintain its leading position by adding capacity to existing destinations and studying the possibility of launching new flights to more Chinese cities. It will add three extra flights between Frankfurt and Shanghai in the summer. The CEO, however, refuses to say which Chinese city is likely to become Lufthansa's next destination in China.

"Of course I wouldn't inform my competitors what we have in mind," he says.

His cautious reply is a reflection of the heated competition between European airlines in China. Top European carriers such as Air France and British Airways have either increased or launched flights to China recently.

Smaller carriers such as Air Europa are also keeping a close eye on China. The Spanish airline started flying to China last May (in 2005) and plans to launch daily flights to Beijing and Shanghai within the next three years.

With such a large number of daily flights to China's three largest cities — Beijing, Shanghai and Guangzhou — the choice for the next destination requires careful consideration, Mayrhuber says.

"We always want to be on the frontline, but we don't fly routes where we lose money," he states. "We don't go for market share, but for profitability."

Other Opportunities

Passenger airlines, cargo and MRO are Lufthansa's biggest profit sources, followed by catering, IT services and leisure travel.

"I think development has only just started," says Mayrhuber. "The opportunities

in China are so big that we need to have a vision of where it will go."

Lufthansa Cargo's most recent joint ventures are International Cargo Center Shenzhen (ICCS) and Jade Cargo International, both established in 2004.

ICCS is a 50-50 joint venture between Lufthansa Cargo and Shenzhen Airport Co Ltd, and operates the international airfreight terminal at Shenzhen International Airport.

Lufthansa Cargo holds 25 percent in Jade Cargo International, which is the maximum for a single foreign investor under Chinese regulations. The joint venture, which is 51 percent owned by Shenzhen Airlines, is expected to start operating this year (2006). The cargo carrier will initially serve domestic destinations and intra-Asian routes, followed by European and American destinations, using six Boeing 747-400 freighters.

Ameco Beijing was the first stop on Mayrhuber's recent business trip. Ameco was set up in 1989 as China's first MRO joint venture. Air China holds a 60 percent stake, and Lufthansa holds the rest.

"It's my baby. I have a very strong feeling for it," says Mayrhuber.

Mayrhuber has spent over 20 of the last 30 years he has been with Lufthansa in a range of management positions in the company's MRO division. He was elected chairman of Lufthansa Technik AG when it became an independent company in October 1994, and he played an influential role in its ongoing evolution into a leading global supplier of MRO services.

"I was there (at the establishment of Ameco) from the very beginning," says Mayrhuber.

Ameco's annual sales have been growing by double digits for four consecutive years, thanks to the fast expansion of airlines fleets in China and the increasing tendency for European and US airlines to outsource maintenance services for their fleets. The MRO joint venture was expected to bring in 1.7 billion yuan ($210 million) in revenues in 2005, a 20 percent year-on-year growth.

LSG Sky Chefs, the catering arm of Lufthansa, now owns 11 percent of the Chinese air catering market. The company is hoping to increase that market share to 30 percent within the next two years, according to HK Cheung, Executive Vice-President of LSG Sky Chefs Asia Pacific. The in-flight caterer has kitchens in Shanghai, Xi'an, Nanjing, Hangzhou, Chengdu, Sanya and Hong Kong. It set up a joint venture with Guangzhou Baiyun International Airport in 2004. LSG Sky Chefs holds 30 percent of the shares.

IT services and leisure travel are Lufthansa's smallest arms in China. It provides flight scheduling systems to Shanghai Airlines. Thomas Cook, Lufthansa's travel company, has not yet established an office in China, but is organizing trips to the country.

Global Giant

Lufthansa received regulatory approval last July (2005) to merge with Swiss International Air Lines. The complete integration is scheduled for 2006 to 2007, the company's website shows. More mergers or acquisitions are possible, Mayrhuber says.

"But we are very selective and we don't want to make mistakes," says the

CEO. "I still believe that this industry has to consolidate itself because there are too many players in the market that can't sustain their businesses over the long term."

He says this is particularly true in Europe, where 60 to 80 percent of the market is within a flying time of one and a half hours.

"There are many, many small countries with many, many airlines," he adds. "If the airline industry should be driven by market forces, you need to be big enough to be globally competitive. If you want to be a global carrier, you need to have the sky. This means you have to grow both organically and through acquisitions."

Mayrhuber says cooperation with other airlines is also vital for Lufthansa to act as a global leader.

"A lot of the costs can be reduced by cooperating," he adds.

Lufthansa achieved profits (after tax) of 416 million euros ($499 million) in the first nine months of 2005, a jump of 154 percent year-on-year. Mayrhuber would not give his forecast on the full-year performance, however.

"We are happy with the 2005 results."

He says Lufthansa is still profitable amid surging fuel prices because of a combination of cost reductions and solid investments in quality products that appeal to customers. The airline launched a cost reduction campaign two years ago to cut 1.2 billion euros ($1.4 billion) by the end of 2006. Mayrhuber says the program is still on track.

The company also restructured businesses that were losing money. In the catering business, for example, 8,000 jobs were axed over five years and non-core activities were sold off. It shut down 11 kitchens in the United States.

"We believe that each business unit should focus on its core competencies," says Mayrhuber. "So things that are not working are sold off. If it doesn't make money, fix it or close it."

Lufthansa invested a lot in 2005 to improve its passenger airline services, including onboard Internet, new business class seats, and in-flight entertainment on long flights. Terminals also began offering special services to first class passengers, and fast lanes were established in airports for business people.

"If you save 100 million euros ($120 million) in cost reduction, you can have 50 million ($60 million) to reinvest," says Mayrhuber. "The investments of today are the profits of tomorrow."

Future Still Bright

In celebration of the company's 80th year in China in September 2006, Lufthansa Chairman and CEO Wolfgang Mayrhuber led a delegation of senior executives and other VIP guests to the country for a series of events highlighting Lufthansa's confidence and commitment to China.

While in China, Mayrhuber was able to spare some time to talk to reporters Lu Haoting and Wang Yu about Lufthansa's ambition and strategy in China.

Q: Lufthansa's business in China now covers passenger flights, cargo, aircraft MRO (maintenance, repair and overhaul), catering, and aviation information technology services. Which one is your largest revenue source? And which areas will Lufthansa focus on developing in China in the near future?

A: Lufthansa, as an aviation group, has an active engagement in China. Each business unit is a leader in its own sector in the service chain of air transportation. Lufthansa will continue to enhance its investments in the market working closely with its partners.

Currently, our passenger business plays the major role in generating group revenue. In China, we now run passenger, cargo, aircraft maintenance, catering and IT systems service. And they are all top runners in their respective fields.

Last Month (August 2006), we inaugurated Jade Cargo, and recently Ameco

Beijing announced plans for a A380 hangar and hosted the Cornerstone Ceremony. Our prospects are very bright.

Q: What kind of role does China take in Lufthansa's global strategy?

A: For us, China is an extremely important market with a great future. Today, no other European airline already offers such a wide range of connections between Europe and China. In the last five years, we have more than doubled services to the Chinese mainland and Hong Kong, from 24 to 52 flights per week. Lufthansa today flies more frequently to China than to Japan.

In terms of the number of intercontinental connections, China is number two in the Lufthansa network behind the US. We want to strengthen our position in the next few years and expand together with our partners. Our cooperation with Air China has really proved itself and Lufthansa has acquired a high level of market competence in China in recent years, which will pay off in the future.

Mutual reliability, professionalism and a high degree of fairness are the foundation of our joint venture with Air China. It is an outstanding example of successful German-Chinese cooperation. Lufthansa is well prepared to face the competition with our extensive flight schedule, operative stability, reliability, punctuality and the many connections for ongoing flights into China's interior which we offer.

At Lufthansa we have the right blend of services to continue to grow further and faster in China's airline business than our competitors.

Q: Will Lufthansa increase its capacity in China in 2006? What is Lufthansa's core strategy in China?

A: Lufthansa already has a strong presence in the Chinese market. We have daily direct flights from Frankfurt and Munich to Beijing, Shanghai and Hong Kong, and from Frankfurt to Guangzhou — a total of 52 flights per week. Via code-share agreements with our new Star Alliance members, Air China and Shanghai Airlines, Lufthansa can offer flights to another twelve destinations.

Among European airlines we are the market leader in flights from Europe to China, with a share of 14 percent of the total seat capacity. The target we will set ourselves over the next few years is to consolidate our leading position and grow faster than our competitors.

The quality of our network planning will be the deciding factor as to whether this goal can be accomplished.

Q: What are your plans for Lufthansa's future expansion in China?

A: Lufthansa aims to participate in the growth of China's aviation industry by exploring the many opportunities offered in one of the most dynamic markets in the world. The airline remains committed to its investments and will continue to enhance its bilateral partnerships.

Lufthansa continues to pursue major objectives in its involvement in China.

The airline wants to grow further and consolidate its position as the leading foreign airline. To this end, as soon as it goes into service with Lufthansa, the huge new Airbus, the A380, will be used to increase the capacities of our Chinese routes, probably on routes to Beijing and Shanghai.

In addition, Lufthansa is giving strong support to the integration of Air China and Shanghai Airlines as members of the Star Alliance. Lufthansa is also continuing to push for the further development of code-share agreements, in order to open up China even more effectively for European visitors.

For the 2008 Olympics Lufthansa expects a further significant increase in passenger volume.

Q: In 2005 when we interviewed Ameco Beijing, we heard that the company's new multi-bay line maintenance hangar, which can simultaneously accommodate two A380s, two Boeing 747-400s and two 777-300ER aircraft, will be completed in 2006. How is the project going? What kind of maintenance services will Ameco Beijing provide to the A380s at Beijing Capital International Airport?

A: As Beijing airport opens a third runway and third terminal in 2007, Ameco will also be opening a new maintenance hangar, especially for its main customer, Air China. The new hangar has been designed right from the start to accommodate our new flagship, the A380.

The Airbus A380 will have a special role in the traffic between Europe and China and that is experts' unanimous opinion. Therefore, Lufthansa is planning to be the first European airline to operate the new mega-liner on its high-volume routes to China. Network strategists are currently examining three possible destinations in China for our A380s: Beijing, Shanghai and Hong Kong.

Q: Ameco Beijing is a major joint venture between Lufthansa and Air China. How do you feel about its development over the past 17 years?

A: Ameco Beijing was established in Beijing in 1989. It is a leading maintenance, repair and overhaul (MRO) facility and it is Lufthansa's most successful project, and the biggest cooperative project, in China.

The founding of Ameco was the start of a success story for both Air China and Lufthansa. The co-operative project has developed into the largest MRO operation in China. Within the first 15 years of its existence, almost 1,000 major overhauls of commercial aircraft were completed, 126 jets were painted, more than 2,000 jet engines serviced and more than 200,000 components repaired.

In 2004, Lufthansa and Air China signed an extension to their contract for a further 25 years. On the one hand, the contract offers Air China optimal reliability and, on the other, offers Lufthansa Technik interesting opportunities in the growth market of Asia.

An investment program worth about $300 million has been planned. Additional hangars, material stores and equipment workshops as well as extended services for maintenance and jet engine repairs will be introduced.

By Lu Haoting

(2006-02-13, 09-26)

Industry Overhaul

An Interview with Hans Schmitz,
General Manger, and Chai Weixi,
CEO of Ameco Beijing

Exciting doesn't even begin to describe it. Ameco Beijing plans to cut a lot of red ribbons in 2006.

The aircraft maintenance, repair and overhaul (MRO) supplier will hold groundbreaking ceremonies for four major projects this spring. The four major projects scheduled for 2006 include a multi-bay line maintenance hangar, which will be able to simultaneously accommodate two A380s, two Boeing 747-400s and two 777-300ER model aircraft. It will be built near Terminal 3 at the Beijing Capital International Airport. Also on deck this year are a new single-bay overhaul hangar, a new plating workshop, and a new warehouse center.

These new undertakings are expected to double Ameco's capacity by 2008 when all the projects are completed before 2008.

"This is only the first part of a long term development plan," says Hans Schmitz, General Manager of the company. "We need to be prepared for the growing market."

The joint venture between Air China and Lufthansa German Airlines seems to be enjoying some of the good luck of the two auspicious symbols of its parent companies: the phoenix and the crane.

Ameco's annual sales have experienced double-digit growth for four consecutive years, and the MRO supplier is expected to record 1.7 billion yuan ($210 million) in revenue in 2005, a 20 percent year-on-year growth.

"A major reason for this," says Schmitz, "is because Chinese airlines are rapidly expanding their fleets. Air China's fleet experienced fast expansion in 2005. Other domestic customers all grew in a similar fashion. This generates an additional workload for us."

China's air travel market has been growing by double digits annually. Domestic airlines are busy renewing and expanding their fleets to meet rising air traffic demand, which will make China the world's second largest aviation market after the United States within the next two decades, according to an Airbus forecast.

The fleets of Chinese airlines should double in the next five years, says Chai Weixi, Ameco's Chief Executive Officer and General Manager. There are currently more than 800 aircraft in service in China.

"Fleet expansion is making China the fastest growing MRO market in Asia," says Chai.

Asia is currently the world's third largest MRO market after North America and Europe, but at 7.4 percent annual growth, it is expanding faster than any other part of the world. China's MRO market is expected to be worth $2.5 billion in 2014, AeroStrategy Management Consulting estimates.

The global MRO market is to grow 5.6 percent on average each year from 2004 to 2014, according to AeroStrategy.

Rising domestic demand is great, Schmitz says, but he is also confident about US and European airlines' increasing tendency to outsource maintenance services for their fleets. Airline profits have been rocked by sky-high jet fuel prices. Four out of the seven major airlines in the United States are now flying under bankruptcy protection, and European airlines are also under cost pressures. More and more airlines are reducing their own in-house MRO capabilities and looking for alternatives.

As the size of the Airbus fleet has grown over the past decade, MRO suppliers have picked up much of the slack, according to figures from Airbus. That trend is expected to continue over the next 10 years, it adds. MRO companies provided 39 percent of Airbus aircraft maintenance in 2005. By 2015, MRO companies will likely handle 47 percent of Airbus aircraft maintenance.

United Airlines assigned the maintenance of its entire fleet of Boeing 777s exclusively to Ameco in August 2005. The five-year contract, worth more than $30 million, is the largest single order Ameco has received from North America, the world's largest MRO market.

In the next five years, United Airlines' Boeing 777 fleet will come to Ameco for heavy maintenance visits (HMVs). More than 50 HMVs are planned for the first three years, and the contract covers about 80 aircraft.

"Many other major airlines in the world are closely watching how we will handle the order from United Airlines," says Chai. "The quality of our services will directly determine our workload after 2008."

The first two United Airline aircraft have been delivered on time and the third one is expected to be completed as scheduled.

Low labor costs in China are giving Ameco an advantage in offering aircraft maintenance and overhaul services. Labor accounts for about 70 percent of total airframe heavy maintenance costs, with materials taking the rest.

"We have a good starting point and we can make very competitive offers," says Schmitz.

He adds that price is only one advantage, however.

"We need to prove we are capable of producing the same quality services and show we can offer competitive turnaround times," says Schmitz.

One additional day of downtime for a Boeing 747 costs an airline $50,000, simply to finance the aircraft.

"Airlines want to fly these assets rather than having them stand in the maintenance hangar," he continues. "That is why turnaround time is so decisive. We need to do much better than average MRO companies to really show we have an overall edge."

Seeing Is Believing

Schmitz has been General Manager of Ameco for more than two years, and is proud to show visitors around the company. His guests have included the chief administrator of the Federal Aviation Administration of the United States and company executives from a number of airlines.

"They are all amazed and surprised at what they see, because they don't expect it," says Schmitz. "In the past foreign customers were very skeptical about the MRO industry in China."

That prejudice certainly existed when Ameco was established in 1989 as China's first MRO joint venture. Air China holds a 60 percent stake and Lufthansa holds the rest. The joint venture was initially geared at raising capital, introducing new technologies and management styles to China's MRO industry, and better serving Air China, the nation's flagship carrier.

Ameco's focus has since shifted to a joint approach to serving both the domestic and international market. It now provides complete maintenance services for Air China's entire fleet, as well as other domestic carriers and more than 30 international airlines.

Air China and Lufthansa extended the joint partnership for another 25 years in August 2004, with a capital injection of $100 million over the next four years.

Ameco was named Best Asia/Pacific Independent MRO Operation of the Year at the MRO Asia Conference and Exhibition in Singapore last November.

"We want to be a strong player in the international MRO market by 2008," says Chai. "We are now 'sharpening the knife' to prepare for that target."

Ameco set up a new department in 2004. With a staff of nine, the department will come up with Ameco's development plans for the next 5 to 15 years.

"We intend to develop our facilities in a very efficient and rational way," says Schmitz. "The market grows quickly and we are sometimes under pressure from new developments, so we need to look far enough ahead to develop plans."

Along with the expanded production capacity, another major project for Ameco is to enlarge its training capabilities.

"With this kind of expansion, we need to develop our human resources as well," says Schmitz.

Ameco has been increasing its staff by 5 percent annually over the past several years. In 2005 alone, it hired about 400 people, or 10 percent of its total workforce.

"It is easy to build new airports and new hangars, but it is not easy to find enough pilots, and to find and train experienced engineers and mechanics," says Schmitz. "This can be one of the obstacles China's MRO industry faces."

Sixty to 80 graduates per year came out of Ameco's training center up until three years ago. In 2005, 120 students graduated from the center, which is responsible for training mechanics and technicians. Ameco is also cooperating with the Civil Aviation University of China, Beijing University of Aeronautics and Astronautics and the Northwestern Polytechnical University, to find young talent.

"Beijing's population is twice that of Sweden," says Schmitz. "There are a lot of young people looking for jobs in the aviation industry. There should be enough young talent for us to attract and train. I don't see a shortage coming up."

By Lu Haoting
(2006-01-09)

Super Link

1. Key Role for Cargo JV

Jade Cargo International, the first Sino-German joint venture airline, is expected to play a vital role in Lufthansa's overall expansion in China, top executives of the German aviation group said yesterday.

"We want to enhance all aspects of our China business, and Lufthansa will be a strong brand in China, so that when you want to do business with Europe (in aviation), Lufthansa will come to your mind first," said Wolfgang Mayrhuber, Chief Executive Officer and Chairman of Deutsche Lufthansa AG, during his visit to Jade Cargo's headquarters in Shenzhen.

Lufthansa holds a 25 percent stake in Jade Cargo, the maximum share a single foreign carrier is allowed to hold in a Chinese airline. Shenzhen Airlines controls 51 percent of the joint venture, while the German Investment and Development Company has the remaining shares.

The maiden flight of the Shenzhen-based cargo joint venture took place from Shenzhen to Amsterdam on August 5, 2006.

It will have a fleet of six Boeing 747-400 freighters by 2008 and plans to develop a network spanning European, intra-Asian and trans-Pacific routes.

Stefan H. Lauer, a member of Lufthansa's executive board, said that Shenzhen-based Jade Cargo would not be adversely affected by its proximity to Hong Kong, a major cargo gateway to the Chinese mainland.

"We are not taking cargo traffic away from Hong Kong — the Pearl River Delta region is a world manufacturing base, which ensures enough cargo business for three airports in the area, namely Hong Kong, Guangzhou and Shenzhen," said Lauer.

He continued, "Shenzhen airport is currently under-utilized and we hope the launch of Jade Cargo will give it a real chance to play the important role in logistics that the airport deserves in this region."

Lauer added that most cargo carriers are currently focused on the Yangtze River Delta region.

Shanghai's cargo-handling capacity is increasing as a result of new start-up joint ventures. For example, Great Wall Airlines Ltd, in which Singapore Airlines holds a 25 percent stake, launched a scheduled flight from Shanghai to Amsterdam in June. It operates two B747-400 freighters.

Shanghai Airlines Cargo, a joint venture between Shanghai Airlines and two subsidiaries of Taiwan-based Evergreen Group, started flights to Los Angeles last month. The company, which currently has three freighters, plans to expand its fleet to 10 by 2010. In addition, Air China plans to establish a cargo joint venture with Cathay Pacific in Shanghai.

Lauer also denied rumors that Lufthansa would purchase a stake in Shanghai Pudong International Airport's new freight zone. But the German carrier's existing joint venture with Shanghai Airport Group, PACTL, will "extend its current services and play a role" in the new freight facilities, he said.

PACTL, or Shanghai Pudong International Airport Cargo Terminal Co Ltd, was established in 1999, and is 29 percent-owned by Lufthansa. China is Lufthansa's largest market in Asia and accounts for 15 percent of its global revenue. Passenger airline service, cargo and MRO (maintenance, repair and overhaul) are its biggest profit sources in China, followed by catering and IT services.

By Lu Haoting
(2006-08-17)

2. Giant Jet Set

Deutsche Lufthansa AG has ordered 15 A380s, and has an option for five more, which will result in the largest A380 fleet in Europe. The German airline will take delivery on its first A380 in the summer of 2009, with the rest to follow until 2015.

It is the first and exclusive commercial route-proving partner of Airbus. During a 12-day program in March 2007, Lufthansa teamed with Airbus to conduct the first-ever service tests on the A380 under normal operating conditions: 500 passengers and 23 Lufthansa flight attendants.

Holger Hatty, member of the Lufthansa Passenger Airlines Board, talked to the reporter during a test flight from Frankfurt to Hong Kong on March 23. Hatty oversees Lufthansa's airline and network strategy, alliances and portfolio management, as well as information technology, purchasing and the overall introduction of the Airbus A380 into the Lufthansa fleet.

Q: Which routes will Lufthansa fly with the A380s? When will Lufthansa's A380 fly to China?

A: The Lufthansa A380 fleet will be particularly employed on the heavily frequented routes to Asia and North America. We are now focusing on about 20 destinations worldwide. The possible final destinations have one thing in common: the passenger volume is already so high today that the capacities of a Boeing 747 or the Airbus A340 family, which are currently available, are not sufficient.

The A380 will fly to Asian destinations in 2010. I am pretty sure Beijing and Shanghai will see the A380. In fact, if we could have gotten the aircraft early enough, as we had ordered, we would have seen it during the 2008 Olympic Games in Beijing.

Q: How is Lufthansa getting itself prepared for deployment of the A380?

A: Since 2003, Lufthansa specialists have been intensively preparing for the introduction of the A380. We created a team of 20 people who are coordinators for the A380 program.

We were already the exclusive partner of Airbus in various test and development phases for the A380, for example with the important evacuation test at the end of March last year (2006), as well as on the first Airbus-internal early long flights in September 2006.

We are also building an A380 hangar in Frankfurt. Since all Lufthansa A380s will have their home base in Frankfurt, the necessary maintenance capacity must be ready in good time. The new hangar, being constructed in the southwest section of the airport, will accommodate four A380s or six B747s.

Q: With the introduction of the A380, will the Boeing 747 fleet retire from Lufthansa's fleet?

A: Deploying a new aircraft does not necessarily mean retiring others. Markets develop over the time. You have certain destinations that need smaller aircraft and others that need larger ones. When the small market develops into a big market, you deploy a large aircraft and put the small aircraft into a new market. It is like life. You are born, you grow up and one day you are an adult. This is a picture we see in the airline industry as well.

In fact, we also ordered 20 B747-748s, the next generation of the B747 jetliners, which are scheduled to be delivered in 2010. So we will have two (types of) new large aircraft in our fleet at the same time.

We usually take aircraft out of the fleet when they are older than 15 years. Some of our B747s are getting to this stage and we will do a rollover.

Q: Do passengers have to pay higher fares for flying with the A380, which boasts a more comfortable cabin?

A: No. We will not offer special prices for the A380. If you buy an economy ticket, it is the same price to a certain destination, whatever aircraft you take. In fact, we have seen, for many years, the fares going down. I am pretty sure this trend will continue in the future. Airlines must find a better cost structure. It is inevitable for us to have this large aircraft, both for our passenger comfort and for cost reasons. The cost per seat of the A380 is much lower than other airliners.

By Lu Haoting
(2007-04-16)

Battle of the Bulge

An Interview with Jim Skinner,
McDonald's Global CEO

The first thing one notices about Jim Skinner: he exudes confidence and enthusiasm. His energy and passion are evident from the moment he bounds into the conference room.

If one had any doubts about Jim Skinner's commitment to McDonald's, its products, or the ubiquitous golden arches they are represented by, these suspicions are quickly dashed when he reveals that he eats the much-maligned fast food everyday.

"I like the taste and know the quality is reliable, so I feel really good," says the fast food chain's global CEO with a grin. He is sincere, yet one gets the nagging feeling that every McDonald's executive, whether global or regional, says the same thing to the press.

McDonald's has always paid close attention to food safety and health, Skinner says. He became global CEO in November 2004, following the departure of two of his predecessors, both of whom left their positions due to health problems. James Cantalupo, 60, died of a heart attack on April 19, 2004 and 44-year-old Charlie Bell quit after being diagnosed with cancer. It's debatable whether their health problems had anything to do with their diets, but media reports implying this connection certainly haven't helped the company's image over the past several years.

Things really got bad for the company when the smash-hit US documentary

Supersize Me chronicled the declining health of a man who attempted to eat nothing but McDonald's for a month. Critical reports that the chips contain carcinogens only added further fuel to the fire. The past few years haven't been kind to poor old Ronald.

Sixty-one-year-old Skinner has worked for McDonald's since 1971, and has aggressively defended the tarnished image of the world's top fast food brand. Many of these public relations initiatives have focused on adjusting menus and providing health tips to customers.

"We all believe there is no bad food in the world, just bad menus," says Skinner. His comments neatly summarize the intentions behind the changes that have occurred at McDonald's outlets across China since October 2005.

Calcium-enriched berry yogurt and bottled water have been added to the menu, and yogurt has been introduced as a side option for McDonald's Filet-o-Fish and Spicy Chicken Wings Happy Meals. These packages are specifically aimed at children, and bottled water, orange juice, and milk are now offered as alternatives to sugary soft drinks. Every McDonald's restaurant in China now provides easily understandable nutritional information. These booklets offer data such as the number of calories in different food items, as well as protein, fat, calcium and iron levels.

"As an industry leader, we understand all of our customers' need to make informed choices when it comes to the food they eat," says Gary Rosen, Vice-President and Chief Marketing Officer of McDonald's China.

Insiders say these moves are a response to criticisms leveled against the conglomerate. Other analysts perceive the changes as necessary to McDonald's hopes of maintaining its popularity in the Chinese market. Chinese consumers are becoming more concerned about nutrition, and thus the company needs to show to the world that its food isn't as evil as some have made it out to be.

Zhai Fengyi, an employee at Mcdonald's Hualian Restaurant in Beijing, says that the yogurt has become the most popular new item, and that middle-aged customers and health conscious young women tend to favor the bottled water.

"I like the yogurt," says Wu Manling, a 25-year-old office worker, adding that the menu should be diversified even further.

Fan Ming, a mother of a three-year-old, says the nutritional information is particularly helpful.

McDonald's dramatically changed its business structure in China in 2005 by dividing market operations into four zones — north, south, east and central — from the previous two. The reorganization led to a series of management and menu changes.

Jeffrey Schwartz, President of McDonald's China, says 80 percent of the menu in the four zones did not change, but that the remaining 20 percent will differ throughout the four areas to reflect regional tastes.

"Perhaps we could offer sour and spicy soup in the western provinces and seafood soup in East China," says a McDonald's public relations official.

Professor Cai Meiqin, Director of the Department of Nutrition at the Shanghai Jiaotong University Medical Institute, says the important thing to remember is that a balanced diet is the key to healthy living.

"It's okay to eat fast food sometimes, it does no harm to either adults or children," says Cai.

Li Meng'en, Vice-Chairman of the China Students' Nutrition and Health Promotion Association, says that all Western fast food chains tend to use too much oil and fat, and the food is usually low in fiber. This can lead to health problems such as obesity and cardiovascular diseases. Often used by restaurants and in packaged foods, trans fats are thought to cause cholesterol problems and increase the risk of heart disease. McDonald's Corp. stated that the french fries sold by the company in China contains no trans fat, following revelations that its fries sold elsewhere contain a third more of the potentially artery-blocking substance than previously thought. In a news release on February. 14, 2006, the Oak Brook, Illinois-based McDonald's said it used only fatty acid-free palm oil to make french fries in China.

Yet despite all the bad press, McDonald's is still the best-selling fast food brand in the world. It has over 30,000 outlets in 121 countries and regions, with 815 in China by the end of August 2007. Kentucky Fried Chicken (KFC) is its biggest competitor in the Chinese market. The chicken chain, at the same time, has about 11,000 restaurants in 800 nations and regions, with over 1,900 in China.

Skinner declines to comment on how McDonald's will deal with competition from KFC in the Chinese market, but praises the work of his colleagues in China.

"We still have a long way to go," he adds.

Industry observers say the quest for market dominance will only intensify in the future, with increased competition from both foreign and domestic competitors. Malan Noodle and Shanghai-style Chenghuangmiao, for example, have several years of experience in the market, and their food is better suited to local tastes. Their traditional Chinese fare is also seen as healthier than Western fast food.

By Liu Jie
(2006-01-16)

Will Drive-thrus Drive McDonald's Growth?

An Interview with Jeffrey Schwartz,
CEO of McDonald's China

Jeffrey Schwartz, CEO of McDonald's China, receives his takeaway from a sales assistant at the fast-food company's new drive-up store in Shanghai.

To customers in China, McDonald's is more than just a fast food chain. As the first fast-food behemoth entering the country, it not only brought in fast food culture and service, but a brand lifestyle as well.

By the end of September 2006, the company's sales growth at its 764 restaurants in over 120 cities throughout China was larger than anywhere else in the world. Although the corporation has been rocked in recent years by criticism of its allegedly unhealthy fare, it still works on innovative ways to push into the country's ever-expanding market. Drive-through outlets are now a key element of the firm's strategy for further growth.

Jeffrey Schwartz, CEO of McDonald's China, told the reporter that drive-throughs will be a major weapon in the company's future expansion.

Q: Having established a presence in almost all the major cities in China, do you think McDonald's still has room for growth?

A: We will have 800 restaurants by the end of 2006, and by the start of the 2008 Olympics, we will have 1,000 outlets in China. But we are not only concerned about increasing quantity, we also place great emphasis on the quality of our locations.

Q: Have you introduced a new set of criteria to choose new locations?

A: What interests us most are those "A" locations, the best trading areas able to serve customers in the best way. We are particularly interested in establishing drive-through outlets.

Nationally, the company has just opened its fourth drive-through store, in Zhoushan, East China's Zhejiang Province, adding to the three already operating in Dongguan and Foshan, in South China's Guangdong Province, and Shanghai's Waigaoqiao Free Trade Zone. Within the year, we expect to add 10 more drive-throughs and in 2007 they will account for 50 percent of new outlets, rising to 70 to 80 percent later on.

Q: Are you testing drive-throughs in some particular cities before opening them in other parts of the country?

A: Drive-throughs are clearly a major part of our future development. We won't confine drive-throughs to any one city and we'll spread them throughout China. Right now, we are running businesses in 120 cities in China, so we are looking at virtually every city we do business in.

Q: Drive-throughs have been around in the United States and other markets for many years. Why have you picking this moment to introduce them in such a big way in China?

A: China's growing car ownership prompted us to expand the drive-through business. Changing lifestyles and a growing acceptance of more diverse foods are creating a fertile environment for the drive-through business.

Q: What are the cost advantages or disadvantages of drive-throughs as compared to your traditional restaurants?

A: The costs for drive-throughs — which will feature space for 30 to 50 cars, indoor seating and Wi-Fi equipped restaurants — are higher than for conventional restaurants. But we expect that the return on drive-throughs will more than justify this increased investment, with research suggesting there is huge demand for the service in China.

Among customers visiting our drive-throughs, 30 percent choose to use the drive-through facilities instead of going inside the stores, compared to 65 percent in the United States, where we have had a drive-through service since 1975.

Q: *What are the future prospects for the development of drive-throughs in China?*

A: We have signed a contract with Sinopec to jointly explore locations for drive-through stores. With more than 30,000 existing petrol stations in the country and an average increase of 500 stations per year, Sinopec is the perfect partner to help us expand our drive-through business in China.

Q: *Will the focus on drive-throughs take business away from your traditional restaurants?*

A: Drive-throughs will not benefit in any way at the expense of McDonald's traditional restaurants, with additions to the menu — including the recent arrival of the quarter-pounder — benefiting both our conventional and drive-through businesses.

Q: *Several international fast food chains are in fierce competition for the Chinese market, and many more are expected. How do you deal with this increasingly intense competition?*

A: The threat from competitors doesn't concern me much. I believe that McDonald's will be okay as long as it listens to its customers. The key measure of our success is customers' satisfaction.

Q: *Any major obstacles to McDonald's development in China?*

A: Obstacles no, opportunities yes. McDonald's will grow with our customers, gaining more and more momentum and evolving along with our customers' changing lifestyles and expectations.

By Liu Jie
(2006-10-11)

MCDONALD'S 207

Super Link

1. McDonald's Takes a Bigger Bite

McDonald's, the world's largest fast food corporation, aims to open more than 100 new outlets in the Chinese mainland in 2005.

Tim Lai, Senior Vice-President of McDonald's (China) Co Ltd, told this reporter that the company's performance in China was running parallel with expectations and was developing steadily.

"We will go anywhere, the key cities, the second-tier cities or middle and western regions, so long as the demand exists," said Lai. "But the most important prerequisite for our expansion is convenient logistics, which can guarantee that our food and raw materials are transported as fresh and safe as we require."

McDonald's is also planning to further expand its franchise business in the country. Its first franchise outlet was opened in Tianjin in 2004, and has since posted good figures.

"A batch of franchise restaurants are expected to be launched in the coming months," said Lai, but declined to disclose their locations.

The vice-president pointed out that McDonald's China is a localized company in terms of sourcing and product development. Ninety-five percent of the raw materials used by McDonald's is purchased from local farms and Chinese-style food catering to local tastes has been promoted in recent years.

On March 8, 2005 in New York, McDonald's debuted its new campaign with the tagline: It's what I eat and what I do. I'm lovin' it. According to Lai, McDonald's will create new packaging with tips for healthy eating and also enlist Olympic athletes such as Yao Ming and Guo Jingjing to promote nutrition, exercise and an active lifestyle.

"McDonald's will diversify the menu to offer more choices to consumers and call for a balanced life," said Lai.

Insiders say McDonald's is working hard to improve its image, and shake off the perception that it only offers poor quality food. The company is facing a lawsuit brought by New York teenagers who claim it hid the health risks of items such as Chicken McNuggets, and that the chain's food made them obese.

Lai reiterated that McDonald's has long been dedicated to offering each customer safe and fresh food.

"Quality and health are at the forefront of our minds," he said.

The company has more than 31,500 locations in 119 countries and regions, and caters to over 50 million customers every day.

By Liu Jie
(2005-03-28)

2. McDonald's Workers Set Up Trade Union

McDonald's first trade union branch was set up in Shenyang on Friday, June 29, 2007, succumbing to pressure from the Chinese Government which requires that all companies comply with China's trade union law.

According to the law, a company with more than 25 employees must have an individual trade union organization. In an effort to prevent employee-management confrontation, the All-China Federation of Trade Unions (ACFTU) has been lobbying for foreign companies to allow the establishment of union branches in their China operations.

Yang Saidan, 26, Deputy Manager Assistant of the Pengli outlet in downtown Shenyang, capital of Northeast China's Liaoning Province, was elected chairwoman of the trade union committee.

"It is a good start for the company. I will do my best to protect workers' rights and interests according to law," said Yang, who has been working in the outlet for six years.

So far, 13 of the 41 employees have joined the union.

"After about a month's negotiation with local trade union authorities, McDonald's agreed to have trade unions in each of its 16 outlets in the city," said Li Jinsheng, Director of the Organizing Committee with Shenyang Federation of Trade Unions (SFTU).

The move will promote harmonious labor relations and sound business growth for the company, said Ju Xiuli, Chairman of SFTU.

The fast-food giants have been criticized for underpaying their part-time employees in Guangzhou by up to 40 percent below the local legal minimum wage of just under $1 an hour. Guangzhou-based New Express reported in March that McDonald's was "violating labor laws" by underpaying workers, most of whom are college students.

The government of Guangdong Province, of which Guangzhou is the capital, has set the minimum wage for part-time workers at 7.5 yuan an hour, but the fast-food giant pays only 4 yuan.

A senior official with the ACFTU said, "No company should enjoy special privileges in China. Irrespective of how big and strong a company is or who owns it, no company should be allowed to have in-house rules that violate the country's law."

By Liu Jie
(2007-06-30)

Self-Service Giant Feels Right at Home in China

An Interview with Bill Nuti, President and CEO of NCR

NCR Corporation is a leading global technology company. Its ATMs, retail systems, self-service solutions and IT services provide relationship technology that, it says, can maximize the value of customer interactions, and help organizations create a stronger competitive position. NCR has built a strong foothold in the China market with an increasing number of Chinese customers. During his visit to Beijing in August 2007, Bill Nuti, President and CEO of NCR, sat down for an exclusive interview with the reporter.

Q: How, according to you, can Chinese banking and financial institutes prepare themselves in order to enhance their competitiveness in terms of self-service, given the fact that foreign banks are now allowed to enter the market and expand rapidly?

A: I think Chinese banks are much like large global banks, focusing a great deal on the quality of their ATM channels. In terms of service channels, it is very important to have the ATM channel available nearly 100 percent at the time. Chinese banks are also focusing on the quality of the venders they do business with, the quality of products they deploy and the service level that they provide their customers.

Q: What do you think are the key issues that multinational companies like NCR are facing in China in terms of branding, financial governance, strategic growth, innovation and industry competitiveness?

A: The key issue for us is that we view NCR China as a Chinese brand. We need to make sure that we continue to make NCR a China brand as much as we do a global brand. For us, it is to continue to make progress in that area. We are going to have to manage all of the investments we have made in China and continue to make in China.

Here in Beijing, we have a manufacturing center. We just surpassed over 23,000 ATMs that have been manufactured here in Beijing. These are ATMs that are not just being shipped in China, but around the world. So managing a global supply chain out of China is going to continue to be a work in progress.

We have professional services and software engineering services. We will continue to add staff to those centers over time. Managing the growth of our staff and development of our people here will be a challenge.

Third, entering a new market, and some new industries that are dealing with these changes in customer interaction. Today NCR is the No. 1 market share leader globally in ATMs and the No. 1 market share leader for ATMs in China. But self-service as well has opportunities in many other industries. Those are a few challenges.

Q: You delivered a speech entitled "The Intelligent Self-service Revolution" at the Retail Finance Asia Pacific Conference in March 2006, and emphasized the importance of data warehouses on enterprise decision-making. How do you view China's intelligent self-service potential? Is NCR well prepared for it?

A: We are a company that has been investing in self-service for 40 years, with the invention of the ATM. Since then, we have made significant investments in other self-service solutions to cater to customers' needs and to keep our business momentum in the market. The simple principle is that self-service is for consumers who want to serve themselves when and where they want; for businesses it cuts costs and increases profits. So it is a win-win solution. For consumers, they can do self-service at the ATM machine, for example, and for the bank it can lower its costs and improve working efficiency.

As for intelligence self-service, it is a combination of finance devices, ATMs, point-of-sale machines and some other kiosks. Intelligent self-service aims to create personal experiences for customers to use those financial devices. In Singapore, for example, the Oversea-Chinese Bank (OCB) uses our ATM and

databank analytic technology. So, if you go to the ATM machine at the bank, you swipe your card, it knows who you are, it knows the typical transaction you like to do, and it also knows what language you want to use, and provides offers based on your previous buying record.

Intelligent self-service has also been used in some other sectors like airports and hotel check-in systems. American airports, for example, use our technology to make things easy and speedy.

Q: You talk about entering new markets and some new industries; what industries do you mean outside banking? Could you foresee the market size of these areas in China?

A: If you think about today, self-service is becoming more popular in banking, and that is where we lead. We expect our self-service capability for check-ins at the airport will be a very popular self-service application in the future. You are very well aware that the queue problem in China is a significant issue. Self-service technology eliminates long queues and increases productivity.

We also see self-service in hospitality becoming more mainstream in China, whether it is hotels that are using kiosks for check-in or check-out, or quick services restaurants, for example, ordering via a kiosk. In the gaming area, particularly in Macao, we see opportunities, and we are working with a variety of casinos on self-service opportunities.

China is also determined to improve healthcare. We have self-service applications that have been deployed in other parts of the world, which have dramatically reduced the cost of delivering healthcare. In the public sector, we have interaction via kiosks for automating many high-cost and low-value transactions in government, the ability to apply visa, driver license, taxation and other applications in the government. The richness of the self-service software behind the kiosk is what NCR is focused on. It does reduce government bureaucracy and improve the relationship.

I would lastly say retail. In retail, we have good opportunities both in the area of customer interaction and self-service.

Q: Which industries have the biggest potential for NCR?

A: For us, the No. 1 potential remains banking. The No. 2 is in retail and the No. 3 is travel. Overall, they all have good opportunities.

Q: What are your views of China as a market. Do you think China is playing a strategic role in NCR's global business? What benefits does China's economic growth bring to NCR in China and the entire NCR group?

A: China is a very important market to NCR. If you look at the growth in China, the growth of the banking sector, the growth of the retailing sector and the growth of Chinese industries, they are incredibly strong. Our goal is to continue to localize our products in the Chinese market. The reason we have made a long-term investment in China is because we are going to be peers of Chinese companies in the China market. We are a global company but with a local Chinese sense. That is key for us.

Q: Currently NCR holds the leading position in the global ATM market. But many local companies are catching up, like GRG Banking Equipment Co Ltd, which is the first and largest domestic ATM maker. How does NCR perceive their efforts, and how will the company react to the potential threat of Chinese companies?

A: We have many global competitors, and we have been competing for many years. NCR has been in the ATM business for 40 years, we have more experience in ATM space. With that, we have more experienced staff than most of our competitors. There might be one advantage for Chinese companies: that they are viewed as local companies. But I must also say that we are also a local company. We have a manufacturing center in Beijing, we have local staff and much larger organizations. If you look at our organizations in China, you will find it is entirely Chinese nationals, from the leaders to ordinary employees. We view ourselves as a local company.

Q: Do you think that the Summer Olympic Games in 2008 and the World Expo in 2010 will drive NCR growth in China?

A: I think it is great for China, and I will be there. The events are going to allow China to be seen on the world stage. That has never been done before and it will help, to speak frankly, break down the barriers of ignorance that may exist there. We are going to be participating in the 2008 Olympic Games and the World Expo in 2010, as a platform to drive our business growth. During the past few years we witnessed many reforms in the Chinese economy, and that was fun to watch, which means it is exciting to see China emerge as an economic power. For me, it is pleasing, as I remembered telling leaders of my company in the 1990s that this was a country that one day was going to be a great power economically, a great power socially, and a great power in terms of business.

Q: What are your secrets for running a successful business? How much does previous experience help in your current business success?

A: The secret is to build a great team. You will not succeed without great people around you. There is no one person who can make the company great. It is a group of people that runs the company. Frankly, the talents that exist all the way through the company would make the company great, and a good leader's job is to build a great team which will build a great team, and so on through the company. But the secret is all about the people who run the company, not any single person.

By Zhang Ran and Wu Yunhe
(2006-10-16, 2007-08-30)

Super Link

Teradata Opens Global Service Center

Teradata, a global leader in business data warehousing, applications and services, opened a global consulting center (GCC) yesterday in the port city of Dalian in Northeast China's Liaoning Province.

Teradata was a division of US-based NCR Corporation, a leading global technology company that helps businesses build stronger relationships with their customers.

As one of the world's top 500 companies, NCR employs about 29,300 people worldwide. It services leading companies in industries such as banking, telecommunications and aviation.

Located in the Dalian Software Park, the new center will provide professional multilingual service support to Teradata customers throughout north Asia, including China and Japan, according to NCR Global Vice-President Hideki Hosoi.

"The center is a critical component of the planned growth of Teradata's global professional services consulting. The GCC team in China will be an extension of Teradata Professional Services, the world's leading data warehouse consultancy," he said.

The center's staff will specialize in data warehousing and business intelligence software, and will offer superior capability in end-to-end business data warehouse implementation, according to Hosoi.

The center will serve customers throughout north Asia and complement other consulting centers recently opened in India and Pakistan.

(2006-08-17)

New Nokia CEO to Keep Up China Push

An Interview with Olli-Pekka Kallasvuo

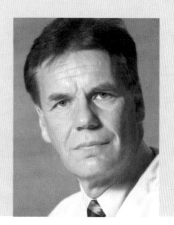

The world's top mobile maker, Nokia, has increased its handset sales in China by 40 percent year-on-year, almost twice its average global growth rate. It is a surprisingly strong performance, beating even Nokia's estimates in a handset market that has become overcrowded with more than 70 manufacturers and nearly 2,000 models on the shelf. Continuing gains in China have put Nokia firmly in the top spot in the global mobile phone industry.

In the past month, Nokia has also experienced a major reshuffle. On June 1, Olli-Pekka Kallasvuo, former head of the mobile phone division, replaced Jorma Ollila as the company's Chief Executive Officer.

Last week, the company appointed Colin Giles, head of Nokia's customer and market operations in China, as the new President of Nokia China. Giles will replace David Ho, who will move to the planned new company Nokia-Siemens Networks as Chairman of the China region.

Furthermore, on June 19, 2006, Nokia formed a 50-50 joint venture with Siemens by combining their respective network equipment business, which is expected to be operational January 1. The company hopes the moves will better align Nokia's operations both globally and in China.

On November 9, 2006, Kallasvuo spoke to this reporter about how Nokia plans to penetrate deeper into both the mobile phone and telecoms equipment markets in China.

Q: When announcing Nokia's third quarter financials in October, you said, "China was surprisingly strong in the quarter." Emerging markets such as China and India are contributing a lot to Nokia's global operations. What are the new growth opportunities in China for Nokia?

A: China is an interesting market with regard to mobile devices. On one hand China is an emerging market because there is a lot of potential for new penetration. We estimate that by 2010, there will be 160 million new subscribers to the network. In that way, it is a market where there is a lot of penetration potential. But then if you look at the market on the other hand, it is also very sophisticated regarding devices and what people want to buy in the marketplace.

The Chinese consumer is interested in all segments of the market. And all price points are relevant in China. For example, there is a strong market for multimedia, high-end and high-tech devices. We don't call these phones, but multimedia computers. In that way, China is a developed market as well. It is an interesting combination: an emerging market and a very developed market.

In Nokia, we are working at all price points and in all market segments. I think we have a very well-balanced portfolio of products. This is especially important in China.

Q: Apparently Nokia was not the first in the market for some models with cool features such as super-slim designs and e-mail capabilities. How is Nokia maintaining its lead despite this?

A: Looking at the market, new features are important and we must be very active to ensure that our new features are the first in the market. That's where we can become even better. And we have a lot of ongoing activities to gain even more speed in product introduction. At the same time, I have to emphasize that it's very important, especially in China, to have a full and complete product portfolio.

We have done a lot of work, in order to understand consumers in different markets, to come up with a complete segmentation model, and to know about different consumer segments in different markets and know what appeals to these consumers. We have interviewed more than 40,000 people, and have more than 6 billion data points. We use these when deciding and marketing our products.

Consumers are different. That's true for China, India and the United States. And even inside China consumers are different. At all times we have to get a portfolio of different products to sell to different consumers. This is very important. So, getting products, getting more speed, managing a complete portfolio and having insight into consumers are very important.

Q: We know Nokia is very conservative about commenting on competitors. Still, what is your comment on Motorola's ambitious goal to overtake Nokia within 1,000 days? What is the gap between Nokia and Motorola? Earlier this month, Nokia won a major equipment contract from Guangdong Mobile. That marks a breakthrough for Nokia in Guangdong's mobile market, a territory previously dominated by Ericsson.

A: We take all competition very seriously, and there is a lot of competition in the marketplace and in the networks market. If you look into the third quarter, our share of the global handset market was 36 percent, and that is a lot bigger than that held by our closest player. On the Chinese mainland, we have gained market share during 13 consecutive quarters, so we have made very good progress in China.

I continue to be very conservative in commenting on competitors. But we must take every competitor very seriously. When it comes to Guangdong, I am very happy that we were able to break through and penetrate that province, and it is a good illustration of the very good momentum that we have there. And of course, we are working very hard to build on that momentum.

Q: Nokia's increasing penetration in the low-end handset market has caused concerns about the decline of the ASP (average selling prices). What do you think of this trend?

A: I strongly believe that to be the market leader you must be active in every area. You have to be active in low end, high end, and intermediate as well. That continues to be our strategy. If you are strong in one part, that doesn't mean you will be strong in other areas. Because of that we will push all phones at all levels.

Think about it: if you sell the first phone to somebody, an entry-level phone, and then the consumer is happy with the quality and the design, you celebrate brand opportunity. When upgrade time comes, the consumer will remember that and you can generate brand loyalty in helping to go forward.

It is very interesting, if you look at brand loyalty. A survey by Media advertising and marketing magazine Media and research company Synovate found Nokia is the No. 1 brand in Asia, beating every other brand in world. I am really happy about this amazing achievement.

Q: The telecoms equipment market appears to be increasingly competitive. Do you have plans for new acquisitions or mergers in the near term?

A: After combining the network business with Siemens, we are very much in the same league as Alcatel-Lucent and Ericsson. Our ambition is, of course, to be the No. 1 in the market. All in all, Nokia-Siemens Networks is an illustration of Nokia's continued willingness to invest into this business.

When it comes to the acquisitions question, we, in this new world where there is much complexity and opportunity, will definitely continue to look at partnerships and acquisitions quite actively, especially in the areas of multimedia, on one hand, and enterprise business on the other.

By Li Weitao

(2006-11-15)

Moving On

An Interview with Jorma Ollila,
Chairman and Former CEO of Nokia

In many ways, Jorma Ollila does not resemble the heads of most major technology companies throughout the world. Big names such as Bill Gates, John Chambers and Steve Jobs can talk passionately on stage to large crowds about future technologies, sometimes even launching fierce attacks on their rivals.

But Ollila, Chairman and former Chief Executive Officer (CEO) of Nokia, tends to be a bit quiet and shy. He speaks slowly, deliberately, and always avoids commenting on any of the Finnish company's competitors.

Yet he remains one of the most successful and admired CEOs in the technology industry. The 55-year-old executive transformed Nokia from a diversified conglomerate in a small country into the dominant mobile phone maker in the world. He held onto his top job for 14 years, the longest tenure in the red-hot mobile communications sector.

His humble and observant approach, coupled with a strong work ethic and tough-mindedness, has contributed a lot to the runaway success of Nokia, as well as his own career, says Ollila. He touched down in Beijing late last month, just a week before he handed over the reins to his successor on June 1.

"(In the 1990s) we realized the mobile phone would be every man's device, not only a toy for kids. We believed it would be a global phenomenon," says Ollila.

This foresight "really paid off", he adds. Anticipating the mobile phone boom, Nokia decided to establish "truly global organizations" much earlier than its rivals, Ollila recalls.

"Investing heavily in China early enough, in both manufacturing and research and development (R & D)" was the best decision he made with regards to Nokia's strategic approach to the country, which is now the world's largest mobile market by subscribers.

China was where Nokia first built its presence when seeking an entry point into the Asian market. In 1985, Nokia established its first representative office in Beijing as its first foray into the mainland. It then established four major joint ventures in the 1990s in Beijing, Dongguan in South China's Guangdong Province and Suzhou in East China's Jiangsu Province.

In 1994, it became the equipment supplier of China's first GSM (global system for mobile communications) network to Beijing Telecommunications Administration. Former Chinese telecoms watchdog Wu Jichuan successfully dialed up the country's first GSM mobile phone call with a Nokia handset N2110.

"We came out strong when GSM was introduced in China," says Ollila. "When technology made a difference in the country, we invested a lot. We are proud that Nokia is the leading player in creating the (mobile communications) industry."

R & D Facilities

By the end of 2005, Nokia had invested a total of 3.3 billion euro in China and had set up a number of R & D facilities. A product development center established in Beijing in 1999, for example, designs a large portion of the handsets Nokia Mobile Phone Business Groups ships throughout the world. Last October, the number of mobile phones manufactured by Nokia factories in China, since 1995, exceeded 200 million units, and a large number of these are exported.

China now has more than 410 million mobile phone subscribers. Twenty years ago, the country's total telephone penetration was below 0.6 percent. Times have changed, and now people throughout the country seem to have mobile devices permanently glued to their ears.

"There is a strong 'use culture' in China," says Ollila. "And China brought us a greater understanding of the Asian lifestyle, which is so different from that in Europe and the United States. The local market is very fashion-oriented and consumer preferences very unique."

The ability to quickly spot and set trends in the industry has helped Nokia score big in China. The company was the first to introduce a number of innovative handset models throughout the country.

In 1995, it launched the Nokia 5110 in China, which enables users to change the external shell. The small, user-friendly model helped popularize mobile phones, which used to be bulky, by turning them into a mass-market commodity. In the following years, Nokia was the first to launch some of the most innovative models on the market, including devices with mobile Internet access and MMS (multimedia messaging services).

But the company also made its share of mistakes. A reluctance to develop clamshell mobile phones and its slow entry into the CDMA (code division multiple access) market forced it to hand over the handset crown in China to Motorola. This was a huge setback for Nokia, because its global market share was double Motorola's.

Nokia was also in big trouble because it was facing challenges from hard-charging local rivals.

"We don't like to lose. We knew we could do better and implement better," says Ollila, noting that Nokia was quick to correct its mistakes.

In 2003, Nokia secured a license from the Chinese Government to make and sell CDMA mobile phones. This has helped increase its total market share. It also launched a number of clamshell models and even Chinese-specific models to fix holes in its product portfolio. Clamshell phones are particularly popular in Asia, especially in China.

The company also merged its four major joint ventures in the country to improve operating efficiency.

"We always have a strong will to win. It's not difficult to find 'be tough-minded' in most management books, but we did it," says Ollila.

Under the leadership of the tough-minded Ollila, Nokia "made a substantial effort to improve distribution and product range over the past three to four years. That has been paying off very well. We are addressing the market segments much better than five years ago."

Market Share

The improved distribution network is also crucial to Nokia's performance in China. Before 2003, Nokia's retail coverage spanned only 50 cities. Today, it covers over 300 cities.

In 2004, Nokia wrested the handset crown back from Motorola. Now it controls more than 30 percent of the market, placing it far ahead of its US rival. Nokia sold 32.5 million mobile phones in China in 2005, up 72 percent year-on-year.

Its net sales of both handsets and network equipment on the Chinese mainland, Hong Kong and Taiwan, surged by 29 percent to 3.85 billion euros ($4.6 billion) in 2005. This robust growth has turned China into Nokia's largest single market. Now the company is expanding into even smaller cities, as well as into the vast countryside, which it now views as a huge emerging market.

Ollila predicts China will have more than 600 million mobile phone subscribers by 2010, from 410 million at present. Most of the new subscribers are expected to come from underdeveloped areas.

That will create huge opportunities, but the diversified and complicated Chinese market will be a big challenge for all industry players.

"Technology is always evolving and the pace is so fast," says Ollila, who will still stay on at Nokia as the Non-Executive Chairman, a position he also holds at Anglo-Dutch oil group Royal Dutch Shell.

"In the coming five to seven years, the impact of the Internet on the mobile communications industry will be significant. This will change business models, handsets and infrastructure," he says.

By Li Weitao
(2006-06-12)

Nokia-Siemens Telecom Network Merger Swings into Action

An Interview with Beresford-Wylie,
Executive Vice-President and General Manager of Nokia Networks, and CEO
of Designate of Nokia-Siemens Networks

Nokia and Siemens announced the merger of their telecom net work businesses in June 2006, a move which could set them up as the No. 3 player in the world's telecom infrastructure market.

The 50-50 joint venture Nokia-Siemens Networks is expected to be operational by January 1, 2007, as part of its ongoing consolidation in the world's telecom market. Its estimated annual revenue of 15.8 billion euros will put Nokia-Siemens on a par with larger rivals Ericsson-Marconi and Alcatel-Lucent in the global telecom equipment market.

The two companies appointed the new entity's worldwide regional operation heads in August, including for China, which was listed as the only single country market for Nokia-Siemens Networks.

Simon Beresford-Wylie, Executive Vice-President and General Manager of Nokia Networks, and Chief Executive Officer Designate of Nokia-Siemens Networks, spoke to this reporter in September 2006 about the merger and pending regulatory approval.

Q: Nokia Networks has been focusing on mobile networks, and we know Siemens is strong in the fixed-line business as well. So what is the role and value of fixed network technology for Nokia-Siemens Networks?

A: When we looked at the merger, originally the logic very much was based on convergence. In the last couple of years, it's becoming increasingly clear that fixed-mobile conversions is a major industry trend. With the merger with Siemens, I think we have a beautifully balanced convergence portfolio.

On June 19, when we announced this I commented that 22 percent of our portfolio from a revenue perspective was based on fixed and 78 percent based on mobile. Currently there are 2.4 to 2.5 billion mobile subscribers (globally). Our expectations are that by 2008 it will grow to 3 billion and will touch 4 billion in 2010.

Other growth areas are very much in broadband, the fixed broadband, and around the convergent call. So fixed actually has, if you like, a nice dovetail from a growth point of view on broadband access and convergent call with the mobility business, so we see a wonderful complementary here.

We feel great about the balance in our portfolio, because as Nokia-Siemens Networks we may start as the No. 3, but we aspire to be the No. 1, and we think our portfolio gives us a great foundation to reach that goal.

Q: China will be the only single country market for Nokia-Siemens Networks. Why do you put China in such an important place, and what are your expectations for this new entity in the China market?

A: When we looked at our business in the structure, we settled on six business units and seven regions, and one region is China. And why is China a region? Well, because it's a huge market. It's a fast-growing market. It's a market full of opportunities and it's big enough and different enough to warrant actually treating it as a region.

Q: What will be the major challenges for the merger?

A: I think the size is obviously very large and with size comes complexity. As we are two large businesses present in many countries and we have to bring these activities together, we have to bring our portfolio of products together and that brings complexity. Also we have to bring different cultures together as well. There are also some very practical issues.

We have about 100 days to make Nokia-Siemens Networks go live. This new company will have around 60,000 employees, around 300 mobile customers, around 150 fixed customers. So what that means is, in January we need to make sure that we can pay 60,000 people, that we can receive orders from 450 customers, that we can deliver equipment and services to 450 customers, that we can issue invoices to 450 customers, that we can collect the receivables from 450 customers.

And actually that is a remarkably complex undertaking that we have to have in a very short amount of time ... but we will do it.

Q: Talking of cultures, some people say there are similarities because Siemens and Nokia are both European companies, while others claim there is still a big difference as German and Finnish cultures are somewhat deep-rooted. How will you address this challenge?

A: It's a very good question. Siemens is a 160-year-old company and Nokia is a 140-year-old company, and when you are dealing with companies that have such long histories there are cultures that build up.

Every company, every country, has its own culture. But there are some strong similarities. If you look at the 60,000 people that will work in the company, two-thirds of them actually or thereabouts will work outside of Finland and Germany and many of us actually including myself come from either Finland or Germany, so both companies are outward-looking and global. Both companies are very fine engineering companies. Both companies are very pragmatic, grounded, direct, and open in their culture.

But we're different, because one has its roots in Finland and one has its roots in Germany. But in a globalizing world the diversity actually can be a competitive advantage. We don't live in a homogenous world. I think as I look at the differences, the one that jumps most into mind is that at Nokia we are more informal while Siemens is more formal. But that is a difference, rather than a good or bad thing. But I don't see this as a major issue or challenge.

Q: It seems there is still a way to go before you become No. 1. How do you plan to reach this ambitious goal?

A: First of all, it's not a long way to go. The distance separating the top three isn't very great. Secondly, I think one of the secret sources we have is our convergence portfolio. Thirdly, and I think the most important, there is a will, a desire to win that I can feel everywhere.

We have to keep the customer absolutely at the heart of our business. There are only 450 and they are like precious pearls. So, if our employee base has that fighting spirit to win, and keeps the customer at the center of reason of being, then we will get there and I know we will get there.

Q: Siemens has sold its mobile phone business and now seems to be also getting rid of its network business. Do you think there will be any change to the future shareholding structure at Nokia-Siemens Networks?

A: As the CEO designate of Nokia-Siemens Networks, I stood between the CEOs of Nokia and Siemens on June 19, and I watched them and I heard them say that they love this business. And I really believe they meant that.

And I think there is no exit planned (for Siemens). They both love this business, and provided we, the leadership and the employees of this company, deliver what we have committed to I have no reason to believe that either will leave. I think they like it and they want to stay.

Q: In the first half of this year, China's telecom revenue growth has been slowing down, even lower than the GDP growth. What do you think of the trend?

A: I wouldn't comment specifically on the market. We sort of giving guidance on 2006 globally that we're expecting a moderate growth and that's all I can say.

Q: Nokia and Siemens have announced there will be a 10 to 15 percent layoff. How is this going to impact China?

A: We expected to find 1.5 billion euros in synergy savings. And 90 percent of those (savings) would likely come within the first two years, and the path of this is a 10 to 15 percent decrease in the headcount. And that's all now part of the planning process, so I have no specific comments beyond that.

Q: We have seen a slew of mergers such as Alcatel-Lucent and Ericsson-Marconi. And recently Alcatel also announced it would buy Nortel Networks' 3G business. Do you believe the consolidation is going to continue as a global trend?

A: It's hard, difficult for me to make that call. I have to say that at the moment I'm now very focused on a couple of things. One is keeping our customers and two is making this integration work. There's been a lot of this (M & As) in the last few months, and I think it's difficult to know what will happen in the future.

By Li Weitao
(2006-09-12)

Super Link

1. Countryside Connections

Soren Petersen traveled to Chiang Mai, a city in Thailand, during a business trip last month.

Petersen, the Senior Vice-President of Nokia's mobile phone business, met a night guard in a village who earned $8 a month and owned a "third-hand" Nokia mobile phone.

"He was the third person to buy it, as he trusted the quality of Nokia phones," says Petersen. "People there know they will get 75 percent of their money back a year later if they buy a Nokia mobile phone and then sell it."

The visit confirmed his belief that the rural market will become increasingly wired up, set to provide a new business opportunity to handset manufacturers. And quality, instead of a low price, matters most, even for a farmer.

That is a similar case in China, which has much more extensive rural areas, says Petersen in an interview in Southwest China's Chongqing, on the sidelines of a global launch ceremony targeting first-time mobile phone users.

Nokia, the world's largest mobile phone supplier, is now looking for growth in China's largely untapped rural market, as penetration in cities is already very high. In the coming years, many people living in China's countryside and less-developed areas will buy mobile phones for the first time, says Petersen.

"We hope their first mobile experience will be linked with Nokia," he says.

Nokia expects the number of global mobile phone subscribers to hit 3 billion by 2008, compared to approximately 2 billion currently.

And half of the next billion will come from Asia-Pacific and China, says Petersen.

Nokia is now aggressively introducing not only low-priced but also feature-rich phones to crack the rural market. Those phones, labelled by Nokia as "entry-level," are typically sold for less than $100.

When addressing the rural market, it will be "a huge mistake" if manufacturers introduce shoddy and feature-less phones, notes Petersen.

"In fact, it is also a quality-driven and aspiration-driven purchase," he states.

Nokia is betting on a host of handset features such as easy-to-use functions, FM radio, flashlights and long standby time tailored to farmers to boost its mobile phone sales in the countryside.

One of the most striking things is a graphics-led phonebook targeted at less-educated farmers.

"For instance, if some don't write, they could choose a football for their son (representing the son's telephone number) in the phonebook," says Petersen.

The latest entry-level Nokia 2610, designed in China, even offers a unique rubberized finish which serves to combat dust and improve grip. It is perfect for farmers, especially those in areas such as Chongqing, a city in the heart of China, where it is incredibly hot and moist in summers, says Petersen.

"Such small details make a big difference," he adds.

A mix of cheaper, feature-rich and quality mobile phones is helping Nokia boost its market share in China. The firm already owns more than one-third of the total market.

China's rural mobile phone market started taking off in 2000, and home-grown brands have had a stronger impact, with a combined share of more than 60 percent by 2003, according to Pang Jun, an analyst with data tracking firm GFK China.

But the figure dropped to less than 40 percent by the end of last year, due to the increasing aggressiveness of foreign makers such as Nokia.

Colin Giles, Senior Vice-President of Nokia's customer and marketing operations in Greater China, says the strong brand awareness of Nokia will help it achieve a bigger share of the rural mobile phone market.

"I had thought Nokia's brand was not strong in rural areas," he says. "That understanding was incorrect."

In China, many people in the rural areas have yet to own a phone, but many have access to TV services, especially from CCTV, the largest TV station in the country, Giles explains. Nokia's aggressive marketing campaigns on CCTV have fostered a strong brand awareness across the country, including the rural areas. The entry-level model Nokia 1100 is the best-selling in the rural market, according to GFK China.

The lure of the rural market is big for manufacturers such as Nokia. The growth of new subscribers in affluent east China is tapering off, and even recorded a year-on-year decrease in the first two months of this year.

The less-developed central China signed up more new subscribers than east China in January-February, while new subscriber growth in the poorest western China area was 30 percent, according to statistics from the Ministry of Information Industry (MII).

. According to GFK China, 75 million mobile phones were sold in China last year. And Pang estimates 30 to 40 percent were sold in the rural areas and small towns.

One of the priorities for Nokia this year is to expand its presence in the so-called "fourth and fifth-tier cities" in China, as a way to further penetrate the rural market, says Giles. Nokia has been aggressively expanding its after-sales networks to better serve the rural market, he adds.

"That helps differentiate Nokia from competitors, other than (good) products," he says.

"Nokia is looking into ways to co-operate with Chinese operators to better address the rural market."

A good thing for Nokia is that China Mobile, the country's largest mobile phone operator, has already identified the rural market as a priority. Chinese operators have been reluctant to invest aggressively in rural communications, which were hardly profitable in the past. But now they are realizing the rural market promises great opportunities, especially given that handset penetration in cities is already very high.

In Beijing and Shanghai, the handset penetration stands at 97.8 percent and 82.9 percent, according to China Mobile Chairman Wang Jianzhou. And in Guangzhou, it is 117 percent, meaning some people already own more than one phone.

"Relatively low penetration in rural areas indicates huge potential, and the state's supportive rural policy is stimulating potential demand in the rural market," said Hong Kong-listed China Mobile in a presentation while releasing its annual results last month.

Operators' expansion in the rural market is endorsed by the central government, which has been promoting the communications service to the remote areas, under a project called "Cun Cun Tong," or "connecting each village".

China Mobile said it would "guide handset vendors" to launch low-price mobile phones in the rural areas.

Nokia's network business unit has also launched the Prepaid Tracker, an innovative solution that lets prepaid subscribers keep track of their prepaid balance and call expenses. Such an innovation could be a favorite for operators.

China now has more than 400 million mobile phone users and more than half are prepaid subscribers. Yet, expanding into the vast rural areas could be a tough job for handset manufacturers, says GFK's Pang.

"In China's third-tier cities, non-chain stores selling mobile phones account for 50 percent," he says. "And in the country and town-level markets, the figure is as high as 80 percent. That means manufacturers have much less control of the distribution in the rural market."

And that could be the thing thwarting manufacturers' penetration in the countryside.

"You can't underestimate the distribution (system) in emerging markets, where consumers tend to be price-sensitive," says Giles.

By Li Weitao
(2006-04-10)

2. The RIGHT Number

In the fast-changing mobile phone market, the popularity of a single handset model is apt to wane quickly. This is especially true in China, where the handset replacement rate is typically rapid.

But the Nokia 6108, introduced to the country two years ago, is an exception. It has been ringing the cash registers for Nokia.

"Even today, it (Nokia 6108) is one of the top-10 selling models," says Colin Giles, Nokia's Senior Vice-President for Customer and Marketing Operations in Greater China.

Giles has good reason to be proud of the pen-based model, as it has played a part in the firm's success story of wresting the crown in China's incredibly competitive handset market. Designed with a built-in touch pad and a stylus, the Nokia 6108 recognizes the handwriting of both Chinese and Latin characters for message sending and taking notes.

The phone, also equipped with a Chinese-English dictionary, has become a big favorite among many Chinese fascinated by short-text messages.

Localized product design is behind the success of models such as the 6108. It was developed at the Nokia Product Creation Center in Beijing. The 6108 has boosted Nokia's brand building in China.

"Designs and products carry brand messages too," Giles tells the reporter.

Indeed, strong design capability is crucial to success in China's mobile phone market. Style comes first in the minds of most Chinese when they are ready to buy handsets. This is somewhat different from the Westerners.

Nifty-looking phones that appeal to local tastes are highly favored. And phones that have both good looks and cool features, such as the Nokia 6108, are even bigger hits.

Some other foreign players, such as Siemens and Alcatel, have been losers in the Chinese market, in part because many of their models catering to Westerners are clumsy.

"Nokia has always been the trend-setter in the design and fashion category," says Giles.

For example, Nokia has been pushing a new and sophisticated fashion collection — with a striking palette of contrasts and red, black and white colors — in the Chinese market.

"We have been really successful with this fashion collection in the market. And you can expect more to come this year (2005) as well," says Giles.

Nokia has been maintaining the No. 1 position in China's handset market since January 2004, when it wrested the crown from Motorola.

According to latest statistics by Beijing-based Sino Market Research, Nokia has a 20.5 percent share of the Chinese handset market, with Motorola taking a 12.6 percent share.

Nokia's first quarter results show that China overtook the United States to become the No. 1 market for the world's largest mobile phone maker. The firm sold 7.1 million units of mobile phones in China, including Hong Kong and Taiwan, in the first quarter of this year, compared with 5.9 million units in the previous quarter and 4.1 million units a year ago.

It sold altogether 4.3 million units in North America in the first quarter.

Strong brand recognition contributed much to Nokia's success, says Giles.

"Nokia has one of the best known, and respected, brands in China," he says. "We have been investing heavily and consistently in brand development throughout the last decade. We have also been pushing our brand penetration to third- and fourth-tier cities."

Extended Coverage

Small cities and rural areas have been largely ignored by most foreign players for years. That explains, in part, why Chinese makers held a larger, combined share of the market two years ago.

"Due to the complexity and huge geographical coverage in China, I'd say distribution was one of the biggest challenges for us a few years ago," says Giles.

But Nokia was quick to flex its muscles in the remote areas.

Giles says Nokia has "the best distribution channels and retail coverage in the industry."

It has balanced national distributors, provincial dealers/fulfillment distributors, direct retail partners, and Nokia professional centers.

"Early on, we relied mostly on national distributors," says Giles.

Before 2003, Nokia's retailing covered only 50 cities. But, today, it covers approximately 300 cities.

Liu Fengxi, Assistant Manager of Shenzhen Konka's Mobile Phone Division, said earlier this year he was amazed Nokia had more than 40 salespeople in a very small city in Central China's Hunan Province.

Small cities and rural areas, where most consumers are first-time buyers, have become an emerging market for handset makers. Many foreign players have been trying to crack the emerging markets. But that involves huge investments, especially in manpower-heavy sales.

To make it easier to extend its own sales network to the small cities and rural areas, Siemens in 2004 teamed with China's top domestic handset maker, Ningbo Bird. Bird promised to open its nationwide, 30,000-shop dealer network in China to Siemens, which, in exchange, committed to invest 10 million euros ($12.5 million) to jointly develop and market handsets in China.

Such a deal underlines the growing desire of foreign players to extend into the more promising markets.

"Nokia sees many opportunities for growth existing in the mobile voice market, and we will continue to focus on this area," says Giles.

Going Low

Nokia estimates that the number of global mobile phone users will hit 2 billion by year's end (2005), and reach 3 billion by 2010.

More than 80 percent of global mobile subscriber growth will come from new growth markets, such as China, India, Russia, Brazil, Mexico, Indonesia, the Gulf and Africa, where mobile phone penetration is around 30 percent.

"And 25 percent of the new growth will come from China in the next five years," says Giles.

Nokia has been making a big push into the low-end market in China, with several entry-level models. Last June (2004), the firm strengthened its entry-level portfolio with the first color screen models, Nokia 2600 and Nokia 2650.

This year (2005), the firm is expected to announce two additional models, whose prices could be as low as 65 to 85 euros ($81 to 106).

Nokia has also teamed with chip maker Texas Instruments to develop a low-price chipset for mobile phones.

Such moves, which have boosted Nokia's sales volume, have put great pressure on local players, which have traditionally relied on low-price strategies. Most Chinese makers are now coping with declining profit margins, and even heavy losses. Sino Market's statistics indicate the combined share of China's local makers dropped to 42 percent in the first four months of this year (2005), compared with 47 percent at its peak last year (2004).

And some foreign makers, such as Panasonic and Mitsubishi, are also having a tough time.

Such underperformance and consolidation in the industry are "not surprising," says Giles.

"The mobile phone industry is a volume game. Players need to have strong economies of scale in order to survive," he adds.

By Li Weitao
(2005-06/20)

Face Value

An Interview with Daniela Riccardi,
President of P & G Greater China

Daniela Riccardi, President of P & G Greater China, says her goal is to get China to exceed the United States and become P & G's largest market in volume.

"Maybe it will take 10 years, but my staff, my company, and I, are very clear that it will eventually happen," says the Italian executive, who has been in P & G's top China position since early last year.

The company is the largest consumer product manufacturer in China and worldwide. With a product line that includes Tide, Olay and Safeguard soap, P & G's annual sales in China are more than $2 billion and its total China investment is over $1 billion. China is its second largest market in volume.

"Now our strategies are designed to touch as many customers in China as possible, step by step," says Riccardi.

Having established itself in Taiwan and Hong Kong, Procter & Gamble entered the mainland in 1988 with its joint venture in Guangzhou, in South China's Guangdong Province. Like other multinational companies, P & G first targeted China's major cities, then kept expanding.

"Our objective is to try to reach towns and villages where there are hundreds of millions of people," says Riccardi.

Laurent Philippe, former President of P & G Greater China, laid a solid foundation for Riccardi, developing multi-tier product lines and strengthening management over distributing channels. He brought P & G to a leading position in nearly every sector it operates.

Riccardi's experience in developing markets in East Europe and Latin America made her the right person to carry on P & G's expansion in China.

She reveals that the company will start testing product sizes and packaging in the six months after October this year, in a bid to better penetrate second tier cities and even smaller markets. The company will also determine how to diversify its distribution channels, from hypermarkets and supermarkets to millions of stores in villages.

In China's consumer product market, P & G is not only facing challenges from international rivals, but competition from growing domestic enterprises as well. To maintain its market share, Riccardi insists the company will focus on the beauty care sector and stick to the concept of reaching the maximum number of consumers.

"The beauty segment is and will continue to be the biggest part of our business in China," says Riccardi.

In most P & G markets, beauty care products account for 30 to 35 percent. But in China, 65 to 70 percent of last year's sales volume came from beauty care products.

P & G's Olay, which is targeted to the mass market, is the biggest skin-care brand in its category in China, far ahead of the number two brand. P & G's branding strategy differs from L'Oreal, its closest rival. Besides bringing its dozen international brands to China, L'Oreal took over two local brands — Mininurse and Yue-Sai targeting Chinese teenagers and middle-aged women respectively — to broaden its product line in China.

P & G decided to take advantage of Olay's leadership by diversifying the product lines under the brand. Olay products have been developed to tap female consumers, from teenagers to middle-aged white-collar workers. Riccardi says the decision was based on extensive market research.

Following Riccardi's appointment to China, P & G started bringing more international beauty care products to China to build market share against intense competition.

At the beginning of 2005, P & G launched CoverGirl, a mid-tier color cosmetics brand that included lipstick, nailpolish and eye make-up. The company

introduced CoverGirl in Beijing and other north China cities, before a full-scale China launch.

Riccardi is confident that P & G will fill the gaps in color cosmetics, although L'Oreal and Maybelline have cornered more than half the market share.

In April, P & G Greater China introduced Illume, a Japanese brand, after changing its packaging and product concept for the Chinese market.

"In the past we mainly focused on female consumers, but now, after acquiring the male shaving brand Gillette, we have the opportunity to tackle the other half of the population in China," says Riccardi.

She is also preparing to optimize international perfume brands, such as Hugo Boss and Lacoste, in the Chinese market.

Perfume is one of the company's core businesses, Riccardi says, but in China such brands are "not sold in a well organized way."

"We are trying to understand the attitude of Chinese consumers towards fragrances; here there is a big difference from what we see in the rest of the world," says Riccardi. "We are proceeding carefully before we go to major activity in this segment."

She is positive that in the next few years, there will be an explosion of designer fragrances in the Chinese market.

The beauty care market in China is also full of traps. Sales of SK-II, the company's top skin-care brand, were suspended in China when the country's product quality watchdog detected some products with chromium and neodymium, both banned for use in cosmetics.

The suspension marked an unprecedented blow to P & G's top skin-care brand in the Chinese market. Sales resumed one month after the suspension, but Riccardi declines to comment.

She says a major challenge the company faces in China is the problem of counterfeiting. Fakes now account for 20 percent of the so-called P & G products in the market, an even higher percentage from several years ago.

"We have been working hard on the fight against counterfeiting and have made some progress. But not as much as I would like to see," says Riccardi.

Acknowledging the efforts the Chinese Government has made in the campaign, she would still like to see modifications in government regulations.

"We hope the value of the counterfeited goods will be judged by their market price instead of their actual cost," she says.

She also hopes that the police will confiscate the equipment used to manufacture fake products, preventing the producers from "returning, weeks later."

By Jiang Wei
(2006-11-20)

Super Link

1. P&G Working to Consolidate Market Position

The world's leading consumer products maker, P & G, is striving to further consolidate its co-operation with retailers, in a bid to both further cement its position and promote corporate philanthropy in China.

"Though P & G has achieved great progress in China, an extremely new market for us compared with the US and European markets, we can still go further and faster considering the huge market potential and speedy economic development here," said Christopher Hassall, General Manager of External Relations, P & G Greater China, during an interview last week.

Since entering the country in 1988, P & G has established factories and subsidiaries in Guangzhou, Beijing, Chengdu and Tianjin, with a total investment in excess of $1 billion.

The firm is responsible for bringing to China such well-known brands as Crest, Rejoice, Head & Shoulders, Pantene Pro-V, Clairol, Vidal Sassoon, Safeguard, Oil of Olay, Zest, Whisper, Pampers, Ariel, and Tide.

Kevin Edwards, General Manager of Customer Business Development, P & G Greater China, attributed P & G's success partly to its sound co-operation with retailers.

According to Professor Li with the School of Economics & Management attached to Tsinghua University, P & G was the first manufacturing enterprise to set up an Efficient Consumer Response (ECR) system in China.

"Amidst a batch of disputes and conflicts between commodity providers and supermarkets in China, P & G has a smooth, harmonious rapport with various retailing companies, thanks to the mechanism, which manages the goods supply and co-ordinates relations with retailers directly,"said Li.

On the foundations of sound business relationships with domestic partners, P & G has been able to advance its social causes.

The giant consumer product maker became involved in the Hope School Project in 1996. When a consumer buys a P & G product from an approved supermarket, 0.1 yuan (1.2 US cents) is donated to the program designed to get children in poverty-stricken areas back into the classroom.

On March 21, P & G donated 4 million yuan ($481,000) to the Hope School Project, taking the company's total contribution to this government-backed project to 20 million yuan ($2.41 million).

"The money we donate this time will mainly be used to improve conditions at the 100 existing P & G Hope Schools across China, as well as build five more Hope Schools, together with CenturyMart, CR Vanguard, and Suguo," said Edwards. As supporters of P & G's charity program, supermarkets are now starting to get involved in the project. "We will work towards bringing more retailers into the Hope School Project," said Hassall.

P & G also recently launched its new global platform for corporate philanthropy in China, aimed at helping needy children around the world.

With the theme of "Live, Learn and Thrive," P & G's new platform of corporate social responsibility focuses on helping children up to the age of 13.

The company will provide basic necessities such as safe water and a sound learning environment, and help them to thrive through programs that develop self-esteem and essential life skills.

But some insiders have suggested that P & G's charity work is an effort to improve its image in China, even as the company faces a lawsuit accusing it of false advertising.

P & G currently employs about 100,000 people in over 80 countries and regions around the world.

Last year, it donated $103 million to charities worldwide, and its global sales volume surpassed $51.4 billion in the 2003 to 2004 fiscal year.

By Liu Jie
(2005-03-29)

2. P&G Faces False Advertising Claims Again

Procter & Gamble (P & G) stand accused of making false claims for the second time, after a provincial advertising standards agency ordered a shampoo commercial to be pulled off air.

According to the advertisement, the company's Pantene V shampoo makes hair ten times more resilient than normal — a claim the Zhejiang Provincial Industrial and Commercial Administration (ZPICA) have taken issue with.

But P & G were standing by the claims in the ad yesterday.

"I don't think the commercials should be banned," said Zhang Qunxiang, Public Affairs Manager at P & G China's headquarters in Guangzhou. "We are at the proof-sharing and exchange stage with ZPICA."

Four P & G products — Pantene V and Head and Shoulders shampoos, Safeguard soap and Crest toothpaste — were originally challenged by Zhejiang's Ningbo Industrial and Commercial Bureau, over exaggerated advertising claims.

The latest allegations follow a case in March when a woman in East China's Jiangxi Province sued P & G over claims that their SK-II de-wrinkle cream could "make one 12 years younger."

On Wednesday, the provincial industry and commerce authority issued an emergency ban on the Pantene V commercial to all local media stations.

It said the shampoo commercial — in claiming that it can replenish hair amino acids, thereby making it 10 times more resilient than regular hair — had violated advertising laws.

In a statement on Thursday, P & G said claims were based on laboratory tests and had been verified by an authorized testing organization. However, the company did not say what that organization was.

Wang Gang, an official with the ZPICA, said the agency was satisfied with negotiations with P & G on Friday, as the company had promised to revise the advert. But P & G's Zhang said there was no timetable for amending the commercial.

"Whether the amendment would be made should be subject to further discussion with the State Administration for Industry and Commerce," he stated.

Earlier Beijing media reported that Beijing's equivalent authority had also started an investigation against P & G.

However, a source reached by *China Daily* revealed that authorities there had not yet launched a formal inquiry.

"We're trying to learn more about the case," said Wang Xiaojing, an official with the Beijing Municipal Industrial and Commercial Administration.

The case has drawn attention to the lack of adequate laws governing advertising.

One Beijing expert attributed the dispute to the lack of a clear definition of "false advertising" in the current Advertisement Law and Regulations on Control of Advertisements.

An advertising expert said: "Generally speaking, commercials' artistic exaggerations are separated from the factual results by a layer of mist."

By Liu Jie
(2005-06-29)

Making Sense

An Interview with Gerard Kleisterlee,
Chairman and CEO of Royal Philips Electronics

Chuzhou, a midsized inland city 300 kilometers north of Shanghai, was once *terra incognita* for Frank Chen, Chief Marketing Officer (CMO) of Philips Electronics China. But when he visited in September, the city immediately excited him and his colleagues in the 50-member group.

The team, composed of the CEO of Philips China and heads of all its business divisions, went around the whole city to study everything; they visited government officials, spoke with sales assistants at electronics stores, found out the quality of service centers for Philips and competitors, visited the radiology departments of hospitals, and even toured grocery markets to understand consumption demands.

"I am surprised to see so many lovers of our electronic shavers, but what excited me the most is that we have such enormous potential there to sell almost all of our products — from lightbulbs to TV sets to computerized tomography machines," recalls Chen, a marketing professional for 18 years.

The reason that those senior executives, managing annual sales of $3.7 billion, stayed for three days is just a sign of a significant shift for Philips: China will change from a global manufacturing base to a huge market.

"It (the transformation of Philips) changes our position in China," says Gerard Kleisterlee, Chairman and CEO of Royal Philips Electronics, in an interview in Beijing.

Since 2004, the largest electronics company in Europe has launched a massive remake, trying to become a market-focused, innovation-driven, high-margin business.

In September 2004, the firm changed its brand positioning from "Let's make things better" to "Sense and Simplicity". The goal is to make Philips products easy to use, designed around customers, with advanced technologies.

Last year, Philips, which used to be the world's largest monitor maker, outsourced its traditional cathode ray tube (CRT) display business, to the Chinese display maker TPV Technology. It exited the bloody price wars in the CRT market and turned to the higher-margin flat-panel display segment.

Kleisterlee made his toughest decision in August, selling the semiconductor business to three private equity firms. Both he and his father had worked in this business for years, but he was ready to take Philips out of the deeply fluctuating,

low-margin semiconductor industry.

One month ago, the Dutch firm announced the sale of its mobile phone business to China Electronics Corp, one of its contract manufacturers.

Philips, a 115-year-old company, is changing direction. In an internal survey several years ago, leaders of product divisions were asked to choose where their money for research and development would go. Existing mature businesses were the most favored.

Philips management decided to change that conservative attitude and started to foster emerging areas, such as healthcare, and look to regional markets like China and India.

"The leading theme in our transformation is responding to people's aspirations for health and well-being," says Kleisterlee.

In the past three years, Philips spent 3.5 billion euros ($4.45 billion) to acquire eight businesses in health-care, lighting and electronic appliances.Kleisterlee reveals in Beijing that his company is considering more acquisitions in lighting and healthcare.

Although China is also one of the most deeply impacted markets with the spin-offs of the CRT, semiconductor and handset businesses, the strategic shift requires Philips China to determine local consumer demands and pursue market opportunities.

For most multinationals, China remains a manufacturing base to increase their global competitiveness, rather than a significant market.

The multinationals are located primarily in metropolitan centers like Beijing and Shanghai, as well as coastal areas.

The vast inland areas, where two-thirds of the Chinese live, are relatively uncharted territories, because of low-income levels, high costs in delivery and service support, sharp cultural differences, and sometimes a fear to market to those price-sensitive customers.

An executive with the Chinese computer giant Lenovo Group even boasts that American competitors like HP and Dell will never have a chance to catch up with his company, as Lenovo covers three-fourths of some 2,000 counties and towns in China, some of which have even less than 100,000 people, while HP's presence is mainly in the so-called third and fourth-tier markets with half a million people or more.

But Philips may be ready to venture deeper into the country. Just as Kleisterlee is determined to reform the business lines and culture of his company, Philips is also determined to penetrate China's untapped markets.

"Sometimes we would say that China is our No. 1 priority, but in actual plans of product lines, it was always the third or fourth, because mature markets with bigger revenues got more attention," says Kleisterlee.

In order to tap the emerging markets in China, India and Brazil, Philips will change its organization to better position the company for local needs.

In markets other than these three, heads of product lines usually report to their respective global presidents. In China, the Dutch electronics giant has a management board composed of a president, chief financial officer (CFO), chief marketing officer, and heads of the product divisions like Consumer Electronics, Healthcare and Lighting.

They all work around the Philips China president, have a common action plan, and launch joint campaigns to win strategic customers.

When the Philips Healthcare unit identified a large hospital in Chengdu in Southwest China, the Lighting and Consumer Electronics divisions also maneuvered their resources to support the bid of the healthcare unit.

The units worked together to give a comprehensive solution, while the CFO and CMO gave financial and marketing support. With such a concentrated effort, Philips is more likely to provide total solutions for customers, win orders, and increase customer loyalty.

Besides a China-specific organization, China-specific products are also important to win customers in the local market. Philips has 11 research organizations. The most important task is to find out local demands and develop products to meet these demands. Based on its strong R & D in China, Philips China has generated and registered more than 1,500 patents in China.

With its current strategic focus on the healthcare business, Philips has developed several products especially for emerging markets like China, and can provide town and county hospitals with basic equipment at affordable prices.

By Liu Baijia

(2006-11-13)

Simple Sense

An Interview with David Chang,
CEO of Philips China

Innovation is the lifeblood of most companies, especially those in the technology sector. Firms that spend a large portion of their annual revenues on research and development (R & D) are the ones that stay ahead of the game and outpace the competition.

Royal Philips Electronics is a true innovator, and their sizable R & D resources have led to the development of common consumer goods such as compact audio cassettes and VCRs.

But for David Chang, innovation is more about reinventing the way the global giant does business.

"Innovation should never be limited to the R & D stuff," says Chang, CEO of Philips China. "In fact, it's everyone's job. It's about R & D, product design, marketing and even our work ethic. The ability of a marketing guy to find a business opportunity is also a form of innovation, and it matters a lot more."

Earlier this year, Philips China formed its New Business Development unit, which is staffed by the firm's top talent across its many different divisions, including Consumer Electronics, Medical Systems, Domestic Appliance and Personal Care, Lighting and Semiconductors.

"These guys are in charge of our future business," says Chang.

The New Business Development unit will look for "blank areas", which are promising markets that the 115-year old company has yet to explore.

"This team will also help develop 'Trans-unit solutions' and seek non-organic business growth through M & As (mergers and acquisitions)," says Chang.

The formation of the new unit marks Philips' desire to move away from solely focusing on technologies. As the leading applier of new patents in the World Intellectual Property Organization, the company is now looking at developing a more market-driven, innovative approach to development.

Chang is now pushing the firm's marketing department, and even suppliers to get more involved in its R & D efforts "at an earlier stage", to help identify new business opportunities. The hope behind this is that these new opportunities could drive Philips' future growth in China.

"In the future, our innovation-oriented activities will focus on a well-balanced mix of technological development and response to market demand," he says.

Philips completed trials in India this past February for a woodstove that can be used for cooking in poorer regions. When used properly, the woodstove can reduce fuel consumption by up to 80 percent compared with traditional, three-stone fires.

Efficient burning and high combustion temperatures also reduce the amount of indoor air pollution by up to 90 percent.

The trials were successful and the innovative woodstove could become a big hit.

"There is not much that is particularly special about the technology itself. The crux of the matter is who comes up with the idea and identifies the potential market first," says Chang.

He says he hopes Philips' employees in China will also be able to identify business opportunities similar to the woodstove in India. There could be a lot of these opportunities in China, where energy conservation and rural development are key priorities.

Philips' energy-efficient lighting solutions, for example, could be a big hit in China, where infrastructure — such as highways — is being aggressively built.

"Philips invested a lot in manufacturing facilities when it first entered China, but then it shifted the focus to R & D," says Chang. "We are now investing a lot in local talent, which is one of our top priorities. And we are also trying to develop in-house marketing gurus, not just R & D specialists. Technologies should not be confined to labs."

Over the past several years, Philips has been spinning off its non-core businesses, reducing its divisions from 13 to 5. There have even been calls to cut more, but the company has found that the package of solutions provided by the current five units offers a strong competitive edge in the market, particularly in China. And for Chang, the idea of "packaging" itself is also an innovative concept.

A surgeon in an operating room, for example, might require lighting systems, wireless technologies, and audio and video. Philips' five divisions include Consumer Electronics, Medical Systems, Domestic Appliances and Personal Care, Lighting and Semiconductors. Together, these units can provide integrated solutions for the medical sector and beyond.

"We are trying to provide a package of solutions, because they are urgently needed in China's medical sector," says Chang. "That bolsters our competitiveness, as small companies are not capable of providing these solutions. We will lose the market if we focus on a single product."

Philips has identified the medical and healthcare market, now worth $1.7 billion, as its biggest future opportunity.

Philips' overall business grew by more than 10 percent in 2005, while its medical unit recorded a double-digit increase.

Industry sources expect China to surpass Japan as the world's second largest market for medical equipment in the near future.

"There is an urgent need to improve efficiency in the medical and healthcare market, through the use of information technologies," says Chang.

Early 2006, Philips instituted the Simplicity Award to encourage teams to propose plans that could help the company become more efficient and flexible.

Philips' re-branding efforts have led to its "Sense and Simplicity" idea, a message that is aimed at making technologies less complicated for consumers. It is now focusing on three core business areas: Healthcare, Lifestyle, and Technology.

Chang says brand positioning is not only about product development and design, but also about streamlining Philips' organizations and process. This requires innovative ideas from all Philips employees throughout China.

"Sense and Simplicity should be incorporated into our daily work," he says.

Multinationals, including Philips, have been expanding their offices and joint ventures in China over the past several years. Philips now has 32 joint ventures and solely funded enterprises in China, with more than 60 offices and 13 R & D centers.

Chang says multinationals need to start thinking differently.

"The more simple an organization is, the more flexibility it will have," he says. "We will cut the number of our legal entities in China, as well as our offices."

This does not mean that Philips is slowing down its expansion plans. The company is instead attempting to expand its China business in a more aggressive and innovative manner.

By Li Weitao
(2006-05-15)

Super Link

Health in Hinterlands

For most overseas medical equipment makers, the Chinese market in 2006 was nothing but a chilly winter.

As the government tightened its budget for high-end healthcare equipment, Chinese hospitals spent only 1.32 percent more on imported apparatus than a year earlier. Yet Philips Medical Systems, the world's third-largest medical equipment maker, managed to register a sales growth of more than 10 percent in 2006, a number that may make most of its foreign peers envious.

"We see an important part of growth coming from the lower-end markets," says David Jin, CEO of Philips Medical Systems China. "And in the coming years, we will make more effort to meet the health care needs of the rural market."

Philips Medical Systems, a leading healthcare player in China, is one of the early arrivals to realize the opportunities in moderate and low-cost equipment. By introducing products for rural hospitals, the company is trying to carve out a larger slice of what is projected to be the world's second-largest healthcare market."

The country's medical equipment purchases have been expanding at more than 10 percent annually for years, due to its huge population and rising income levels.

In 2006, the nation spent more than 5 billion euros for healthcare equipment such as X-ray and CT scanner machines, the third-most globally. In the next five years, the nation is expected to overtake Japan as the world's second-largest market for medical equipment.

Overseas equipment makers, including Philips, General Electric and Siemens, have been dominating the high-priced market, as public hospitals in cities quickly adopt the latest equipment to meet rising healthcare demands in urban areas. At the same time the rural market was largely overlooked as more than 70 percent of the country's healthcare budget was channeled into cities.

The nation has now decided to shift its focus on healthcare needs in rural areas. In 2006, the central government pledged 6.77 billion yuan to offer high-quality medical services to rural people before 2010, as part of its effort to establish a cooperative medical care system in vast rural areas.

The Ministry of Health has also announced plans to tighten control over its medical equipment procurement, especially expensive high-end products, as part of efforts to combat corruption in the medical industry.

Overseas equipment makers have already felt the pinch, since their products, usually imported, are often too expensive for the rural market. Customs figures show the volume of imported healthcare equipment only grew 1.37 percent in 2006, compared with more than 16 percent a year ago.

"Rural areas will be increasingly important for healthcare equipment suppliers," says Jin. "The middle and low-end segments already account for 75 percent of the country's medical equipment market."

Netherlands-based Philips has restructured itself over the past years and decided to focus on "healthcare, lifestyle, and technology". The company's healthcare division is now the world's third-largest medical equipment provider. It has maintained an average revenue growth of 16 percent in China since 2003.

Philips, like many other overseas giants, still sees the bulk of its revenues coming from imported high-end products, but the company has already made attempts to tap into the rising lower-priced market.

In 2004, the company set up a joint venture — its first outside the US and Europe — with Shenyang-based Neusoft Digital Medical Co Ltd, to strengthen its ability to offer lower-cost products in China. The venture develops and manufactures medical imaging systems such as less-expensive CT and X-ray equipment. Philips said earlier that the venture was expected to expand sales revenue by some 30 percent annually before 2010.

"The products will mainly be provided to the central and western regions," says Jin. "It is very important for us to complete a more comprehensive product line in China."

According to Jin, the venture has begun to export products to the Republic of Korea, Southeast Asia, the Middle East and Africa, as demand for low-cost medical equipment is also strong there.

"We are also studying opportunities to acquire local medical equipment makers, which are major players in the low and middle-end market," says Jin.

By Wang Xu
(2007-04-16)

Measured Approach

An Interview with Richard Hausmann, President and CEO of Siemens China

Not long after arriving in China, Richard Hausmann has fallen in love with the exhilaration of driving through the wide but busy streets of the nation's capital.

"You have to think, act and react quickly, and watch out for pedestrians and cyclists," says Hausmann, President of Siemens China. "Otherwise, you'll never even move forward. In that sense, it's kind of like running a business."

With its huge population and gross domestic product growth exceeding 8 percent, China has become one of the world's most desirable investment destinations. Siemens, a world leader in automation, communications, medical technology, transportation, and household appliances is eager to use this potential to its advantage.

Hausmann refers to Siemens' growth model as a blend of organic and inorganic methods. The Germany-based company is working in a range of fields to encourage long-term development in China.

"We focus on the business itself, strengthening our portfolio by expanding our sales coverage, and localizing our business operations in China, especially our R & D (research and development) programs," says Hausmann.

This aspect of doing business is the organic side of Siemens' business strategy. The industrial giant now has 56 regional offices across China, and aims to have 70 in the near future.

In the 14 months since his arrival, Hausmann has spent most of his time traveling around the country.

"I went to 20 provinces last year (2005) to talk with local governments and our customers. We want to get closer to the needs of the market," says Hausmann, emphasizing that Siemens' portfolio is a natural fit for the rapidly growing Chinese economy.

Siemens is increasingly localizing its R & D in China. It has opened an R & D center in Beijing, employing more than 100 people. The facility designs and implements corporate projects targeting the local market.

Siemens has also established an R&D center in Shanghai to develop medical equipment and solutions, and a center in South China's Shenzhen. These two centers design and manufacture medical equipment for both the domestic and international markets.

The other resource that Siemens is localizing is people. China is important for Siemens, Hausmann says, because of both the enormous market potential and the huge talent pool.

"We see China not only as a market, but as a talent pool. We see it as an integral part of our value chain," explains Hausmann.

Over 36,000 people are now working for Siemens China, and less than 1 percent of them are foreigners.

"Every person working at Siemens has the chance to get to the top level," he says.

According to him, Siemens is also looking at inorganic growth through mergers and acquisitions (M & As). The company recently acquired a local small engine manufacturer in East China's Jiangsu Province, for example.

In 2004 it bought US Filter, a water treatment company based in the United States. Siemens has found a Chinese partner to start developing water treatment products for the domestic market. The new business will be based in the north China city of Tianjin.

"We are constantly looking to collaborate with others," says Hausmann.

The company is in talks with a number of local firms medium and large, the company executive discloses, but declines to mention names.

Business Opportunities

Siemens has not had any significant problems identifying new business opportunities in China.

"We see huge opportunities here, especially from the rapid development of

the country's energy sector," says Hausmann.

Siemens' unique technologies could help China realize its ambitious energy conservation plans. The Chinese Government announced last year that it plans to cut energy use by as much as 20 percent within the next five years.

"It's impossible to get everything running just by saving energy," says Hausmann. "You need to have good technologies, because we need energy. The point is you have to use resources properly."

From power generation to distribution, Siemens provides energy efficient equipment. The company is now helping to upgrade many of China's power facilities.

In December 2005, Siemens supplied six compressors and three steam turbines to an ethylene plant in Northwest China's Xinjiang Uygur Autonomous Region. PetroChina, the country's biggest oil producer, owns the facilities.

Renewable energy is also a priority, with a total of 88 Siemens wind turbines already installed in eight wind farms in northern and southern China.

The company is also talking with local governments to improve energy efficiency in office buildings and urban traffic systems. Hausmann says that Siemens is in talks with the municipal governments in Beijing, Shanghai and Shenzhen, to introduce a traffic management system that could streamline the flow of traffic.

Siemens supplied the entire traffic security control system for Athens throughout the 2004 Olympics. The company sees a huge need for efficient traffic management during big events such as Beijing's 2008 Olympics and Shanghai's Expo in 2010.

"A transportation surge like this can't be handled in the usual way," says Hausmann.

By Wang Ying and Wan Zhihong
(2006-02-21)

Energy-saving and Environmental Protection

Leave your work seat for a few minutes, and the air-conditioner in your office will turn off automatically.

This is the advanced technology Siemens has used in its new Beijing office, which is to be completed at the end of 2007. In order to save more energy the German industrial giant has used a number of technologies in the building.

Energy-saving and environmental protection are issues that the company has been paying constant attention to.

"Our company is committed to a sustainable future for society, both in the environmental and energy-saving standards that we practice and in the technologies we provide to our customers," said Richard Hausmann, President and CEO of Siemens China. "In China, with our energy-saving and environment-friendly products, we are committed to helping the nation achieve sustainable development."

The company offers a series of high-efficiency products, equipment, and systems, from power generation to power transmission and distribution, up to energy applications and energy-saving services.

Some of its products are designed for everyday life: the energy-saving lamps consume up to 80 percent less power than normal lamps, and its washing machines save much more electricity and water as compared with normal machines. Besides these, the company also supplies its energy-saving products to many big industrial projects in China. By using Siemens turbines and generators, the Waigaoqiao power plant, a coal-fired power plant in Shanghai, saves one million tons of coal each year.

And the company has also furnished the Shidongkou plant in Shanghai with an ultra-efficient gas turbine, making this the most efficient power plant in the world.

"We strongly believe our portfolio at Siemens fits the needs of the sustainable development of China, especially in the area of energy efficiency, as well as overall pollution reduction," said Hausmann.

The latest two acquisitions validate Siemens' plan to boost its business volumes in the energy and environment-related areas.

"Wind energy is playing an ever-greater role in power generation worldwide," said Hausmann. "With the acquisition of the Danish wind power plant manufacturer Bonus Energy, a leader in the offshore sector, Siemens is now in a position to play a major role in the world market for wind power plants, as an experienced full-range provider."

And this year, after the acquisition of the coal-to-gas technology company Sustec, Siemens signed an agreement with Shenhua Ningxia Coal Group (SNCG) to supply its advanced gasification equipment, a move that marks its entry into China's coal gasification industry.

"The move further strengthens our position in the Chinese and worldwide gasification markets, and the coal-to-chemical business," said Hausmann.

The coming Beijing 2008 Olympic Games is a huge event — as well as a great opportunity — for any multinational worth its salt, and Siemens is no exception.

According to Hausmann, Siemens has a great part to play in the Beijing 2008 Olympic Games, by providing some energy-efficient and environment-friendly products and solutions.

The company's Bei Xiao He Waste-water Treatment Plant will be used to purify the water in the Olympic village.

"The plant will turn waste water into drinking water, without the addition of chemicals," he said.

By Wang Ying and Wan Zhihong
(2006-02-21, 2007-03-24)

Super Link

1. Siemens Denies Graft Charge

German industrial group Siemens yesterday denied an allegation that the bulk of its business in China is run by bribery, and vowed to take a zero-tolerance approach to anyone who violates its internal policy.

Over half of Siemens' businesses in China are tainted by bribery, German media Wirtschafts Woche has quoted unnamed sources as saying.

Investigation into the claim is still under way, said Richard Hausmann, President and Chief Executive Officer (CEO) of Siemens China.

"We are fully collaborating with the investigations, and I have full confidence that we are doing this in the right way, working with the authorities involved," said Hausmann. "The allegation does not hold water."

The German industrial and engineering giant has been embroiled in a bribery scandal since November 2006, when German authorities raided Siemens headquarters and arrested six former and current employees suspected of bribery. "In relation to bribery, I have clearly stated this is my most important agenda, and there is a zero-tolerance policy for anybody violating the internal policy," said Peter Loescher, President and CEO of Siemens AG. "We have a full audit and a full compliance program in place, and always communicate the zero-tolerance policy to our staff," said Hausmann. "We found some cases, and are working on them ... there are clear consequences in those cases." Siemens China, according to Hausmann, dismissed 20 employees in 2006 for "deeds that the company did not accept". Loescher is on his first visit to China after taking over as Siemens AG's president and CEO in July. "China is critical to our strategy of exploring fully the potential growth in emerging markets," he said. The German firm chalked up 50.2 billion yuan sales in China in 2006, a figure the company is aiming to double by 2010. Siemens has poured 10 billion yuan into China in the past three years, and last year pledged to invest another 10 billion yuan in the next few years. The rising population, rapid urbanization and massive environmental challenges faced by China, Loescher said, would translate into huge business demand for Siemens.

"All group units have reached their business goals (in China) in the first three quarters," he stated.

By Zheng Lifei
(2007-08-23)

2. Siemens Joins Hospital Venture in Shanghai

German conglomerate Siemens and hospital operator Asklepios Kliniken yesterday signed an agreement with Tongji University, to jointly build a 1-billion-yuan Sino-German Friendship Hospital in Shanghai.

Tongji University will hold 46 percent of the shares and Siemens 40 percent. The first phase of construction is scheduled to be completed in 2009. It will start operations before the World Expo 2010.

"All the partners contribute their individual core competencies: Tongji University adds its medical and scientific know-how; Siemens adds its expertise in structured finance, clinical workflow and hospital technology solutions; and Asklepios Kliniken adds its experience as an operator of more than 100 hospitals," said Wolfgang Bischoff, Managing Director of Siemens Project Ventures, the equity arm of Siemens and joint-venture partner of the Sino-German Friendship Hospital.

Siemens is making great efforts to provide tailor-made products and solutions to customers in China in both high-end and low-end market segments, said Richard Hausmann, Siemens China President and CEO.

"While the Sino-German hospital project speaks for our capabilities and commitment to the needs of China's leading medical institutions, our recent $10 million investment in the development of rural healthcare solutions, as part of the Clinton Global Initiative, highlights our engagement in the development of basic and widely affordable solutions as well," Hausmann stated.

Siemens will also open a research and development center for medical imaging technology later this year, near the hospital in the Shanghai International Medical Zone.

"Together with our partners, we pave the way for high-quality, patient-centered medical care in China — highly efficient with the best and the most effective processes," said Siegfried Russwurm, member of the Executive Management Board of Siemens Medical Solutions. "The Sino-German Friendship Hospital will impressively show that trendsetting medical technologies and powerful IT for process optimization play a decisive role in reaching this goal."

The joint venture agreement was signed yesterday in the presence of President Hu Jintao and his German counterpart Horst Kohler. In November 2005, they signed a memorandum of understanding for the project in Berlin.

By Wan Zhihong
(2007-05-25)

3. Siemens Seals Coal-gas Deal

Industrial giant Siemens signed an agreement with Shenhua Ningxia Coal Group (SNCG) yesterday to supply advanced gasification equipment to the group, a move that marks the German company's entry into China's coal gasification industry.

Under the agreement, Siemens Power Generation (PG) Group will sell key gasification equipment to SNCG for a coal-based dimethyl ether (DME) project, with a planned annual production of 830,000 tons.

Siemens PG also signed a memorandum of understanding to provide equipment for SNCG's coal-based propylene project that, when completed, will be one of the largest in the world.

"The move further strengthens our position in the Chinese and worldwide gasification markets, and the coal-to-chemical business," said Lutz Kahlbau, President of Siemens PG China. "It also marks the faster pace of development of SNCG's large-scale coal-to-chemical projects."

Kahlbau did not disclose the value of this contract. He stated that the fuel gasification process used by Siemens, known as GSP, was one of the three most advanced technologies of its kind in the world. He added that its designs were efficient and more environment friendly than in the past. In addition to a wide range of coal grades, the Siemens technology can also use biomass, as well as petroleum coke and refinery residues, as feedstocks.

Siemens is tapping into an enormous market for its technology. According to a draft plan for the development of China's coal chemical industry, the sector will see more than one trillion yuan invested by 2020.

As for SNCG, it now has five coal chemical projects under construction, representing a total investment of about 100 billion yuan.

According to Zhang Wenjiang, Chairman of SNCG, the DME phase I project will produce 210,000 tons of DME and 600,000 tons methanol per year, refined from 1.87 million tons of coal. Investment cost is set at about 3 billion yuan.

The company plans later expansion to produce 830,000 tons of DME per year, which will mainly be used as auto fuel and an overall alternative to petroleum.

Zhang said SNCG's coal-based propylene project would require an investment of 13 billion yuan, with capacity projected at 520,000 tons of polypropylene per year, and 220,000 tons of gasoline and liquefied fuel as by-products.

This project is not only the biggest project to date by SNCG, but one of the biggest coal-based propylene projects in the world.

"The cooperation of Siemens with SNCG is a significant milestone for Siemens China, as well as Siemens global," said Richard Hausmann, President and CEO of Siemens China. "We will work hard to look for other opportunities in China's booming energy market."

By Wan Zhihong
(2007-01-18)

Starbucks Still Brewing Up a Storm in China

An Interview with Howard Schultz,
Chairman of Starbucks

In Starbucks' headquarters in Seattle, a group of company executives meet regularly, but not to discuss new items on the menu or what marketing campaign should be adopted. Instead, their topic of conversation is China.

They are part of the "China Club", established by more than 300 senior company officials at the US coffee company. Learning to speak Mandarin recently became a part of their routine.

Starbucks Chairman Howard Schultz is one of the club members.

"In our Seattle office there has been such great enthusiasm and excitement for Starbucks in China. If I am not traveling, I always try to be at the meetings," say Schultz.

Although China accounted for less than 10 percent of Starbucks' $6.4 billion global sales in 2005, Schultz says the country will soon become the firm's largest market outside of North America.

"We look at this market in terms of how quickly Starbucks has been accepted in just a few years. The market response has exceeded our expectations," he says.

Surveys have shown that since the first Starbucks outlet on the Chinese mainland opened in Beijing in 1999, Starbucks has become one of the most popular brands among Chinese white-collar workers aged between 25 and 40.

Starbucks in Beijing has maintained an annual sales growth of over 30 percent in recent years. Starbucks in Shanghai started to make a profit in the second year after the first store opened in the city. Its net profit reached 32 million yuan ($4 million) in less than two years.

But to Schultz this is only "a good start" for Starbucks' long-term expansion plans in China. A more challenging task is to grow even faster, in what is potentially the company's largest overseas market.

Analysts believe finding the best ownership structure is vital if Starbucks is to realize that aim.

To lower the risks in overseas markets, Starbucks uses different types of ownership structures. It either authorizes a local developer to use the Starbucks brand or sets up a joint venture with partners.

Beijing Mei Da Coffee Co Ltd is Starbucks' authorized developer in north China. It is 90 percent owned by a Hong Kong-based firm, of which H & Q Asia Pacific is a major shareholder. H & Q Asia Pacific is one of the largest venture capital companies in the Asia Pacific region. Beijing Sanyuan Group, a leading Chinese dairy producer, holds the remaining shares.

Shanghai Uni-President Starbucks Coffee Ltd is responsible for operations in Shanghai and East China's Jiangsu and Zhejiang provinces. The joint venture used to be 95 percent owned by Taiwan-based Uni-President Group, while Starbucks held a 5 percent stake. Starbucks raised its share to 50 percent in 2003, by reportedly paying $21.3 million to Uni-President.

Hong Kong's catering conglomerate Maxim's Caterers Ltd is Starbucks' joint venture partner in Hong Kong, Macao and southern China. Starbucks in 2005 increased its stake in the joint venture, Coffee Concepts (Southern China) Ltd, from 5 percent to 51 percent.

The three individual companies can seek independent development within their own regions, but cannot help Starbucks' national expansion plans, analysts said. The coffee company has to acquire controlling stakes in its joint ventures if it wants to strengthen management control and "reap substantial profits as the market grows," says Pei Liang, Secretary-General of China Chain Store & Franchise Association.

"Licensing or holding a minority stake is an effective tool when first stepping into a new market because it involves a small investment," says Pei. "But Starbucks, the brand's owner, only receives royalty fees from the licensee. It is unable to regulate cashflow in the business."

Better Pace

To help Starbucks grow more efficiently, Schultz strengthened the management team in China by appointing a number of new executives in April. Based in Shanghai, they directly report to US headquarters and are expected to consolidate Starbucks' operations in China, including in management, logistics and marketing.

Schultz calls them "a team of real professionals," and they include Wang Jinlong, who headed Starbucks' overseas expansion in the late 1990s, Eden Woon, the former CEO of the Hong Kong General Chamber of Commerce, and Shantel Wong, once McDonald's China's Chief Marketing Officer.

"With 400 stores in China, including 180 on the mainland, Starbucks' business in China is large enough already to have a direct relationship with the Seattle support center and the senior team there," says Schultz. "We also believe the opportunities in China represent the largest opportunities we can have outside of North America. It deserves to be a separate business unit unto itself.

One mission of the strengthened Chinese team is to speed up the pace of opening wholly-owned Starbucks stores in cities where its three partners do not operate, while the US company negotiates with its partners about raising stakes.

Since 2005, Starbucks has opened nine wholly-owned stores in Qingdao, East China's Shandong Province, and Dalian and Shenyang in Northeast China's Liaoning Province.

"Expansion will continue," says Schultz. He continues, "The Starbucks growth model has been successful with many different types of ownership structures. From time to time we revise those ownership structures because of strategic opportunities. China is no different from many other markets around the world.

"In 1999, we didn't have the infrastructure that we have today in China. Now we are more prepared and more capable of doing things. That might mean, over time, some changes in equity."

The removal of restrictions on foreign investment in the retail industry at the end of 2004, due to China's World Trade Organization (WTO) membership, also opens the door for Starbucks to be directly involved in the development of the China market, Schultz adds.

"But we must look at how everybody can win. A great partnership is a win-win situation for everybody and that is what we have been doing with Beijing Meida," he says. "And let us not forget to give credit to Mei Da for helping Starbucks enter China back in 1999. Hsu Ta-lin, Chairman of H & Q Asia Pacific, was instrumental in that effort."

Hsu said in 2005 that Starbucks planned to buy a 50 percent stake in Beijing Mei Da. A contract signed by Starbucks and H & Q Asia Pacific in 1999 — when the first green mermaid logo appeared in Beijing — said Starbucks could buy half of the company after five years in operation. The price of the deal has been at the center of negotiations.

With 11,500 stores around the world, 35-year-old Starbucks still opens five new stores every day. Schultz said in February 2006 that the coffee retailer would maintain annual earnings growth of at least 20 percent over the next three to five years.

"We believe over the long term that the market opportunities for Starbucks worldwide mean at least 30,000 stores, with 15,000 in North America and 15,000 outside North America," says Schultz.

He believes that besides the ever-expanding menu of coffee and tea beverages, an array of new products and services would help to turn his ambitions into reality.

The coffee retailer has dished out, among other things, CDs, board games and wireless Internet access. It recently joined forces with a major Hollywood talent agency to find movies that could be promoted in its coffee stores.

The first movie to get the Starbucks treatment is *Akeelah and the Bee*, which debuted last month, and is about a Los Angeles girl who becomes a spelling champion.

Starbucks will introduce a book written by "a world-renowned author" in the fall, Schultz says. The book will be sold at Starbucks outlets.

By Lu Haoting
(2006-06-13)

Super Link

1. A Cup of Java, with Extra Venture Capital

A medium Starbucks Mocha, with a side of Ta-lin Hsu — "the John Doerr of Asia."

The combination, on first thought, might be unthinkable.

But hawking Starbucks coffee in northern China has become Hsu's most stable profit source for venture capital (VC) investments in China. That, interestingly, proves the wisdom of that age-old saying, "Don't put all your eggs in one basket."

Hsu, Chairman of H & Q Asia Pacific, stakes his money in three major areas — high-tech manufacturing, the consumer market for brand-name products, and financial services.

He believes the Chinese mainland is the hen laying the golden egg for VC investment, despite the lack of a VC exit mechanism.

"A venture capitalist must always try to lower risks and find a way out. High-tech projects bring great returns, and great risks," said Hsu. "A second board is an ideal exit mechanism," he added. "But, unfortunately, I cannot predict when it will appear on the Chinese mainland."

Diversifying investments is wise.

"VC does not necessarily go to high-tech projects," Hsu said. Selling coffee to China's tea drinkers sounded like a mission impossible a few years ago.

"But today's Chinese have diverse ways of consumption, given their improved living standards. And there is a great market here for brand-name products, such as Starbucks coffee," said Hsu last week, on the sidelines of opening ceremonies for the 40th Starbucks coffee shop in northern China.

H & Q Asia Pacific holds a 75 percent share of Beijing Mei Da Starbucks Coffee Co Ltd, which is the franchisee in northern China of Seattle-based Starbucks Coffee International Inc.

At 23 yuan ($2.80) per cup, a medium latte takes a huge sip out of the monthly disposable income — which was 1,128.11 yuan ($135.90) in August 2003 — of an average, three-person family in Beijing, indicate National Bureau of Statistics' figures.

Starbucks does not plan to cut prices.

Starbucks, nevertheless, keeps growing in popularity. The number of Starbucks coffee shops in China has grown in the past three years. A cup of Starbucks' java has become the latest fashion statement in China.

"Top-quality coffee is the basic factor of Starbucks' success, but it isn't the only reason," said Hsu. "Starbucks promotes a new lifestyle and provides a 'third space' to people. And there is a certain group of people here who really crave such a lifestyle and way of relaxation, and this group is growing larger and larger."

Just ask Maggie Huang. The 25-year-old Lenovo employee buys Starbucks' coffee twice a month.

"Taking a taxi in Beijing often costs 23 yuan," she said. "But here, with 23 yuan, I can spend one or two hours sitting on a comfortable couch, reading a book while sipping a cup of delicious latte. It is worth the money!"

Starbucks' first shop in Beijing opened on January 11, 1999. The company now has 34 outlets in Beijing and 6 in Tianjin.

"I am quite satisfied with the business of Starbucks in Beijing. If SARS (severe acute respiratory syndrome) had not swept Beijing, the profits would have been even greater," said Hsu.

He declined, however, to provide exact figures.

When comparing Beijing's coffee-drinking market with that of Shanghai, Hsu said he was confident about his coffee business in the capital.

"Compared with Shanghai, Beijing is much larger, and its downtown area scatters to the east and west," said Hsu. "So do the coffee stores. Each store might have a smaller flow of customers, but that could serve as a strong point for Starbucks in Beijing, because highly condensed coffee houses will compete with each other."

In Shanghai, the modern metropolis in East China, more than 30 Starbucks have opened since March 2000.

Taiwan-based Uni-President Group and Starbucks Coffee International Inc hold equal shares in Starbucks' Shanghai franchise — Shanghai Uni-President Starbucks Coffee Ltd.

Uni-President Group used to control 95 percent of the franchise, but in July it sold 45 percent to Starbucks Coffee International for 176 million yuan ($21.2 million).

Hsu did not say when he would sell his shares in Starbucks northern China.

H & Q Asia Pacific, founded by Hsu in 1987, is one of the largest VC firms in the Asia-Pacific region. It manages more than 17 funds and has in excess of $1.8 billion in committed capital. The firm has invested about $200 million in the Chinese mainland.

H & Q Asia Pacific's biggest investment — more than $50 million — in the Chinese mainland is in SMIC (Semiconductor Manufacturing International Corp). SMIC is expected to list on NASDAQ and the Hong Kong bourse, simultaneously, in March.

The Chinese mainland has greatly affected the way Hsu does business.

"When I conducted business in Taiwan, I seldom thought about the importance of the consumer market, because Taiwan is an export-oriented island," said Hsu. "But since I came to the Chinese mainland at the beginning of the 1990s, I have come to realize the tremendous power of purchasing, and I am now negotiating with possible partners to bring more brand-name products here."

Hsu declined to name the possible "newcomers".

By Lu Haoting
(2003-10-21)

2. Starbucks Acquires Local Coffee Company

Starbucks, the world's biggest coffee chain operator, bought Beijing Mei Da Coffee Co yesterday, its authorized developer in North China, as it steps up its expansion in the country.

The Seattle-based coffee chain yesterday acquired High Grown Investment Group (Hong Kong), the majority shareholder of Beijing Mei Da, from

H & Q Asia Pacific, a private equity firm. Beijing Mei Da currently operates more than 60 Starbucks retail outlets in Beijing and the nearby port city of Tianjin. Both sides declined to reveal the financial terms of the deal.

The latest acquisition, which gives Starbucks a 90 percent controlling stake in Beijing Mei Da, will help the coffee company "achieve greater operational efficiencies and accelerate our expansion in China", said Wang Jinlong, President of Starbucks Greater China. "We are now poised to expand rapidly in this important region two years ahead of the upcoming 2008 Beijing Olympics."

Beijing Sanyuan Company will continue to hold the remaining 10 percent stake in Beijing Mei Da.

The deal comes at a time when the coffee chain giant is accelerating its expansion in China, which its chairman, Howard Schultz, said, "would soon become the firm's largest market outside of North America."

China accounted for less than 10 percent of Starbucks' $6.4 billion global sales in 2005, its chairman said in an interview in early 2006.

"We believe China will eventually be the largest international market for Starbucks going forward," said Martin Coles, President of Starbucks Coffee International, at a press event yesterday in Beijing.

The US coffee chain operator is planning to open 20,000 stores around the world in the coming years, of which half are expected to be in the Asia-Pacific region, according to Coles.

"And in China, the number will be in the thousands," the president said yesterday, declining to give specific figures.

Starbucks had 190 stores in 19 cities throughout the Chinese mainland by October 1, 2006. It opened its first store in Beijing in 1999.

This is the second time the US coffee shop giant has increased its equity stake in a local joint venture.

In 2003, Starbucks reportedly paid $21.3 million to raise its 5 percent stake to 50 percent in Shanghai Uni-President Starbucks Coffee Ltd, a joint venture that was 95 percent owned by Taiwan-based Uni-President Group.

Shanghai Uni-President Starbucks Coffee Ltd is responsible for Starbucks' operations in Shanghai and neighboring Jiangsu and Zhejiang provinces.

The possibility of Starbucks further raising its stake in the Shanghai venture remains, according to Coles, but he would not elaborate.

H & Q Asia Pacific, an Asia-focused private equity firm that has $2.1

billion in assets under its management, bought a majority stake in Beijing Mei Da in 1998 for $10 million, according to Bloomberg reports, citing Vincent Pun, Senior Research Manager at Asian Venture Capital Journal in Hong Kong.

By Zheng Lifei
(2006-10-25)

3. Public Protest Clears Forbidden City of Starbucks

The most controversial symbol of globalization in Beijing has closed its doors.

The Starbucks outlet in the Forbidden City downed its shutters on Friday after months of online protests by millions of people, saying its presence undermined the solemnity of the former imperial palace and trampled over Chinese culture.

The move follows the Forbidden City management's decision to allow shops to operate only under its brand name.

The Forbidden City was the seat of 24 emperors before the end of imperial rule in 1911. It is China's top tourist attraction, drawing about 7 million visitors a year.

Li Wenru, Vice-President of the Palace Management Board, said Starbucks was offered the option of operating under the Palace Museum brand name like the other outlets. But Eden Woon, Starbucks' Vice-President for Greater China, didn't agree to that. *Beijing Youth Daily* quoted him as saying: "It is not our custom to have stores that have any other name, therefore we decided the choice would be to leave."

The outlet was opened in 2000, and the rent it paid was used for maintenance work. But this January, China Central Television (CCTV) anchorman Rui Chenggang initiated an online protest saying that the coffee shop was ruining Chinese culture. Millions of people supported him.

Starbucks, however, denied any link between the protest and the closure.

"It (the closure) is just out of respect for the palace's decision," said Starbucks spokesman Sun Kejiang.

Seattle-based Starbucks Corp has 250 outlets on the mainland, making the country one of its major growth markets.

The Forbidden City management's move is aimed at streamlining commercial activities and recreating the palace ambience, Li said. All shops operating in the palace will have to follow the norms. Several domestic coffee brands will start operating under the palace's brand later this month, he said.

The reaction to Starbucks' closure from sociologists and the public has been mixed. "It may have been just a business choice for Starbucks," said Wang Xiongjun, a sociology scholar from Peking University. "But the important thing is for the palace management board to figure out an effective way to preserve the palace ambience."

Some people, however, felt differently. Beijing resident Liu Yu said: "Coca-Cola and Kodak films, too, are sold at the palace. It's impossible and irrational to sweep all of them out. They reflect cultural pluralism."

By Wu Jiao
(2007-07-16)

Full-Scale Engagement

An Interview with Atsutoshi Nishida,
President and CEO of Toshiba

In 1972, when China and Japan normalized diplomatic ties, Japanese companies and business leaders cast their eyes on their huge but poor neighbor. They had mixed feelings about China: there was the desire to embrace Chinese culture, which had significantly influenced Japan for more than 2,000 years, and revive their long history of exchanges — but other concerns persisted.

This could be why Toshiba held its biggest exhibition in an overseas market in China in 1985. At the event, the Japanese conglomerate showcased its TV sets and VCRs over the course of six days at the Beijing Hotel, which is next to the capital city's former royal palace, the Forbidden City.

More than two decades later, many Japanese business leaders still have mixed feelings about China. There is an interest in sharing the benefits of economic growth in the world's most populous market, but there are very real anxieties about the challenges and risks of doing business on the mainland. Issues such as rising labor costs, difficulties in managing partners and suppliers, and unfavorable political relations between the two countries, have long created obstacles to economic exchange.

But Haruhito Takeda, President of Fujitsu China, simply responds to these worries with a traditional Chinese proverb: If you don't go into the tiger den, how can you catch the cub? Basically, Takeda is saying that you can't get the big prize unless you take risks — which is exactly what Toshiba is doing in the mainland market.

The Japanese giant held its only Toshiba Expo in an overseas market in 2006 on June 7 and 8 in Beijing, featuring all of its latest technologies, including its next-generation SED TV set, fuel cells for computers, voice recognition systems, and a range of robots.

The exhibition also signaled that the company's strategy has shifted to full-scale engagement with the Chinese market.

Toshiba is known among Chinese consumers for its copiers, TV sets, and notebook computers, but few know it also develops cutting edge technologies for nuclear power plants and elevators that can reach the top of a 1,000-meter-tall building in just one minute, for example.

China has become Toshiba's key overseas market in Asia, so the company has decided to expand its presence and raise its market share in all of its businesses: electronic devices and components, digital products, infrastructure systems and consumer goods.

"Given the breadth of the businesses we are engaged in, including leading edge semiconductors, digital products and a diverse range of social infrastructure systems, we believe we can contribute to China across a broader range of areas than we do today," said Atsutoshi Nishida, President and CEO of Toshiba.

The importance of the Chinese market to its operations is obvious. Over the three years (2006-2008), Toshiba plans to expand its overseas business, which accounted for 47 percent of its total revenues at the end of the 2005 fiscal year to 57 percent by the end of fiscal year 2008.

While average annual growth is projected at 7 percent for the next three years, the average outside Japan could reach 15 percent and more than 20 percent in China. At this rate, Toshiba's revenues in the Chinese market could increase from 365 billion yen ($3.12 billion) at the end of 2005 to more than 600 billion yen ($5.13 billion) by 2008.

A proactive strategy in China does not only mean the introduction of all of its business lines onto the mainland, but also the inclusion of more functions and the enhancement of all current operations.

"China has a central position, not only in manufacturing and expanded marketing, but also as a global procurement base," said Nishida.

The company has 64 subsidiaries covering almost all of its business functions, including manufacturing, sales, services, and research and development (R & D).

Nishida said China lies at the core of Toshiba's global strategy; the

company has one-third of its Asian production based in the country.

But other than production, China's huge talent pool is also attractive to the Japanese enterprise. Toshiba has listed software development, voice recognition, and human interface technologies as the main areas for development on the mainland.

Toshiba is not the only company to recognize these advantages. Software behemoth Microsoft, for example, has already selected these areas as the focus of its Microsoft Research Asia Center. It has developed a number of world-class technologies out of the Beijing facility.

The management of sales and marketing channels, a pressing concern for many multinationals, is also a huge challenge for Toshiba.

"As we reinforce all aspects of R & D, procurement, production and sales in China as an overall base, our sales and sales channel policy will play an important role," said Nishida.

Many multinationals in the consumer electronics business face similar problems. Some choose to have their own sales channels for direct control and speed of execution, but at much higher costs and narrower coverage. Others rely on distribution partners, which provides wider geographic coverage, but collaborators often switch to competitors. Still others work with chain stores such as Gome, with more than 400 stores in China, but these enterprises constantly press electronics manufacturers for lower prices, or they simply cut prices themselves, breaking multinationals' pricing systems and squeezing their profits.

Samsung Electronics is giving a large portion of its profits to channel partners, to help it gain tighter control and faster market penetration. But its South Korean peer, LG Electronics, runs its China business primarily through its own sales team.

Toshiba, a top home appliance brand in Japan, only has a small share of the home appliance market, including TV sets, refrigerators and washers. This creates difficulties in finding ideal channel partners.

By Liu Baijia
(2006-07-10)

Another New Era

An Interview with Nobumasa Hirata,
Chairman and President of Toshiba China

"Toshiba, Toshiba, a Toshiba in a new era." So went a TV commercial in the 1980s, a slogan that still lingers in the minds of thousands of Chinese.

Back then, big Japanese names like Toshiba, Hitachi and Toyota were the top brands in their respective areas. A survey at that time showed that six of the top-10 brands in China were Japanese.

However, since the last decade of the 20th century, and with increasing competition from other multinational and local companies, Japanese companies no longer enjoy such overwhelming leadership in the Chinese market.

Now, 10 years after the establishment of Toshiba China Holding and years of adjustment to the Chinese market, the Japanese giant aims to restore its huge reputation.

A Challenging Task

To restore its past glory, Toshiba must maintain growth ahead of its market competitors.

On August 9, 2005, the new Toshiba President and Chief Executive Officer Atsutoshi Nishida announced that his company would start a future-focused strategy.

A core part of the strategy is an increased focus on overseas markets, and the new plan aims to take sales from markets outside Japan, from 44 percent of the company's total at the end of the 2004 fiscal year, to 50 percent at the end of

TOSHIBA

its 2007 fiscal year.

China, a growth engine for many multinationals, has been highlighted in Toshiba's global strategy. Toshiba's China business is required to play the role of locomotive for its global business, with a targeted annual growth of 20 percent.

Nobumasa Hirata, Chairman and President of Toshiba China, says his operation's goal is to grow sales from $6 billion in 2005 to $10 billion in 2008, including both local sales and exports.

"You can say an annual growth rate of 20 percent is pressure, but I would like to see it from a more active perspective and regard it as a challenge," says Hirata, who has been leading Toshiba's Chinese operations for the past five years.

He believes his company's adjustments in the past five years have readied it for new heights, in terms of both the quality and quantity of its Chinese operations.

While Toshiba is working on consolidating businesses in other parts of the world, Hirata says the number of the Chinese operations will not fall, but continue to grow.

"When we invest in a venture in China, we often plan to see 10 to 20 years growth of the venture, so cutting the number of ventures is out of the question," he says.

It is very likely that Toshiba will even expand the number from 63 at present to 70 in the near future, he adds.

The reason is that Toshiba, with its long product lines and increasing opportunities, needs to make its presence felt in many new areas.

While continuing to invest is fundamental to success, it is equally important to raise the quality of the operation of those ventures.

In Toshiba's new global strategy, a key step is to achieve an innovative multiplication effect, which means all units must try to multiply the business results by working together.

Having built its 63 ventures in cooperation with many partners, Toshiba China, says Hirata, has made significant progresses in making its ventures work together.

"We have the management systems in place and have accumulated a lot of experience, so we can say we are ready for that," says Hirata.

Toshiba not only needs to consolidate its position vertically — taking in research and development, production, and sales — but also increase horizontal coordination between its business groups.

A year ago, Toshiba consolidated all its semiconductor-related units under one umbrella, Toshiba Electronics Management (China) Co Ltd, which is based in China and is in charge of coordinating design, back-end engineering, and market sales.

It also established an internal department to manage some 10 further infra-structure-related ventures.

Hirata reveals that similar moves are still under way in its digital device unit and Toshiba China aims to form several groups to unite those entities together.

A Key to Winning

Another challenge for Toshiba in China is an increasingly competitive market.

Being such a diversified company, producing everything from engines for high-speed trains to electric ovens, Toshiba has a huge group of rivals, many of them global players.

In industrial equipment, it competes against General Electric, Siemens, and ABB. In the home appliance market, it goes head-to-head with the likes of Sony and Samsung, as well as a host of smaller Chinese competitors.

German giant Siemens said in November that its order in-takes in China grew by 40 percent in its 2005 fiscal year ending September.

Toshiba's fellow Japanese company Sony said in October that it would aim to grow sales from $3 billion in 2004 to $8 billion in 2008.

While these competitors all have their own strengths, Hirata believes Toshiba should continue to spend more on research and development, especially in developing products for Chinese customers.

He says that in its electronic device business, including semiconductor and display devices, Toshiba's strength lies in technology, but in its other two pillars — digital products and social infrastructure — the key to success is energy-saving and environmentally friendly technologies.

China, facing mounting pressure to save energy and raise efficiency, raised the issue in its 11th Five-Year Plan (2006-2010), aiming to reduce energy consumption by 20 percent from the end of the 10th Five-Year Plan (2001-2005).

"There is not much difference between us and our Chinese competitors in the digital products sector, so our future will depend on our energy-saving technologies," says Hirata.

His company's joint refrigerator venture with the Chinese home appliance giant TCL, which begins operation next year (2006), will be an example of how Toshiba plans to push itself forward, he adds.

By Liu Baijia
(2005-12-05)

Toshiba Draws Up Ambitious Plan in China Market

An Interview with Takaaki Tanaka, Chief Representative of Toshiba Corp in China

Toshiba, one of the most famous Japanese firms in China, has spelt out a hugely ambitious plan to grow its Chinese business to as big as its home market in the medium term. Takaaki Tanaka, former Head of the Overseas Business Development Department of Toshiba, was assigned to lead Toshiba's Chinese business in February 2007. In this exclusive interview, he talks about Toshiba's strategies and goals.

Q: How important is the development of the Chinese market in Toshiba's overseas strategy?

A: Our revenues in fiscal 2006 were 66.4 billion yuan, including both domestic sales and exports. In April 2007, our President and CEO Atsutoshi Nishida visited China. According to his plans, our projected growth will be 19 percent to reach 79 billion yuan. Of course, this growth must come with proportionate profit growth, and every division and department of Toshiba here is working hard to achieve that goal.

Q: Nishida's visit showed Toshiba's emphasis on this market. Did he give out any new instructions on the China strategy or its role in Toshiba's overall overseas strategy?

A: At present, the break-up of Toshiba's revenues between Japan and overseas markets is exactly 50-50, and the proportion of overseas markets will continue to grow. Among all overseas markets, we think China has the most potential and will play a key role in Toshiba's sustained growth.

Since Nishida assumed the current post two years ago, Toshiba's profitability has continued to improve. The targeted annual growth rate from fiscal 2006 to 2009 is about 8 percent, with 2 percent in Japan and 12.5 percent from other regions. During his April visit, Nishida said the growth rate in China should be about 20 percent.

As for our strategy, we have two focuses. First, 60 percent of our sales in China come from electronic devices, 20 percent from digital products and home appliances, and the rest from social infrastructure.

Electronic devices, such as semiconductors, flash memory and small-sized LCD screens, have enjoyed a smooth development, but we must seek faster expansion in the other two.

Secondly, we launched a new brand campaign in the business-to-consumer (B2C) area, which features TV sets, notebook computers and color copier products, etc., and started airing our TV commercials with the Chinese diving star Guo Jingjing as the brand ambassador.

Q: What are the short- and long-term opportunities in tapping the environment-related market in China?

A: A real opportunity in this respect is the recent nuclear power plant contract that Westinghouse, now part of Toshiba, won. Other opportunities include electricity transmission.

Long-term opportunities include water treatment and greenhouse gas emission reduction. The reason why they are long-term opportunities is that these are usually comprehensive matters, and governments need a holistic view and a comprehensive mechanism in dealing with them.

Q: Some Western companies have started developing products in China and selling them here or global markets. GE and Philips, for example, develop their low-cost CT and ultrasound equipment here. What is Toshiba doing?

A: In the global medical equipment market, there are four major players: GE, Philips, Siemens and Toshiba. In the future, Toshiba is going to be a much bigger player.

We have developed a very advanced 256-slice CT, which our competitors do not have. We will bring products like this into China. We'll need time to find out if we can become one of the top three here.

In Dalian, we have a manufacturing company. We have a 200-people development team there, and do researches with our units in Japan. It is working hard to develop products for China-relevant products.

Q: What are the challenges for Toshiba in China? Are these mainly internal or external challenges?

A: For me, working as the corporate representative of Toshiba in China is very exciting but also very challenging. For Toshiba, the biggest challenge is the demands of customers.

China is a huge country and changing rapidly. So coping with fast changes and using our resources effectively and efficiently is a key task. In our notebook business, we have 650 retail iShops in China and our plan is to grow them to 1,000. Through them, we hope to listen to the voices of customers, as they are very important to us.

Q: If we say a big achievement of your predecessor Nobumasa Hirata was to bring Toshiba back from a notebook crisis in 2001 and restore its image among the Chinese, what legacy would you like to leave for your successor?

A: Hirata was in China for six years and seven months, so I think my tenure will also be about six years. In this period, I hope Toshiba China can establish an appropriate structure and become an independent company according to the situation of China, not just a subsidiary of Toshiba.

I hope sales in China will exceed those in Japan ($30.50 billion in fiscal 2007). China has 1.3 billion people, much more than Japan's population. With its fast growth, I think it is quite achievable.

By Liu Baijia
(2007-09-27)

Unilever Demonstrates the Power of One

An Interview with Frank Braeken,
President of Unilever (China)

Frank Braeken, who took up position as President of Unilever (China) in August 2005, says he has seen most of the realities of the Chinese market in the other eight countries he has worked in.

But addressing the Chinese market is still a difficult task that requires a sophisticated answer, he says.

It is bigger, changing faster, and is much more complicated than other countries he has worked in, he says.

"I prefer to looking at China not as one country but as 50 countries. It looks like Europe," says Braeken of his experience in China, in his first interview since he took the top job. "As a fast-moving consumer goods business in China, the most important thing is that you must always manage a double agenda and be aware not to lose the right speed," he adds.

Merely selling as much as the company can sell tomorrow is a strategy that does not work in China, he says.

To meet the challenge of both the short- and long-term visions of the company in China, Braeken took measures last year to reshuffle the organization.

Now, he says, the company comprises a group of people thinking about long-term brand development and a group of people focusing on promoting brands to be sold in the next month. In the past, the two groups were one and the same. He also boosted numbers by 20 percent (based on last year's figures) in the area of long-term development.

Braeken came to China at a crucial time for the consumer goods company, with the global operation of its One Unilever program.

He saw many ups and downs as he reorganized three companies — foods, home and personal care goods, and ice cream — into one.

"The most important thing we have done, and are still working on, is to integrate different distributions the three companies used to have," he says.

When the restructuring is complete, Unilever will have one sales distribution channel for its production in China — with the exception of its Wall's brand, because different rules apply to the distribution of ice cream. According to Braeken, 80 percent of the task has been done.

"Gradually we want to look at where we can integrate, but it cannot happen dramatically overnight," says Braeken.

But the Unilever president says he will not simply forget about expanding even after the company integrates.

Unilever will expand its distribution coverage to keep pace with competition.

But choosing the right speed for distribution expansion is crucial to the process, he says.

"If you are too fast you will lose control, particularly control of your brands. The goods will be sold at a price you don't want to sell at and in places you don't want to have," he adds.

And if the pace is slow, Braeken says, competitors may increase their pace so that there is nowhere for the company to sell its goods.

"It's arrogant to say I have found the right speed here, but I am aware of the importance of checking and rechecking it all the time," he says.

To maintain a certain amount of control, the company will not allow its sales arm to expand too rapidly.

In terms of production, however, Unilever is continuing to be competitive on manufacturing costs.

With an investment of approximately $50 million, the Unilever Hefei Industrial Park will integrate the company's industrial operations, originally in both Shanghai and Hefei, into one site.

The park, covering about 25 hectares of land, opened in November 2005.

Comparing the cost of labor, transportation, land, and different tax policies, costs at the new integrated site could be lowered by 30 percent.

By doing so the company can put more money into the brand-building of an expensive undertaking in a big country such as China, he says.

"The strategy for Unilever in China is to invest for growth, but not to pull out maximum profit," says Braeken.

Although the China operation generates much more money, it re-invests all that money back into the business in advertising, infrastructure, sales and marketing.

China is the No. 1 priority in Unilever's global structure in terms of investment for growth, he says.

Braeken conservatively estimates that the company's turnover increase in China will keep pace with the growth of the country's consumer-spending by 15 percent this year.

"But to be a winning company in the consumer goods market in China, I believe it may (have to) be 20 percent or more," he affirms.

When the Anhui production base is complete, the company expects its export share to substantially increase from the current 10 percent.

Though the company's objective is not the export market, Braeken says it would be "stupid" not to use exports as a way to be more competitive abroad. And the more the factory produces, the cheaper the costs, he says.

Braeken says Lipton teas are the company's most exciting brand: small in terms of turnover and volume but with a big reputation.

"We have an enormous opportunity to have more Chinese consumers drinking it," he states.

By revenue, Omo and Lux are two key brands for Unilever China, and Zhonghua has the most distribution coverage. Unilever has 400 brands across the globe, but in China it has only 15 brands, all of which Braeken says are strategically important.

When he first came to China 10 months ago, he found that working in China requires a lot of energy.

"I feel guilty if I don't work on the weekend, because all of China looks like it's working at that time," he says.

Formerly with Unilever France, a company with a revenue five times that of

Unilever China, Braeken says he likes working here more. He says revenue size is not as important as contribution to growth.

"And I love the idea that when I look back at my career 10 years later (I can think): I really made a difference," he says.

That is easier for Braeken to achieve in China, because the company leader has many things to create and do here and many important strategic choices to make.

Braeken also notes that it is important for him to have the cultural empathy to understand China.

He suggests company leaders that are new to China must be open-minded.

"It's important not to read too much before you come to China," he says.

With ideas formed through reading, preconceptions may be formed and they may think they know the country, he says.

"But why? You might not be curious any more if you think you know it. To be a teacher and a student all the time is important for a foreign company leader in China," he says.

By Dai Yan
(2006-05-23)

China Leveraging

An Interview with Harish Manwani,
President for Asia and Africa, Unilever Plc.

Thirty years on the eastern bank of the river, 30 years on the western side.

Unilever executives firmly believe in the old Chinese adage, with its implied meaning of unexpected changes involving business success and failure.

Unilever, the global consumer goods powerhouse, is preparing for its turning point in the white-hot competition against arch rival P & G in China, by devoting more effort to innovation and localized marketing strategies. Currently Unilever is identified in China with its brands such as Lux and Dove soap, OMO and Lipton.

One regional boss reveals to the reporter that Unilever will gear up its innovation capability in China through building local research and development (R & D) strength.

"We have immediate plans to scale up our R & D capacity in Shanghai. After expansion, the local innovation and research force will serve not only China, but also Unilever's widely scattered global markets," says Harish Manwani, President for Asia and Africa, Unilever Plc, to the reporter in an exclusive interview.

Manwani is keeping tight-lipped on details concerning the R & D expansion plan, including investment figures and specific projects.

"I prefer not to let our competitors get any clue to our future plans in China," smiles Manwani, only revealing that all of Unilever's efforts are geared towards shaping the Shanghai R & D center as a major innovation force for Unilever.

Regarding the R & D expansion plan, Frank Braeken, the Belgium-born Chairman of Unilever Greater China, adds that Unilever's Shanghai R & D center will be moved to a new, larger building. The new facility will involve not only basic research, but also the designing of localization products.

"We will not only bring in our top brands from the global market, but also localize and create more products for the Chinese market," emphasizes Unilever's Greater China boss.

"Our Shanghai R & D center will play a bigger role in this area. Besides fundamental research, people will see more innovations from the Shanghai facility, especially involving the food segment," says Braeken.

Tea and nanotechnology-related research from the Shanghai R & D center have already made prominent contributions to Unilever's product development in China, according to Braeken.

"A large talent pool is fueling our research work in China," says Manwani.

The Shanghai research center is expected to grow into one of Unilever's major global R & D facilities. Manwani does not elaborate on how large the Chinese R & D center will be, compared with Unilever's parallel facilities around the world.

R & D for the World

The boss of Unilever's Asia and Africa division contends that R & D forces in emerging markets such as China and India will play larger roles in Unilever's global innovation strategy.

A native of India, Manwani believes that Unilever R & D centers in China and India should collaborate with each other, rather than compete.

"It should be China plus India, instead of China versus India, when talking about the country-level role in Unilever's innovation strategy," he says. "Despite being an Indian, I am delighted to witness China playing an increasingly crucial role in R & D. I am happy to see anything positive happen for further growth of

Unilever. As an Indian, I am not at all jealous of China's growth." On Unilever's global business radar, China is both a source of innovation and a promising consumer market.

Manwani says that 40 percent of the company's business revenue comes from emerging markets, such as Asia and Africa. More importantly, 50 percent of new business growth is expected to come from Asia and Africa, of which China may account for 25 percent in the future.

"Our targeted consumers now number 300 million in China. We will expand the figure with the combination of enhanced penetration of current brands and introducing new products from overseas markets," says Manwani.

Tapping Vast Potential

Agreeing with Manwani, Braeken says, "We will consider the option of introducing more products to China and even localize their production in the future. But our current top priority is still to further tap the growth potential of our current product portfolio. There is plenty of room for further development of our current brands."

Unilever owns 400 brands worldwide, with only 15 currently available in China.

As to how to snatch more market share from competitors, especially arch rival P & G, the two Unilever executives respond that the company will stay faithful to its own strategy, aligning the strategy with market demand.

"We will not follow our competitors' suit and move with them," declares Manwani. "We will stay focused on our own strategy, which is to access more customers by offering innovative products.

"If our strategy needs additional brands as support, we will introduce them to China. We will keep our strategy consistent."

P & G is leading Unilever in China in terms of overall market share. Besides the high-end sector, P & G is marching into the low- and medium-end of the Chinese market with brands like Oil of Olay and Head & Shoulder.

"I firmly believe that everything is changeable; as the Chinese saying goes: 'Thirty years on the eastern bank of the river, 30 years on the western side.' We are confident in our own strengths and ability to win over any competition," says

Braeken seriously.

The Zhonghua Story

"We will not follow in our rivals' footsteps. In fact, we have always been diversifying our product portfolio to reach more tiers of the Chinese market. Zhonghua toothpaste is an example," says Braeken.

Unilever acquired the Zhonghua toothpaste brand by inking a leasing agreement with Shanghai Toothpaste Factory Co Ltd in 1993. The contract was renewed in 2003. The Zhonghua product portfolio, under Unilever's management, has been enriched, from high-end to mass products.

In terms of local production, Unilever also expects its China manufacturing base to play a more important role in its global business.

"China, with its comparative advantage, will be an increasingly important sourcing place for Unilever," says Manwani.

Investing some $50 million, Unilever opened its Hefei Industrial Park in Anhui Province late last year (2005). The park will eventually consolidate the company's manufacturing sites, currently in both Shanghai and Hefei. According to Unilever, the move will trim production costs in China by 30 percent.

Currently, 10 percent of the products rolling out of the Hefei manufacturing center are for export, according to Braeken. Once it operates at full capacity, Unilever expects the Hefei production base to export more.

In an earlier interview, Braeken said that although the company did not regard China as an export-oriented production base, it would be "stupid" not to use exports as a way to be more competitive abroad.

By Wang Yu
(2006-11-13)

Super Link

HQ Homecoming

Unilever, the world's second largest consumer goods producer, opened its new China headquarters in the city on February 2, 2007, becoming the latest Fortune 500 company to build offices in this economic hub.

Vice-President of Unilever China Zeng Xiwen, however, believes that the construction of the multi-billion yuan complex is simply the last leg of a long homecoming journey for the consumer goods giant.

"When Unilever came to China in 1929, we had our own headquarters building in Shanghai," he says.

But when the company reentered China in 1986, it leased properties for its offices rather than building its own.

"Now we have settled down again in our own home," says Zeng.

While the consumer goods giant recently sold part of its global headquarters in London in order to cut costs, the decision to build its own office in China reflects "our long-term commitment to the Chinese market," says Zeng.

Located in Shanghai's Hongqiao International Business Park, the new headquarters will cover 46,000 square meters, becoming Unilever's third largest office.

The project's first phase calls for the construction of a 22,000-square-meter office area that will accommode 1,150 employees.

Scheduled for completion in 2008, the second phase calls for the construction of 24,000 square meters of research and development (R & D) facilities. The entire project is expected to cost up to $100 million, according to Zeng.

"This huge investment highlights the important position China occupies in Unilever's overall global strategy," he says.

In addition to its historical connections, Shanghai's geographical and economic position in the country, and its favorable policy incentives, also played a major role in Unilever's decision to establish its headquarters in the city, adds Zeng.

"Shanghai is China's economic hub and the leading economic engine of the Yangtze River Delta, so it is natural for us to set up our China head office here," says Zeng.

"Many of our manufacturing facilities are clustered in the Yangtze River Delta region, and many of our supplies are transported through the nearby Hongqiao Airport, which makes it very convenient for us," he adds.

The company has a global production center in Hefei, capital city of East China's Anhui Province. Its Hefei facilities, launched with an initial investment of $50 million, are gearing up for expansion and are expected to soon become its largest production base worldwide.

Zeng says that Shanghai's municipal government doled out favorable incentives for the establishment of the company's headquarters, but he declined to elaborate.

The pool of highly educated and talented human resources available in Shanghai, which Zeng says "is as good as Beijing," in addition to the city's highly developed R & D facilities, made it an attractive destination for its headquarters.

The Dutch-Anglo consumer products giant currently has a global R & D center in the city. This is one of six such centers the company operates worldwide, and will go from being the smallest to the second largest once the second phase of construction is completed.

The company's China office, according to Zeng, is also an office taking care of Unilever's brand development business in the Asia Pacific region.

"It will greatly improve our efficiency and cut our operational costs," says Zeng. "The new office demonstrates our determination to fully explore the Chinese market."

China is currently the third largest market for Unilever in the Asia Pacific region, trailing India and Indonesia, Zeng says.

Its sales revenue in China grew more than 20 percent to reach 5 billion yuan in 2006, making the country the fastest growing market for the consumer goods producer.

Unilever expects that China will overtake India — which currently records 30 billion yuan in sales — in 8 to 10 years, says Zeng.

By Zheng Lifei
(2007-02-12)

Volkswagen Pulls a U-turn in Chinese Market

An Interview with Winfried Vahland,
President and CEO of Volkswagen China Group

W infried Vahland has reason to grin. He has turned Volkswagen's ailing China operations around in just one year.

Since the 49-year-old Vahland launched a radical restructuring plan in October 2005, the German carmaker has regained sales growth and made big progress in cutting costs in China. He was appointed President and Chief Executive Officer of Volkswagen China Group in July 2005.

In the first nine months of 2006, Volkswagen's China sales surged by 28.7 percent year-on-year, selling 524,558 vehicles.

Also Executive Vice-President of Volkswagen Group, Vahland said the company's full-year sales will exceed 600,000 units in China.

The figure, although a little conservative, is up from 570,876 units posted in 2005, which marks a rebound from consecutive plunges over the past two years.

"The 2006 sales," said Vahland, "will enable Volkswagen to lift its market share in China to 17.5 percent from 17 percent in 2005. This is far from the 50 percent share it enjoyed a few years ago, but it is heading in the right direction."

Vahland said Volkswagen has slashed its production costs in China by 20 percent in 2006 from 2005. He anticipated that in 2007, the German carmaker would achieve its 2008 target of cutting costs by 40 percent from 2005.

These achievements are the direct result of Vahland's restructuring plan in China, called the Olympic Program. The company said the program was designed to increase sales, stabilize market share, cut costs and strengthen the position of all of the German carmaker's products.

The plan came as Volkswagen — the sole official automotive partner of the 2008 Beijing Olympics — suffered a tumble in sales and market share in China over the past several years due to strong attacks from rivals, its relatively aged line-up and high costs.

Commenting on the implementation of the Olympic Program, Vahland declared: "Speed is the most decisive success factor."

However, the cigar-smoking executive is not puffed up by his success, but cautiously optimistic.

"There's still a lot of work to do, but we are well on our way to becoming the gold medal winner among carmakers in China," he said.

No doubt that Volkswagen, the biggest player in China's car market since the middle of the 1980s, will face more formidable challenges ahead from both increasingly popular Japanese brands and fast-growing Chinese carmakers.

Volkswagen now runs two car joint ventures — with Shanghai Automotive Industry Corp (SAIC) and First Automotive Works Corp (FAW) — the two top Chinese vehicle manufacturers.

New Products

The German carmaker plans to introduce 12 to 14 new models into the two ventures, from late 2005 to 2010. The venture with SAIC will manufacture Volkswagen's Santana, Passat, Polo, Gol and Touran. It will launch an Octavia compact sedan from Skoda, the Czech unit of Volkswagen, at the beginning of next year. Skoda will also bring its Superb (mid-sized sedan) and Fabia (subcompact) into the venture later.

FAW Volkswagen's existing line-up includes the Jetta, Bora, Golf, Sagitar and Caddy as well as the Audi A6 and A4. Audi is a premium brand wholly owned by Volkswagen. The venture will launch the Volkswagen Magotan (mid-sized sedan) in 2007.

In the past, Volkswagen Group's products made at the two ventures were perceived as competitors with each other.

To alter the scenario, the German carmaker has differentiated the market

positioning of its brands: Volkswagen-brand models made at the venture with SAIC target "young urban people and trendsetters"; Skoda is "the mid-range line for trend-setting urban families"; the venture with FAW's products under the Volkswagen nameplate targets customers with "high social standing who love original German designs"; Audi is the premium brand for the elite.

Vahland, former Vice-Chairman of Skoda, said he expects the Czech brand to kick off production in China in 2007. He says it will be a new "pillar" of Volkswagen Group's local operations as well as the Volkswagen and Audi brands.

In line with the branding strategy, Volkswagen and its two ventures have also restructured sales channels, with each brand having its own dealer network focused on different customer demands for products and services.

To meet the needs of increasingly sophisticated customers in China, Shanghai Volkswagen and FAW Volkswagen have launched their own service brands — "TechCare" and "Total Care with Precision," which have both gotten positive feedback.

According to a recent JD Power survey, Audi ranks No. 1 in terms of customer satisfaction. FAW Volkswagen and Shanghai Volkswagen ranked No. 3 and No. 4. Volkswagen and the two joint ventures now have a total of more than 1,000 dealerships and service stations in China.

Cost-Cutting

In the past, Volkswagen's vehicles were relatively expensive when compared to its rival products in China.

However, analysts said, Volkswagen is likely to be more attractive to Chinese customers, with the German carmaker's persistent cost-cutting efforts. To reduce costs, Volkswagen and its two Chinese ventures have centralized sourcing of all their auto parts. Volkswagen also plans to speed up sourcing of local parts for its China-made vehicles.

It expects that an average of 80 percent of parts used in its China-made cars will be purchased locally by 2008, up from around 60 percent at present. The German carmaker and its two ventures now have a total of 800 suppliers in China.

Despite the rising localization of parts, Vahland stressed that there was "no compromise" on the quality of its products made in China. He said China's parts industry was on a good development trend and would reach a much higher level in the years to come.

Analysts have said that car prices in China would continue on a downward trend as a result of heated market competition. This would add pressure on foreign and domestic carmakers to cut costs.

More Efficient on Lowering Fuel Consumption and Exhaust Emission of China-Made Cars

German carmaker Volkswagen Group announced in March 2007, that it plans to lower the fuel consumption and exhaust emission of its China-made cars by more than 20 percent by 2010, with the introduction of its latest-generation engines and gearboxes.

Under a plan labeled "China Powertrain Strategy", the group will spend $600 million on the manufacture of its most advanced engines and gearboxes with local partners, to equip all of its new cars built in the world's second-biggest vehicle market, said Winfried Vahland, Volkswagen's Executive Vice-President and China CEO.

Vahland said Volkswagen's plan was in response to China's goal to cut energy consumption per unit of gross domestic product in 2010 from 2005, announced by Premier Wen Jiabao at the beginning of March in 2007.

"Volkswagen Group China takes its responsibility as a market leader seriously, to guarantee growth in compliance with environmental protection and ahead of government regulations," he said.

As a first step in its plan, in March 2007 Volkswagen started production of its 1.8-liter turbo FSI, four-cylinder, four-valve engine, in a joint venture in Dalian with the First Automotive Works Corp (FAW), China's No. 2 vehicle group.

The engine produces a maximum power of 118KW/5,000-6,200 rpm and offers a top torque of 250Nm/1,500-4,200 rpm. It will be fitted in two models to be introduced in China — the Magotan mid-sized sedan and the Octavia compact sedan. The Magotan will be manufactured in June (2007) at Volkswagen's car venture with FAW in the northeastern city of Changchun. The Octavia will be launched in May at the German group's other car venture in Shanghai with SAIC Motor Co Ltd, China's top automaker.

The engine venture in Dalian, in which Volkswagen and FAW hold 60 and 40 percent stakes respectively, will have an annual production capacity of 300,000 units by 2011, with a total investment of 1.5 billion yuan. The plant will also assemble a 2.0-liter engine in the future. The engines will also supply Volkswagen's markets abroad.

Vahland said Volkswagen would reveal detailed plans before the end of this year to bring its other advanced engines as well as gearboxes into China's production. The group will also use light-weight material technology in the components of its vehicles made in China, to further reduce their fuel consumption and exhaust emission, he added.

Volkswagen has another engine joint venture in Shanghai. It manufactures gearboxes in the city with SAIC and FAW. The German carmaker also runs a platform spare parts venture in Changchun with FAW.

"We have confidence that we will grow our China sales and profit this year," said Vahland said, without furnishing specific targets.

Volkswagen's sales in China jumped by 24.3 percent year-on-year to 711,298 units in 2006, maintaining its leadership in the nation's passenger car segment.

After posting losses in the previous two years, the group regained profits in China in 2006, thanks to strong sales growth and its aggressive cost-cutting efforts.

Sales of China-made vehicles climbed by a quarter to 7.22 million units last year, including 4.2 million passenger cars, according to industry data.

Vehicle sales this year are predicted to reach 8.5 million units, with passenger cars surpassing 5 million units.

By Gong Zhengzheng
(2006-11-18, 2007-03-31)

Super Link

1. Volkswagen to Increase Sourcing of Spare Parts

German carmaker Volkswagen, taking advantage of China's cheaper costs, has plans to increase the sourcing of spare parts in the country by ten times in 2006 from 2005.

The carmaker expects to purchase spare parts worth $1 billion from China to use in markets outside of the nation in 2006, up from $100 million in 2005, said Winfried Vahland, CEO of Volkswagen China Group. Volkswagen is negotiating with 50 to 70 parts producers in China and one-third of the talks have entered into a substantial stage, according to Vahland.

"Spare parts from China are 20 to 30 percent cheaper than in Germany," he said. "But they must meet Volkswagen's technology and quality standards."

Last June (2005), the carmaker opened its first China material-testing center in Beijing, to accelerate the approval process of spare parts purchased in China. Previously, all testing was carried out in Germany.

Vahland said China's parts industry was on the right track, and would continue accelerating. Volkswagen now has more than 800 parts suppliers in China. China's spare parts exports have increased rapidly in recent years, thanks to global automakers choosing to source these parts, and the nation's increasing vehicle shipment overseas.

Industry statistics show the nation exported $10.9 billion worth of key auto components and spare parts in 2005, up 34 percent from 2004. In the meantime, China's vehicle exports skyrocketed by 158 percent year-on-year, to $1.6 billion. The nation is on the road to becoming one of the world's biggest spare parts manufacturing bases. All of the world's major parts makers have built plants in China. There are more than 1,000 foreign-funded companies producing spare parts in China.

China has set an ambitious target — to export $35 to 40 million worth of spare parts annually by 2010, according to industry sources. Shen Ningwu,

Deputy Secretary-General of China Association of Automobile Manufacturers, said the nation's parts industry, however, was still plagued by fragmentation, lack of strong independent development, and shrinking profits.

There are more than 4,000 spare parts producers in China now and most of them are too small to be competitive internationally.

The profits of China's spare parts sector have been tumbling in recent years due to carmakers' price wars and growing material costs. Statistics indicate that the spare parts sector reported 20 billion yuan ($2.5 billion) in profits in 2005, down 11 percent from 2004.

By Gong Zhengzheng
(2006-02-28)

2. Chengdu Plant Starts Making Jetta

German carmaker Volkswagen AG has found a second site in western China to make its Jetta, one of the oldest but best-selling passenger car models, in the world's second-biggest vehicle market.

A plant in the southwestern city of Chengdu, wholly owned by Volkswagen's partner FAW Corp, started assembling the compact sedan on Thursday with an initial production of 24,000 units a year, the German group told this reporter. The previously idle factory will add to the line of joint ventures between the German and Chinese carmakers, in the northeastern city of Changchun that's producing the Jetta, other Volkswagen models and Audi vehicles, with a total annual capacity of 600,000 units.

Jetta cars made in Chengdu, to be marketed by sales networks of the joint venture, will mainly target the western market in China, Volkswagen said. Top executives from Volkswagen and FAW said the move follows the central government's call to speed up development of western China and will take the Jetta closer to buyers in the region.

The model, produced in Changchun since 1991, has been the top seller for many years despite competition from new models launched by other carmakers. In the first half of 2007, Jetta sales climbed by 3.4 percent year-on-year to 97,547 units, accounting for 45 percent of the joint venture's total sales. But no full-year sales goal for the model has been revealed. In 2006, Jetta sales hit 176,800 units.

Yale Zhang, Director of Greater China Vehicle Forecasts for US consultancy CSM Worldwide (Shanghai) Ltd, said the Jetta was well-received by Chinese buyers for its "excellent durability" despite being a very old model.

"The model has good price value and fuel economy. It's also easy for maintenance due to a high localization rate," said Zhang.

The 1.6-liter Jetta retails between 71,200 and 100,600 yuan. Over 90 percent of its spare parts are locally produced.

"Jetta's persistently strong performance indicates that car demand in China is highly diversified," he said.

He said production of the model in western China would help boost sales further, as there is huge growth potential for car demand in the region.

China sales of Volkswagen, which has another tie-up with SAIC Motor Corp, surged by 24.6 percent to 431,369 cars from January to June, maintaining its two-decade top spot in the country's passenger car sector.

Winfried Vahland, the group's China CEO, said earlier this month that it aimed to move more than 800,000 cars this year (2007) in the country, up from 711,298 units last year (2006).

Sales of passenger cars — sedans, sport utility vehicles and multi-purpose vehicles — are predicted to grow to 5 million units in China this year from 4.2 million in 2006. First-half sales jumped by 26 percent to 2.55 million units, according to industry statistics.

Volkswagen's venture with FAW said last month that it plans to launch at least one new model annually over the next five years.

By Gong Zhengzheng
(2007-07-24)

图书在版编目（CIP）数据

世界 500 强企业 CEO 谈中国攻略＝ World Fortune 500
CEOS Talk about China：Working and Winning in
China：英文／中国日报社编著 . 一北京：
新世界出版社，2008.1
（中外文化交流系列）
ISBN 978-7-80228-497-5

I. 世… II. 中… III. ①跨国公司—概况—世界—英文
②三资企业－概况－中国－英文 IV. F279.1 F279.244.3

中国版本图书馆 CIP 数据核字（2007）第 170817 号

Working and Winning in China – World Fortune 500 CEOs Talk About China
世界 500 强企业 CEO 谈中国攻略（英文版）

主　　编：朱　灵
策　　划：李淑娟　张海鸥
编　　委：王西民　曲莹璞　任　侃　刘伟玲　宋丽军　张晓刚　史允和
执行编辑：刘伟玲　任　侃
主要作者：李卫涛　刘百家　陆浩婷　姜晶晶　戴　琰　吴允和　刘　洁　张　冉
　　　　　龚铮铮　张　璐　姜　薇　王　钰　宛志弘　郑立飞　丁清芬
责任编辑：李淑娟
责任校对：张民捷
封面设计：王天义
装帧设计：清鑫工作室
责任印制：李一鸣　黄厚清
出版发行：新世界出版社
社　　址：北京市西城区百万庄路 24 号（100037）
总编室电话：＋ 86 10 6899 5424　　68326679（传真）
发行部电话：＋ 86 10 6899 5968　　68998705（传真）
本社中文网址：hhttp://www.nwp.cn
本社英文网址：hhttp://www.newworld-press.com
本社电子信箱：nwpcn@public.bta.net.cn
版权部电子信箱：frank@nwp.com.cn
版权部电话：＋ 86 10 6899 6306
印刷：北京外文印刷厂
经销：新华书店
开本：787 × 1092　　1/16
字数：170 千字　　印张：20
版次：2008 年 1 月第 1 版　　2008 年 1 月北京第 1 次印刷
书号：ISBN 978-7-80228-497-5
定价：78.00 元